How to Interpret Literature

How to Interpret Literature

❦

Critical Theory for Literary and Cultural Studies

Robert Dale Parker
University of Illinois at Urbana-Champaign

New York   Oxford
Oxford University Press
2008

Oxford University Press, Inc., publishes works that further Oxford University's
objective of excellence in research, scholarship, and education.

Oxford   New York
Auckland   Cape Town   Dar es Salaam   Hong Kong   Karachi
Kuala Lumpur   Madrid   Melbourne   Mexico City   Nairobi
New Delhi   Shanghai   Taipei   Toronto

With offices in
Argentina   Austria   Brazil   Chile   Czech Republic   France   Greece
Guatemala   Hungary   Italy   Japan   Poland   Portugal   Singapore
South Korea   Switzerland   Thailand   Turkey   Ukraine   Vietnam

Published by Oxford University Press, Inc.
198 Madison Avenue, New York, New York 10016
http://www.oup.com

Oxford is a registered trademark of Oxford University Press

Library of Congress Cataloging-in-Publication Data

Parker, Robert Dale, 1953–
   How to interpret literature: critical theory for literary and cultural studies/
Robert Dale Parker.
      p. cm.
   Includes bibliographical references and index.
   ISBN-13: 978-0-19-533470-8 (pbk.: acid-free paper)
   ISBN-13: 978-0-19-533471-5
   1. Criticism—History—20th century.   I. Title.
   PN94. P37 2008
   801'.95'0904—dc22   2007035122

Printing number: 9 8 7 6 5 4 3

Printed in the United States of America
on acid-free paper

✦ Contents ✦

⇘ Preface ⇙

I wrote this book because my students needed it and asked for it. As college and university literature and cultural studies courses have raised our expectations for teaching critical theory, the number of surveys and introductory theory books has grown. Some of those books have proven very valuable, and, arguably, some of them look like this book. But based on my experience as a teacher, it seems to me that we still need a book that approaches critical theory more historically, showing how different movements in critical theory respond to and build on each other, and a book that covers a good many issues and debates that I do not see adequately addressed in other books on the topic. To name only a few out of many possible examples, as a teacher I wanted a book that did more than other such books to introduce narrative theory, because most students take a particular interest in novels and stories. I wanted a book that introduces the dialogues among different kinds of feminist criticism and a book that introduces queer studies, the debates over essentialism and the construction of race, and the dialogue among critical race studies, postcolonial studies, and international indigenous studies. I also wanted a book that would take formalism seriously while at the same time taking history and cultural interpretation seriously. In that sense, I set out to write a critical theory survey committed to the interpretation of literature—including film—and at the same time committed to cultural studies and the interpretation of culture at large.

This book sets out to do all those things and to do them in readable language that does not assume previous knowledge of the material, yet also in language that takes students seriously and respects their curiosity and ability. In that spirit, I welcome feedback from students, teachers, and other readers.

The primary audience for this book is the critical theory survey course now routinely offered in college and university English and literature departments. I have tried to present the material in a format flexible enough to go along with the ways that different teachers approach a wide range of courses. Teachers, for example, may choose to use this book with a variety of other materials, depending on the course. The book may hover in the background as a supplement to the study of Shakespeare, the modern novel, film noir, and so on, or it may anchor a course in critical theory. For courses in critical theory, some teachers may choose to have this book carry the course, while others may combine it with readings from critical theorists (available in a variety of excellent anthologies as well as in the books and articles where they first appeared), including the theorists whose ideas figure in this book. They may also choose to combine this book with works of criticism and with works of literature and film. Some teachers will want to return to the same works of literature or film across a large part of the course, but different courses and populations of students will lead instructors to choose different works and strategies, so I have opted to leave those decisions to instructors rather than to make this book depend on referring to the same works over and over. Now and then, I offer anecdotes from my own classroom experience. I have found that students appreciate and learn from such anecdotes, and I hope that readers beyond my classroom will find them helpful as well. I do not include samples of student writing, because many instructors find that such samples are not a good match for their own students and lead students to think too imitatively. Instructors who find student examples useful can probably find the best examples for their own students from previous students at their own institutions. Throughout the book, however, I provide examples of how to interpret literature and culture in dialogue with the movements in critical theory that this book presents. I have tried to write those examples to encourage, rather than to interfere with, teachers' and students' readiness to develop their own examples.

In many ways, Terry Eagleton's dated but still valuable classic, *Literary Theory: An Introduction* (1983), inspired this book, more than the various other books that arose in its wake. Though this book differs greatly from Eagleton's, for I bring fewer skills to the task and bring different limits and resources, I hope it can honor Eagleton's legacy, even while I speak from the perspective of a later generation and a different intellectual history. I hope, as well, that this book can lead students to continue thinking about the issues that it puts forward as they move on to other courses and, beyond course work, as they live their daily lives.

ACKNOWLEDGMENTS

For a book like this, it is more than mere formula when I say that no one besides myself is responsible for my mistakes, oversights, and misjudgments. Nevertheless, I am grateful to many people for encouraging this book and helping to improve it. Over the years, I have learned so much related to this book from so many different people that the task of trying to name them all is too daunting to dare. I would inevitably leave out many people by oversight and for lack of space.

But some people cannot go unmentioned. I want to thank my students. They provoked me to think about the issues this book confronts and taught me to ask many of the questions it depends on. They made this book worth writing. More than that, they compelled me to write it. An extra thank you goes out to the student—I wish I could remember who it was—who said something like, "This course should be called 'How to Interpret Literature.' Then students who don't get it would realize how interesting this stuff is and realize that they need to learn it."

I would also like to thank Brian McHale for insisting, from early on, that there was more out there in criticism and theory than I had usually been led to believe, and Zohreh T. Sullivan for helping to convince me, long ago, that literary and critical theory had found ways to reach beyond the formalisms that I cherished but found confining. With pleasure and appreciation, I also thank the long list of challenging and dedicated friends and colleagues who have made it a privilege to work in the Department of English, the Unit for Criticism and Interpretive Theory, and the Program in American Indian Studies at the University of Illinois at Urbana-Champaign. They continually expand my sense of what there is to know and make me question my own thinking. An extra thanks goes to David Wright for helping out in a small crisis. Cory Schneider, Assistant Editor at Oxford University Press, patiently shepherded the manuscript through the production process. I am especially grateful to Janet M. Beatty, my editor at Oxford University Press, for her receptive interest in this book, her canny ability to point me in helpful directions, and her diligence in getting useful responses from the following readers of the manuscript: Nathan A. Breen, Depaul University; Michael Calabrese, California State University, Los Angeles; Lynn A. Casmier-Paz, University of Central Florida; Barry J. Faulk, Florida State University; James Ford, University of Nebraska, Lincoln; George Hahn, Towson University; Brady Harrison, University of Montana; Susan Howard, Duquesne University; Cy Knoblauch, University of North Carolina, Charlotte; Ira Livingston, Pratt Institute; Alan S. Loxterman, University of Richmond; Elsie B. Michie, Louisiana State University; Harry Rusche, Emory University; and Douglass H. Thomson, Georgia Southern University. To those readers, as well, I am immensely grateful. And as always, at the beginning, the middle, the end, and beyond, thank you to Janice N. Harrington.

How to Interpret Literature

⇒ 1 ⇐

Introduction

This book sets out to invite its readers into contemporary conversations about how to interpret literature, culture, and critical theory. It surveys the most influential patterns of thought in critical theory from the 1930s to the present, with a special interest in the role of critical theory for interpreting literature and culture. The study of critical theory has changed rapidly over the last few decades, and though teaching has changed more slowly than scholarship, teaching has now caught up. For many years, I felt impatient with my own field of English because of its attitude toward theory in the classroom. Since the mid-1970s, when I was an undergraduate, and arguably still today, "theory" has been at the center of what English professors do, but at the same time, many English professors worked by the unspoken principle that this thing at the center of what we do had better be kept a privileged secret. The idea was, go ahead and learn all the critical and literary theory that we can, and let it drive everything we do as professors of literature, but *don't tell the students*.

Don't tell the students, because it will scare them. Don't tell the students, because they can't handle it. They're not smart enough.

Fortunately, the fear of teaching theory in the classroom has mostly faded away, and at many schools it is already buried. When students read this book for a class, then, their teacher and perhaps the department their teacher belongs to are part of that change. Indeed, I have written this book because I join with the many critics—perhaps we are now a majority—who think that the idea that students cannot learn critical theory is nonsense. Theory will

1

scare students if we do it in a scary way, and I will admit that many professors discuss theory in ways that can scare off the uninitiated, but we do not have to discuss it that way. Devotees of theory sometimes like to have a privileged territory that they can paint as terribly difficult for everyone else, but it is not usually difficult unless we make it difficult, trying to make it sound sophisticated so that we can tell ourselves, and others, that we are sophisticated. In fact, most students are already sophisticated theorists. They just don't use the same vocabulary of theory that English professors do. While students may not know English professors' vocabulary, they have their own specialized vocabularies that most English professors do not know, and many of them theorize with their specialized languages enthusiastically. Does that mean that English professors are not smart enough to understand them? It only means, of course, that people who do not know a given vocabulary cannot speak the language that uses that vocabulary. And theory is a language with its own vocabulary of words and ideas, whether in the latest mix of youth music and technology or in the scholarly, college, and university dialects of "literary theory," "critical theory," and "cultural criticism."

Since the early 1970s, the growth of "critical theory" (the broader category) and "literary theory" (the narrower category) has revolutionized literary criticism and cultural criticism. For a time, the swiftly accumulating changes came wrapped in scandal. How dare they contaminate—or even replace—the study of literature with "theory," opponents asked. In the late 1970s many English and other literature departments splintered into pro- and antitheory factions. It was partly a generational difference, for to some people, theory seemed like the newfangled fad of the young. But the younger generations were learning the theory from older generations, and in its broadest sense theory goes back as far as the ancient philosophers, so it was never just a matter of people's age. Eventually the sense of scandal disappeared, for no one asks theory to replace literature. And it is hard to argue convincingly that theory is bad, because by saying so, opponents of theory end up proposing another theory— the theory that theory is bad—so that they end up endorsing what they thought they were objecting to. Gradually, from the late 1970s through the 1980s, theory went mainstream, sometimes over the objections of theorists themselves, who often fancy their role as troublemakers or gadflies.

Though the varieties of theory described in this book hit their first big threshold in the debates of English and literature departments, they also drew on and then came back to influence ways of thinking in philosophy (which of course was always theoretical), linguistics, political science, history, communications, anthropology, film studies, sociology, and many other fields. Eventually, the growth of critical theory generated a common language that allowed people in different disciplines, and in widely varying precincts of the same disciplines, to talk to, understand, and learn from each other across their differing backgrounds and interests. Students and faculty from political science, for example, found that they could talk about their interests with students and faculty in English in ways that they never could before.

That helps give the lie to the complaint, still occasionally heard, that theory is so arcane that it makes literary study irrelevant at a time when relevance and connection to the troubled, practical world has a desperate urgency. In fact, and as we will see as this book moves along, theory is about nothing if it is not about the interweaving of literary study, critical study, and the everyday world where all of us live. This book—and the ideas it presents and discusses—set out not to make literary study less meaningful in our daily lives, but to make it more meaningful. So much so that, as you read this book, you might start to find connections between what this book discusses and a great many other things you care about, such as politics, art and beauty, the environment, music, movies, social policy, identity, and on and on, including, for students, a wide range of classes in literary studies and other fields. Literature connects to and is part of everything else around us, and literary criticism, critical theory, and the study of literature also connect to and are part of everything else. This book sets out to bring all those things together: literature, criticism, theory, cultural studies, and everything around us. In short, this is a book about how, every day, we interpret—and can enjoy interpreting—the dialogue between art and daily life.

   *   *   *   *   *

Students sometimes ask what we mean when we refer to *criticism*, because criticism does not usually carry the same meaning in literary and cultural studies as it carries in casual conversation. When we use the term *criticism* in casual conversation, it refers to saying what we dislike. But that is not what the term means in this book, and it is not what the term typically means in critical writing or in college and university literature, film, and cultural studies classes. Instead, as this book uses the term, and as cultural, film, and literary critics typically use the term, it refers to interpretation and insightful commentary.

Film and book reviews sometimes see it as their role to judge whether a film or book is a good or not-so-good film or book, but critical writing focuses far more on interpreting and usually lets judgments about a work's value remain implicit or peripheral.

Even so, there is a difference between *criticism* and *theory*. Criticism tends to focus on interpreting a cultural practice, such as something from popular culture, film, or literature. Theory tends to focus, by contrast, on proposing or interpreting models for how to do criticism. Nevertheless, theory and criticism overlap, because theory includes criticism and criticism draws, at least implicitly, on theory. Still more, as I discuss later, theory and criticism depend on each other and can even merge into each other.

Some criticism, however, focuses less on theory, and some ways of thinking about models for criticism do not usually find room under the umbrella of critical theory and thus are not included in this book. For example, this book does not discuss poetic form (*prosody*) or offer suggestions about how to craft a critical essay. Such concerns can influence how we think about, understand, and write criticism; but other, easily found books already address those concerns well, so this book concentrates more on the topics typically associated with critical theory.

It can probably help, as well, to ask what we mean by the term *literature*. The truth is, there is no exact, definitive, and widely agreed-on meaning for the term *literature*. For the purposes of this book, literature is simply those things we refer to by the word *literature*. For more traditional critics, literature refers to poetry, drama, and fiction and perhaps sometimes to more self-consciously artful essays or autobiography. In recent years, however, as we will see through the course of this book, the term has opened up considerably. It can include any writing that people wish to study with the same critical intensity and appreciation that critics traditionally bring to poetry, drama, and fiction, and not only writing, but also film. More broadly still, especially under the influence of cultural studies, critics increasingly see the textuality of literature as overlapping with the textuality of all language and with the textuality, loosely speaking, of popular culture and other forms of communication, whether written (a magazine article, a poem), aural (music, speech), visual (photography, painting), kinetic (sports, dance), or some combination of those (film, new media). While in the narrow sense of the term, literature often continues to refer to poetry, drama, fiction, and perhaps essays and autobiography, critics seem comfortable moving back and forth between narrower and broader uses of the term, without worrying over definitions and flexible categories. In that way, then, this book takes heed of film and popular culture as well as poetry, drama, and fiction.

     *   *   *   *   *

The progression of chapters in this book follows a shape that it may help to lay out explicitly at the beginning. For the most part, the sequence is chronological, and in a sense it is also circular. If you look at the Contents, you might object that it does not look chronological, because even readers who do not yet know much about the ways of thinking referred to in the Contents will sometimes know, for example, that psychoanalysis began before structuralism or deconstruction, that feminism began before psychoanalysis, or that Marxism began before queer studies. But that is not what I mean when I say *chronological*. Rather than organizing the chapters in a sequence according to when each way of thinking began, I have put them in a sequence that follows when each way of thinking reached its threshold in the history of literary criticism (which is usually roughly when it reached its threshold in the history of critical theory in general). The exception is the chapter on reader-response criticism, the shortest chapter, which comes at the end simply because it refers to issues from other chapters in ways that will be clearer if it comes after those other chapters. In the process, the chapter on reader response can serve as a coda for the rest of the book. Otherwise, I have chosen a chronological sequence, not out of some sterile notion of counting the years, but because it tells a story across the book.

That is to say, each movement in criticism and theory draws on and responds to the movements that preceded it, and so to understand each movement, it helps to have studied the movements that came before it. For that reason also, as we move forward in the book, our patterns of thought will build on each other and make the discussion cumulative. Beginning especially with Chapter 4, on deconstruction, as we work with each new movement we will use the movements that preceded it. Deconstruction, as we will see in Chapter 4, is partly a response to structuralism, from Chapter 3. And structuralism (not in its roots, but in its use by literary critics, especially in the United States) is partly a response to new criticism, from Chapter 2. Psychoanalysis began with Freud's work before new criticism, structuralism, and deconstruction, but it did not grab powerful hold of literary criticism until after it had structuralism and deconstruction to work with. Feminist criticism, then, responded profoundly to psychoanalysis, and so on through the rest of the book. In that way, the book tells a story. But also in that way, the chapter boundaries are not as firm as the Contents might suggest, because when we study any one method, we will continue to study the methods before it.

As we study the earlier ways of thinking, I will risk making things a little more difficult, now and then, by peeking forward to begin (just briefly) to make comparisons to ways of thinking that came later. While in the short run that risks confusing readers, in the long run it makes things easier and clearer, because it would be artificial to pretend, while studying a set of ideas from the past, that other ideas from later on have not influenced the way we can understand the older ideas. In discussing new criticism, for example, I will draw (a little) on historicism, because now that critics have developed a new range of skills for reading historically, it would be false to pretend that historicist insights cannot help us read new criticism, even though the new critics themselves (as we will see) were not especially historicist.

At the same time that the sequence of chapters has a chronological shape, in another sense it has a circular shape. That is to say, at the end we will return to where we began. The new critics whom we will begin with wanted to make criticism more formalist (we will see what that means soon, in Chapter 2), and in making it more formalist they tended to make it less cultural and historical. The structuralists and deconstructionists, then, whatever their differences from the new critics and from each other, extended that interest in formalism. Then eventually, as we will see, many critics reacted against formalism and sought to take criticism back to a focus on the cultural and historical. In that sense, the story this book tells is circular. But when critics returned to the cultural and historical, they returned in the light of the intense developments in formalist criticism under the new critics, structuralists, and deconstructionists, which meant that, in their hands, cultural and historical criticism looked dramatically different from how it looked two or three generations earlier, before the new critics. That is the story that this book will tell.

Along the way, the book will introduce a great deal of vocabulary, because, as we have already suggested, studying critical theory is not only *like* studying a language, it *is* studying a language. And so this book will go a good distance toward introducing the language of critical theory. Sometimes the terms are specialized and stuffy, and other times they are lively and provocative. Either way, the terms are out there, and learning them can at the least help us follow other people's use of them. At the most, it can help us learn and use the concepts of criticism, because each term provides a handle that helps us grasp the idea it represents and that may help us turn that idea to use, whether we respond to the idea skeptically or enthusiastically. (Key terms appear in **bold** when they are introduced and explained, which is usually the first time they appear in the book. In the index, those terms are also bolded, along with the numbers for pages that introduce and explain them.) Along the way, as well, the approach of the book will change a little after the first few chapters. Chapters 2 and 3 run longer, not because new criticism and structuralism are more important than the topics in later chapters, but because, besides introducing new criticism and structuralism, those chapters also introduce the overall book. Later chapters can sometimes be shorter, because the earlier chapters will already have introduced many of the key concepts and terms that later methods of criticism rely on.

In the process, this book attempts to include two different approaches. Some scholars, teachers, and students of critical and literary theory favor an approach that studies theory for the sake of theorizing, while other scholars, teachers, and possibly a majority of students favor an approach that addresses theory for the sake of interpretation, such as the interpretation of literature or film. Rather than leaning in one direction or the other, this book respects both impulses and is willing, at any given point, to irritate either of them, if that helps get across a concept. I see the opposition between theory and interpretation as a false dichotomy, what deconstructionists call a *false binary*. Without trying either to balance them or to lean in either direction, this book welcomes the conflict between theory and interpretation as a fruitful provocation. I try to speak in practical, accessible, and provocative ways both to theory itself and to the interpretive "application" or "use" of theory without the skepticism that each of these interests sometimes brings to the other, for I see theory and interpretation as versions of each other, two faces of the same coin.

Readers will get the most from this book if, when possible, they read the texts or watch the films that the book takes as examples to discuss in more detail. Even so, I have tried to provide enough quotation or context to help readers unfamiliar with the works, and for longer texts, such as films, plays, and novels, I have kept in mind that readers who do not already know the works may not find it convenient to read them or watch them. But many of the sample texts are so short that they are included within the book or are easy to find and read (such as Kate Chopin's "The Story of an Hour," to name just one example), because they are readily available online and in libraries.

A word to the wise: Most critical and literary theory after the new criticism comes from the political left, and most of it is secular. I say this up front, not to scare off readers who may not come from a left or secular perspective, but instead to welcome them to the conversation. I believe that it is better to make that explicit than to try to sneak it in. Most people who teach and write about the material discussed in this book approach it as if all their readers and students will share their left and secular perspectives. While I recognize that many readers of this book will share those perspectives, either more or less, I do not assume that all students, teachers, and other readers will join me in such views. I also believe that left and secular positions need have no monopoly on the ideas and debates discussed in this book. Even Marxist strategies of interpretation (if not Marxist goals) seem to me mostly adaptable to right-wing thinking. In many respects, the ideas in this book can be debated, endorsed, or applied by readers on the right just as well as by readers on the left. It would be healthy for critical theory to have the right and left join in more dialogue, and more mutually informed dialogue, about the debates that this book reviews.

I have written this book in part because I find that the courses I teach that evolved into this book make more difference to students than any other courses I teach. They make so much difference because learning about critical theory helps us think about everything else we do, and it often helps us think about those things in dramatically new and exciting ways. While this book sets out to help its readers think and write about literature, including film, it also assumes a give-and-take relation between literature and everything else so that it tries to help readers discover ways to build what they can do as critical thinkers in general. That, in turn, can feed back into our thinking about literature, which then can feed our other thinking all the more, which comes back yet again to energize our thinking about literature, and so on in a cycle that can inspire our commitment to and pleasure in literary and cultural interpretation.

⇻ 2 ⇺

New Criticism

The new criticism is now the old criticism and the bogeyman that every later critical method defines itself against, but when the new criticism emerged in the 1930s and 1940s, it was revolutionary. It radically changed critical practice, especially in the United States. Though it is far out of fashion now, the new criticism continues to wield enormous influence, even on many critics who reject it.

When I introduce students to new criticism, I like to ask how many of them, in their previous experience in literature classes, have heard any of the following phrases, which all come from new criticism: close reading, evidence from the text, pay attention to the text itself, pay attention to the words on the page, unpack the words. Every time I ask that question, sometimes to classes as large as seventy students, every single student raises a hand, even students from continents far beyond the United States. It has a powerful effect when students look around the room and see that every one of them shares that experience. Then I ask how many of them have heard of new criticism? Suddenly, all but a few hands drop. Sometimes I ask if the few people whose hands have not dropped think they might be able to define new criticism (telling them, of course, that I won't actually put them on the spot and ask them to define it), and usually their hands drop too, or if they don't drop, they wobble.

In short, across an enormous range of different schools, in colleges and high schools, many English teachers have taught students these principles but not told them about the larger set of ideas that the principles come from. I want to take the opposite approach here. This book sets out to bring students behind the curtain and invite them to join the sometimes-hidden discussions about critical theory that drive the study of English.

In fact, though some teachers do not tell students this, everything the students have done in their English classes over the years has followed, and owes its ideas to, a selection of specific *methods of interpretation*. By keeping quiet about those methods in front of students, teachers make it harder for students to criticize what we do in English classes and also make it harder for students to learn what their teachers are doing and to figure out ways to do it themselves. By contrast, if we make the methods visible, then students can evaluate those methods (and how the teachers use them). That might make it harder for teachers, if the teachers do not want their students to think critically about what the teachers do, but to my mind getting students to think critically about what their teachers do is a good thing. And in the process, for most students, the study of critical method—of critical theory—will make English easier, and far more interesting, and even more *fun*. In that way, this book sets itself against the view that critical theory is too difficult for students. We make literary study too difficult if we cloak its premises in mystifying secrecy, but we make it more accessible—and more honest—if we yank open the curtain to reveal the squeaky machinery behind it.

Students may find it helpful, as they read this book or after reading it, to use what they read about here to help themselves ask, in every class (not just English classes), what methods of criticism (or thinking, or experiment, or research, and so on) the class is using. What are the specific characteristics of those methods? Why would people choose those methods, or not choose them? Why would other people choose other methods, and what other methods might they choose? How would different methods produce different results? How have the methods changed over time, and why? If it were up to you, what methods would you choose? These are the questions we will ask about literary and cultural criticism in this book. The assumption is that readers will get far more out of their interests in literature and criticism and their interests in artistic and cultural expression in general (movies, music, paintings, websites, politics, sports, and so on) if they step back and think about the methods at stake when they think about literature, art, and culture. Critical theory, in short, is simply thinking about thinking. We can think more expansively— and enjoyably—if in the process of thinking we also think about thinking.

The new critics were the first modern Anglo-American critics to set up a programmatic, deliberate method for interpreting literature, and in that sense they begin the story that this book tells. Moreover, since everything we will study later in this book defines itself, in part, as an alternative and response to new criticism, it will help us understand more recent ways of thinking about how to interpret literature and culture if we first get a good grounding in new criticism.

While for the most part this book begins with new criticism, we can better understand new criticism and today's criticism if we look briefly at the state of things before new criticism, at the practices that the new critics invented new criticism to replace. New criticism succeeded so widely in taking over the critical landscape that even now, when every later critical method sets itself against it, new criticism has come to seem so natural that students often find it hard to imagine alternatives to new criticism or to understand how it seemed new from the 1930s to the 1950s. New—as opposed to what?

Before the new critics, the classroom study of English literature routinely focused on history, on what the new critics sneered at as "impressionistic" responses to literature, on moralizing, and on reading aloud. The new critics set up their ways of reading literature in direct opposition to each of these previous routines.

History: Teachers and critics who focused the study of literature on history often concentrated on the writer's biography. Sometimes, they focused on the writer's "milieu," meaning the writer's circle of friends and of other writers and artists. Many historical critics gave special attention to studying a writer's influences and sources. For example, they might note that the British Victorian poet Alfred, Lord Tennyson, uses lyrical language that often echoes the lyrical language of his predecessor, the British Romantic poet John Keats, and sometimes they would go to great lengths to trace individual words or phrases, pointing out that Tennyson's words and phrases echo or repeat words and phrases from Keats or perhaps from an earlier poet, such as Edmund Spenser. After new criticism, this kind of source and influence study can seem arcane or dry, and, despite a gossipy exception here and there, it does not usually hold students' interest for long. Biography continues to interest readers, but many critics, influenced by the new critics, believe that biography tends to stray from the point, for they believe that the point is the literature itself, in the "text" that new critics ask us to read "closely." (We will address biography again later in this chapter, when we talk about the *intentional fallacy*.)

Impressionism: The new critics wanted a rigorous, systematic, theorized approach to literature. They looked down on more casual approaches, which they dubbed mere impressionism. To say that Tennyson's "Marianna" is the saddest poem in the English language or that the humor of Shakespeare's Falstaff or the suspense of Jane Austen's *Pride and Prejudice* can keep us cheerful on a rainy day would seem anti-intellectual to the new critics. Remarks like that are the kind of fluff that new critics sought to replace with concrete methods of criticism. To some readers, the new critics suffered from what we might call "science envy," and we can understand why. Literary studies and science both held considerable prestige, but they did not hold the same kind of prestige. In the university environment of the first half of the twentieth century, the hard or social sciences might seem more established than English. They had methods, and their methods gave them an identity. If professors taught or wrote about sociology, they were sociologists. If they taught or wrote about botany, physics, or chemistry, they were botanists, physicists, or chemists. But if you crossed the university lawn to the professors who taught or wrote about English literature, what would you call them? There was no term for it and no concrete sense of what they actually did as scholars or teachers. The new critics, who sometimes wrote anxiously about the relation between science and literary study, sought to change that fuzziness of definition by proclaiming that the work of literary study is criticism and that criticism has its own methods, just like chemistry or sociology. To the new critics, criticism was not about vague impressions or feelings. It was about methodical interpretation.

In that context, moralizing had no place in criticism, the new critics thought. The point of studying William Wordsworth's "I wandered lonely as a cloud" is not to teach us how to behave better. We do not—or should not—read Emily Dickinson's "Further in summer than the birds" for the purpose of learning to appreciate the environmental value of crickets or even to gain a profounder understanding of loneliness. The point of Jane Austen's novels is not to teach us when to speak out and when to hold our tongue, and the point of Nathaniel Hawthorne's *The Scarlet Letter*, for a new critic, is not to teach us the danger of adultery or to instruct us in sympathy for our neighbors. To new critics, criticism should look for the art or artistic form of the story, not for the moral of the story.

It would get hard for new critics to insist on that distinction for literary works explicitly devoted to moral or ethical causes, such as

Harriet Beecher Stowe's *Uncle Tom's Cabin* or Upton Sinclair's *The Jungle*, but they would happily escape that bind by seeing such works as propaganda and not as great art fit for serious critical analysis. To be sure, not everyone agrees about that distinction between propaganda and art, especially for more self-consciously literary works that still speak directly to politics, such as Charles Dickens's *Hard Times*, Richard Wright's *Native Son*, Elie Wiesel's *The Gates of the Forest*, Joy Kogawa's *Obasan*, or Pat Barker's *Regeneration* trilogy. But new critics would avoid such examples, or they would see the combination of art and political commitment in such books as coincidental, with the politics not illuminating the art. Such examples can start to show the theoretical rectitude that often attracted people to new criticism and that also made many people skeptical of an aesthetic fastidiousness and social aloofness in the new critics. Readers may continue to see both sides of that dilemma as this chapter goes along.

Before the new critics, many literature classrooms took no interest in the goals of criticism as the new critics understood those goals. Teachers and students cared more about the appreciation and the performance of literature than about the criticism of it. That pattern continues in some classrooms, especially in the lower grades or, at some colleges, in general education courses for nonmajors. In that vein, and especially before the new critics, many classes gave little or no heed to criticism and concentrated on reading the literature out loud. New critics might not object to reading aloud, but they would see it as just a beginning, as incidental to their critical goals, rather than see reading aloud itself as the goal.

Let me give an example. In about 1980, I heard Maynard Mack, a distinguished critic of Shakespeare and eighteenth-century British literature, tell a story about what college classes in English literature were like before the new critics, based on his recollection of his time as a student. (He graduated from Yale University in 1932.) He said that a Shakespeare class might begin with the professor asking the students to write an account of how they once felt the way that Romeo feels in Shakespeare's *Romeo and Juliet*. (At Yale in those days, all the students were male. I wonder how things might have gone if they were asked to recall a time when they felt the way Juliet feels or if they were given a choice between Romeo and Juliet.) A class like that usually strikes today's college students, when I tell that story, as far from what they would expect at the college level today, and in that way it gives us a feeling for the impressionism that the new critics rebelled against and for how dramatic a change they brought to the study of literature.

Instead of history, impressionism, moralism, or reading out loud, the new critics called for the study of literature to focus on rigorous, systematic *interpretation*. For the new critics, the best response to a literary text was an interpretation of that text. And the best way to develop interpretation, according to the new critics, is through **close reading**, which means detailed, careful attention to evidence from the text itself, to the words on the page.

The study of history, philosophy, religion, and politics, they believed, is acceptable for background, but it is no substitute for close study of the text itself. After all, they reasoned, we can explain nonliterary writing by studying its history, ideas, beliefs, and politics, but literary writing (poems, plays, stories, and novels) differs from other writing—and to the new critics, literary writing was its own special category. They saw literary writing as primarily about literary art and only secondarily about ideas and beliefs. The art, they insisted, rests in the literary form, in the way that literary texts use words, as opposed to resting in the ideas that the words express. They dismissed literary commentary that focuses on history and culture as **extrinsic criticism**, as not really literary criticism, because it concentrates on matters they saw as outside the literary text, and they called instead for **intrinsic criticism**, criticism that focuses on the text itself.

They also believed that good literature is unified. The new critics were not the first to exalt unity in literature or art. In Plato's *Phaedrus* (c. 370 BCE) Socrates argues "that every discourse ought to be a living creature, having a body of its own and a head and feet; there should be a middle, beginning, and end, adapted to one another and to the whole" (Plato 3: 172–73). Similarly, in his *Poetics* (c. 350 BCE) Plato's student Aristotle argued that "Tragedy is an imitation of an action that is complete, and whole.... A whole is that which has a beginning, a middle, and an end ..., the structural union of the parts being such that, if any one of them is displaced or removed, the whole will be disjointed and disturbed" (Aristotle 65, 67). While such ideas have long been commonplace, the new critics intensified the focus on unity as a defining feature of great art. They often grounded their thinking in what they called **organic unity**, the belief that an admirable literary work forms an **organic whole**. The term *whole* suggests completeness and self-sufficiency, as if, to interpret a work of literature that forms an organic whole, we need to read only the work of literature itself. The term *organic* (referring to living organisms, such as plants and animals) suggests that the unity is natural and complete and that an admirable work of literature, like a plant, grows naturally into its full expression and beauty, with each of its parts tied to each other part. As Samuel Taylor Coleridge, the Romantic poet and critic, famously put it, "a *legitimate* poem . . . must be one, the parts of which mutually support and explain each other; all in their proportion harmonizing with, and supporting the purpose and known influences of metrical arrangement" (Coleridge, 2: 13).

By now, that view of unity is embedded in our typical cultural assumptions about art and the value of art. Most readers can probably remember conversations about a movie when someone said that he or she liked the way one part of the movie went with another part, maybe through foreshadowing, or echoing, or simple repetition or consistency. Readers can probably also remember conversations when someone said that she or he did not like a movie because part of it did not fit with another part. Perhaps the movie's ending clashed with something in the middle, or viewers saw a troubling inconsistency in character, plot, mood, or cinematography. In cases like that, viewers are judging by a principle of unity, assuming that if a work of art is unified, that is good, and if it is not unified, that is bad.

Most readers can probably remember similar discussions in literature classrooms, when students or the teacher pointed out unities or disunities, working from the assumption that unity is good and disunity is bad. Many an English class takes the form of students arguing about, or students or the teacher pointing out, how different features of a literary text fit together or explain each other, working from a taken-for-granted assumption that unity is good and that pointing out unity in a work of literature might convince skeptical students to appreciate and enjoy the work as literary art. Eventually, we will see ways to question the assumption that a literary text should be unified and to question the assumption that our purpose as critics is to find the unity in a good text (or the disunity in a not-so-good text). But for now, the point is simply to underline the focus on unity or organic unity as a new critical assumption that grew so **naturalized** (so taken for granted, as if it were simply natural) that we do not usually even recognize it as an assumption.

HOW TO INTERPRET: KEY CONCEPTS
FOR NEW CRITICAL INTERPRETATION

The new critics' commitment to interpretation revolutionized the study of literature. In the process of pursuing interpretation and arguing for a systematic approach to literature, they popularized four key, overlapping concepts—paradox, ambiguity, tension, and irony—along with intense attention to patterns and symbols. These terms and concepts have grown so familiar that most students have no idea that we owe much of their routine use in literary interpretation to the new critics.

Paradox, ambiguity, tension, and irony, for the new critics, typify the connotative art of literary writing, as opposed to what they saw as the denotative straitjacket of scientific writing. A **paradox** refers to an expression that combines opposite ideas, such as when Shakespeare's witches tell Macbeth that "Fair is foul, and foul is fair." Similarly, Shakespeare's Sonnet 138 proclaims, "I do believe her, though I know she lies" (Shakespeare 1360, 1868), and William Wordsworth tells us, in "My Heart Leaps Up," that "The Child is father of the Man" (Wordsworth 62). Sometimes paradoxes are witty, such as famously in the poems of John Donne (a new critical favorite). In "The Canonization," Donne wittily and paradoxically merges religious and erotic language. He argues that the love between his lover and himself can "canonize" them (make them into saints), saying (in a punning paradox on the renaissance notion of orgasm as a little death) that "Wee can dye by it, if not live by love." **Ambiguity**, similarly to paradox, refers to suggestively multiple and unsettled meanings. The end of Zora Neale Hurston's story "Sweat," for example, leaves the blame for Sykes's death ambiguous. His battered wife, Delia, could have prevented it, but readers might want to blame Sykes for Delia's inability or, ambiguously, her unwillingness to prevent his grisly demise. "The Canonization" leaves it ambiguous whether Donne exalts or spoofs religion by comparing it to sexual love, and ambiguous whether he exalts or spoofs sexual love by comparing it to religion. **Tension** refers to connected ideas that pull away from each other without reaching resolution. The term *tension* often confuses students who are new to its use this way, as a term about language or literature. It does not refer to tension as in "My roommate's crazy habits make me really tense" or "This critical theory stuff makes me tense." It is not an emotional tension, though sometimes it includes emotional tension. Instead, it is a suspended set of conflicting possibilities that will not settle into resolution, as in Emily Dickinson's paradoxical insistence that "Much Madness is divinest Sense" (Dickinson 278). "The Canonization" evokes a tension between religious exaltation and erotic exaltation, especially in such lines as "Wee can dye by it, if not live by love" and "all shall approve / Us *Canoniz'd* for Love" (Donne 11–12), where the off-rhyme between "love" and "approve" can evoke an ambiguous blend of assertiveness and modesty or hesitation. To take one more example, we can see an ambiguous paradox in the tension between opposed meanings of the scarlet letter in Nathaniel Hawthorne's novel about Hester Prynne, who wears an "A" on her breast, a scarlet letter that over the course of the novel comes to stand for many possibilities, ranging from adultery to angel and even—it might seem for a new critic—to ambiguity itself.

To most readers, **irony** is probably a more familiar term. Though deeply linked with new criticism, it has a life of its own before and after new criticism and remains too common a term for the new critics to have it to themselves. *Irony* refers to an expression or event that means something different connotatively from what it means denotatively. The same words can easily gain or lose irony, depending on the context and on the way they are read or spoken. Is Donne's "The Canonization" ironic? A new critic might say that the poem's paradoxes set up a linguistic tension that makes it ambiguous whether the connection between sex and religion is ironic or straightforward. But often we know irony when we see it. We see irony in Charles Dickens's *Great Expectations* when we learn the secret that Pip's mysterious benefactor is the last person Pip would otherwise feel beholden to. Or we might find it ironic in William Faulkner's *Absalom, Absalom!* that Charles Bon, the very man who offers the possibility of fulfilling Sutpen's dreams, also threatens to destroy those dreams. (We might also find it ironic that Bon threatens to expose the tragic way that Sutpen founds his ambition on horrendous misconceptions about class, race, and men's abuse of women. But that would take us into critiquing social structures, which, as we will soon see, the new critics tended to shy away from.)

By this point in the description of new criticism, some readers might smell a rat. How can the new critics believe that the same poem, novel, story, or play they describe as fraught with paradox, ambiguity, tension, and irony is also unified? That paradox in new criticism dramatizes a key issue for the new critics, an apparent contradiction that threatened to topple their entire system, because paradox, ambiguity, tension, and irony might seem to make the literary text a seething stew of conflicts, which sounds like the opposite of unity. But the new critics managed to make that apparent contradiction integral to the system that it threatened to topple.

They proposed that eventually, at least in great literature, the paradoxes, ambiguities, tensions, and ironies all balanced each other out, suspending the competing energies in a unifying harmony. That way of reading takes what might seem like a fatal contradiction between unity, on the one hand, and paradox, ambiguity, tension, and irony, on the other hand, and turns the apparent contradiction into a unity-making machine, into the very definition of great literature, and turns the work of finding that balance into the purpose and goal of literary criticism.

Even readers learning here about new criticism for the first time have probably seen and heard criticism work according to that new critical model many times, in the classroom, in criticism they may have read, and perhaps even in papers they have written (or papers they may have seen by other students). The usual pattern is pretty standard now, but the new critics invented it. First the critic, whether a professional critic or a student writing a paper, finds a problem. For the new critics, the problem, as we have seen, often took the form of a paradox, ambiguity, tension, irony, or a combination of those overlapping categories. Then the critic traces the pattern of that problem as it repeats itself across the text. For example, we might find a series of moments in Donne's "The Canonization" that suggest a paradoxical, ambiguous, potentially ironic tension between the language of religion, or love of God, and the language of eroticism and earthly love. (This is exactly what Cleanth Brooks, one of the founding new critics, did in an influential discussion of Donne's poem called "The Language of Paradox.") Then, at the last possible moment, just when the text seems ready to crash into unresolvable chaos and the new critical method seems ready to collapse, the new critic rescues the critical method, and the text itself (and maybe the student critic's grade on a paper), by brilliantly pointing out how the balanced suspension of competing possibilities makes a larger argument about the relation between, in this case, two different kinds of love, or the mysteries and multiple possibilities of literary language, and perhaps even about poetry itself (or about fiction or drama or whatever the critic is writing about). In this way, the new critics offered a systematic critical method, interpretations of individual texts, and also a claim that literary language itself depends on a balanced tension of ambiguity, irony, and paradox.

In the process, two other characteristic strategies of new criticism emerged that later commentators have not called attention to as much as they have to paradox, ambiguity, tension, and irony, namely, the new critical preoccupations with **patterns** and symbols. We have already begun to see the new critical interest in patterns through the way that the new critics traced patterns of paradox, ambiguity, tension, and irony and discussed how the various conflicts balanced each other to form a unity. That interest drew on and contributed to a broader interest in literary patterns at large. Repetition makes patterns, whether for a predictable category like description (a color, perhaps), language (a favorite word or image), an event (such as scenes at a window or two characters meeting), a habit (such as a character's repeated gesture), or a structural feature (such as chapters or scenes that begin in a similar way), and so on with endless possible variations. Most students and teachers of English have read or written literary criticism or sat through a class that traces a pattern across a work of literature. But the point is not just to say that the pattern is there; the point is to interpret the pattern. The interpretations vary as widely as the interpretive methods discussed throughout this book, but the habit of looking for patterns and treating them as evidence gained enormous momentum from new critical practice and from the new critical assumption that a repeating pattern indicated a unified artistic vision across the breadth of a literary text.

The new critics have no monopoly on **symbols**, but new critical practice fit snugly with an interest in symbols and helped expand that interest to the point that symbols became almost definitional of what many people think they are supposed to find in a literary text and what they expect to hear about from English classes and English teachers. The concept of symbols seems ready-made for new criticism because a repeated symbol (Hawthorne's scarlet letter, Herman Melville's great white whale, Homer's rosy-fingered dawn) makes a pattern and because patterns and symbols lend themselves to the new critics' commitment to interpretation. It has reached the point where we might say, without much fear of exaggeration, that generations of high school students and beginning college students terrified of their English classes have learned that the safe path through the gauntlet of interpretation is to play a game of *find the symbol*. If they fear their English class, they need only to find a symbol, and then everything will turn out ok. We can often hear the pride in achievement when beginning students start to talk about symbols, and they deserve credit for learning the lesson that English teachers have taught them. But by the time students get to college—or beyond (for the symbol treasure hunt sometimes continues into graduate school and professional criticism)—they owe it to themselves to set a more challenging goal. The best criticism has little to do with that kind of symbol mongering, so it is now long past time for teachers to tell their students, at least once they get past high school, that the resort to symbols as a crank that they can turn to produce an interpretation has come to seem like a parody of literary criticism more than an enactment of literary criticism.

The problem comes in the assumption that a symbol bears a one-to-one relation to a meaning that it symbolizes. As it happens, such famous symbols as the scarlet letter and the great white whale bear anything but a one-to-one relation to their meaning, for in many ways the whole point of *The Scarlet Letter* and *Moby-Dick* is that readers cannot determine the meaning of the symbol, that it defies any one meaning. Moreover, it was exactly that ambiguity, that tension between competing meanings, that excited the new critics. The usual use of symbols in new critical writing, however, or perhaps even more in the imitators of new criticism, including the classroom discussions and the papers of generations of English classes, implies that a symbol expresses a single meaning that rescues us from the seething uncertainty of literary language, and in that way the usual search for symbols seems far too simple. Symbol hunting is a travesty of the mysteries of literary meaning and even, arguably, an over-simplifying travesty of new criticism. The way most people use the word *symbol* seems to suggest that they think they have solved and done away with the mystery of a text, instead of helping us see and participate in its mystery.

HISTORICIZING THE NEW CRITICISM: RETHINKING LITERARY UNITY

Some of the new critics were friends, but they were not a set group or organized movement. They were mostly Americans and often Southerners, though the new criticism has loose analogues in other traditions, including French "explication de texte" and Russian formalism (discussed in Chapter 3). Several influential British critics associated with Cambridge University, I. A. Richards, William Empson, and F. R. Leavis, often draw comparison to the new critics. Richards's *Principles of Literary Criticism* (1924) and *Practical Criticism* (1929) anticipate many new critical ideas. In *Practical Criticism*, Richards experimented with showing readers poems without the poets' names on them and then interpreting the readers' responses, a project that relates roughly to the new critical interest in focusing on the text itself more than on its cultural, historical, and biographical context. Empson's quirky *Seven Types of Ambiguity* (1930), written while he was an undergraduate, influenced the new critics' sense of complex literary language. F. R. Leavis, working closely with Q. D. Leavis, called for a close scrutiny of literary works that in some ways parallels the new critics' interest in close reading. But F. R. Leavis was more concerned with the social role of literature than the new critics were, and his critical writing, rather than providing the close reading that the new critics called for, favored broadly impression-istic evaluations about which writers and works of literature are "great" and which are not great. Some of the best-known figures more directly associated with the new criticism include R. P. Blackmur, John Crowe Ransom, and Allen Tate, as well as René Wellek and Austin Warren in a book called *Theory of Literature* (1949) that was often required or expected reading for English graduate students, though it gets little attention today. The term *new criticism* comes from the title of a 1941 book by Ransom. To my mind, however, the most influential new critics, through their critical, theoretical, and textbook writing, were Cleanth Brooks and Robert Penn Warren.

In 1938, Brooks and Warren published a revolutionary new crit-ical textbook called *Understanding Poetry*, which went through many editions and was soon matched by a corresponding book called *Un-derstanding Fiction* (1943) and another called *Understanding Drama* (by Brooks and Robert B. Heilman, 1945). In later years, Warren would become the only person to win Pulitzer prizes for both fic-tion and poetry, and he would serve as the first poet laureate of the United States. *Understanding Poetry* revolutionized the teaching of introductory poetry courses, but at first it met outraged resistance. Determined to teach the skills of close reading, Brooks and Warren organized their book according to principles of interpretation and poetic form, instead of according to the historical sequence of the poems and poets. To their detractors, they took the life out of lit-erature by dehistoricizing it. To their advocates, they cut back the drab recitation of secondary background information and focused

Cleanth Brooks (1906–1994) (left) and Robert Penn Warren (1905–1989), about 1980.

instead on the glories of the poems themselves and of the interpretation of poems. Their method came to represent the cutting edge of new criticism and gradually became the norm. For a generation or more, students trained through the *Understanding* books became the teachers of high school and college students and future generations of teachers. Brooks also contributed two key books of new critical interpretation and theory, *Modern Poetry and the Tradition* (1939) and *The Well Wrought Urn: Studies in the Structure of Poetry* (1947), which included his famous essay on Donne's "The Canonization." Brooks's book takes its title from a phrase in "The Canonization," and it perfectly expresses the characteristic new critical confidence in the polished completeness and unity of the works they saw as great literature.

In seeing works of literature as complete, unified, and ripe for interpretation through close reading of the words on the page, through what they sometimes called "unpacking" the figurative language of paradox, ambiguity, tension, and irony, and through image patterns and symbols, the new critics replaced predominantly historical criticism with what we call **formal** criticism or **formalism**, terms that sometimes confuse beginning students. To call new criticism formal does not mean that it is stuffy or wears an evening gown or a tux. It simply means that it focuses on the form of literary works, that is, on such matters as the literary structure and language. For the new critics, the focus on form meant a declining focus on history, cultural context, biography, and politics. The turn from history and culture is a lightning rod for the opponents of new criticism, who often misrepresent how the new critics actually understood the relation between literary interpretation and history and culture.

As readers will soon see, I can be highly critical of new criticism, but the common idea that new critics reject history and reject the study of the culture that literature comes from is so exaggerated that it is fair to say that it is just plain wrong. They were extremely knowledgeable about history, and they often drew on literary and cultural history as background to their interpretations of literature. But they asked for criticism not to focus on history and culture. They asked for criticism to focus, instead, on the literature itself (those words on the page). In focusing on literature itself instead of on history or cultural context, they implied that literature has a relatively independent existence apart from its culture. In the wake of new criticism, for many critics an interest in formalism came to seem opposed to an interest in history and culture, an oversimplification as unfortunate as the mistaken idea that the new critics rejected history and culture. In any case, the turn away from history and culture, partial though it was, has stuck out notoriously for later generations of critics.

Indeed, from the perspective of a later time (a time that Brooks and Warren lived long enough to see), a time far more interested in reading historically and culturally (as we will see later in this book), it can help us understand the new critics to read them with the resources of an interest in history and culture that, contrary to popular opinion, they did not reject but that they certainly underestimated. If we read them historically, we can see a relation between the new critical interest in form and unity and their relative lack of interest in the relation between history or politics and literature. That requires characterizing the most influential new critics.

The most influential new critics, including Brooks, Warren, and Ransom, emerged out of a group of conservative, Southern, white, male writers and cultural commentators at Vanderbilt University called the Fugitives (after their magazine, *The Fugitive*), who evolved

into a group known as the Agrarians. In 1930, the Agrarians published *I'll Take My Stand* (Brooks was not a contributor, though he
was close to the Agrarians), which attacked modernism and industrialism and called nostalgically for a return to the lost sense of
community and harmony in the preindustrial, agrarian South.

This nostalgic view of the old South should, I think, give us pause.
The old South romanticized by the Agrarians was not the long-
standing center of Western humanism, harmony, and community
that they imagined, influenced by the wave of turn-of-the-century
novels romanticizing the old South (soon to culminate in the novel
and movie *Gone with the Wind*). It was a land teetering on the edge of
slave resistance and class conflict. The unsteady profits wreaked from
that land, as the economy swung back and forth between frenzies of
boom and bust, depended on the forced, unpaid labor of black slaves,
and for much of the South (especially in North Carolina, Georgia,
Alabama, and Mississippi), far more than most Americans realize,
that economy fed off agricultural improvements made by American
Indians and their slaves. Whites stole the Indian-owned farms while
pressing the federal government to drive Indian people from their
land. The old South was not the idyll of humanistic letters celebrated by the Agrarians, isolated from the market economy, but
rather a place of riotous land speculation where most people, black,
white, and red, suffered horrendous poverty and had little or no
access to books and where an environmentally exploitive, revolv-
ing class of coastal entrepreneurs who desperately painted themselves as patricians and a newer set of inland upstarts eventually
cobbled together a generation of shaky prosperity before the Civil
War. The Agrarian movement, in short, was founded in self-serving
delusion and denial.

In the community of shared values that the proto-new critical
Agrarians imagined, people always knew their place and accepted
their place, but when I look around at my students or family, I see
hardly anyone whose ancestors fit into the imaginary world of the
Agrarians. In short, scandalized by the social disunity they saw around
them, fearful of what others might see as the excitement as well as the
dangers of modernity, the Agrarians called for us to return to a phony,
fantasy past where people always knew and accepted their place, but
where, in fact, only people like the Agrarians themselves might want
to go. And from there it appears that they projected their deluded
vision of social unity, and of escape from the strife of contemporary
culture, onto a model of literature and literary criticism that sought

to prop up their ideal of harmonious unity and divorce it from the cultural and historical cauldron that threatened their position of privilege.

And so when the new critics see unity in the literary text, whose unity do they see? By choosing not to give weight to social issues, they deny, or we might even say suppress, the role of social conflict in literature, as if the symbols and patterns, the paradoxes, ambiguities, tensions, and ironies, were all about language in a tunnel-visioned way that isolates language from history and culture. On the contrary, the language and literary form that the new critics so lovingly caressed have everything to do with ideas and social meanings that the words in that language and form represent, and ideas and social meanings have everything to do with language, which we use partly to express them, including literary language. Readers and critics can choose to pay less attention to social meaning, but they cannot fence it into the mere background of literature. Even the new critics' effort to exile social meaning carries (ironically) a social meaning, for it suggests their fear of the changing social world, of conflicts across race, gender, and class. Their vision of unity has no place, literarily or socially, for most of the rest of us.

We might go so far as to question the cherished notion of literary unity altogether. Unity is not something *in* a text, intrinsic to a text, but something we project onto a text if we follow a method of reading, like the new critics' method, that seeks unity. Readers can find unity in any text, if they want to. Even if it is disunified, that is a kind of unity. Readers can always find some connection between different parts of a text, if they want to see them connected. After all, the new critics' almost-audible sighs of relief when they marshal the panoply of paradoxes, ambiguities, tensions, and ironies into an orderly balance to prop up organic unity should tell us just how precarious that balance can look from another critical perspective. It might not look like balance at all. It might look like chaos, exactly what the new critics feared and sought to exile from the works they were willing to see as great art—as well as from their agrarian social fantasy.

When we see disunity in a work that someone else reads as unified, that disunity might come from a paradox, ambiguity, tension, or irony, or from a social conflict or a conflict of ideas, or from any variation in form. Here, for example, a stanza of poetry rhymes, and there it doesn't rhyme. Here a line of poetry follows a perfect iambic rhythm, and there another line varies the rhythm. In one place a story sees from a character's perspective, but in another place it looks from an exterior narrator's perspective or from the perspective of a dramatically different character. Here a play or a movie proceeds at a pace that makes the time on the stage or screen match the amount of time it portrays, but there it suddenly skips ten years. In one scene the cast faces the audience or the camera and the set shines with yellow light, but in another scene they face each other or the lighting bathes them in blue. Here a work uses colloquial language, and there it uses formal language, and somewhere else it mixes the colloquial and the formal, perhaps spicing them with shifts between italic and roman fonts, or shifting between dialogue and description, or jumbling together French and English. The possibilities that we can read as disunity are endless. And one instance of disunity will trump a pattern of unity, because as soon as we find one disunity, then we no longer have unity.

As readers, we can choose to put more weight on the unities we see than on the disunities, perhaps choosing to look at connections between different characteristics of a text more than we look at the disconnections, but that is a choice we make as readers. It is not an inherent, intrinsic property we discover in the text, but a preference we project onto a text.

Why care about the new critical infatuation with unity? Because the cultural habit of supposing that one goal of critical discussion must be to find the unity (like finding the symbol) hugely limits the possibilities for criticism, as we will see again when we get to deconstruction in Chapter 4. The critique of unity will also help prepare us to study deconstruction. (Indeed, readers experienced with later methods of criticism or readers who have skipped around in this book may hear the influence of reader-response criticism or deconstruction in this critique of the new critical notion of unity. While readers do not need experience with those later methods to follow this discussion, the critique of new criticism here gives a hint of things to come.)

In these ways, the critique of unity has everything to do with the critique of the new critics' turn away from history and culture, which went hand-in-glove with their idea of aesthetic unity. To most contemporary critics, the new critical turn from history and culture did great damage to our sense of critical possibilities and even our sense of what literature we might read. The new critics could only sustain their notion of unity if they focused on literary works that allowed them to deny the social conflicts seething around them. That made it possible for them to sustain the historical preference of most white men of their education and class for writing by other white men, to the exclusion of writing by the rest of the world. As the study of English has moved beyond new criticism, so also, in recent decades, has it vastly expanded the social range of literary works that critics and English classes read and study.

In the 1930s, when the new criticism emerged amidst the Great Depression and a fervor of political activity from both the left and the right, there was a burgeoning new interest in writing from beyond the traditional boundaries of race and class that had come to typify college reading lists. The new critics' narrower sense of what might make great literature helped put the brakes on that emerging receptiveness until the 1970s. Meanwhile, their resistance to political interpretation, especially to Marxist or leftist interpretation, had a quietist, antipolitical cast that fit well with the conservative, anti-Communist America of the Cold War 1950s. That itself carries a certain irony, since the new critics' fantasy of a retreat from modernist industrialism and back to a lost idyll of Agrarian harmony was anticapitalist, and the new critics might even seem like the kind of intellectual eggheads that 1950s anti-Communist McCarthyites scorned. Still, by separating the study of literature from the unruly politics that readers often found in plays, novels, stories, and poems, the new critics managed to contain (in the Cold War sense of the term, meaning to contain or limit Communism) ideas about art, literature, and literary criticism that might prove disruptive to conservative Cold War pieties. But as American politics changed with the rise of the Civil Rights movement, the war in Vietnam, and the growth of feminism, students, teachers, and critics increasingly rejected the new critical impulse to separate literature from its social meaning.

We might wonder, in these contexts, whether the new criticism has grown so maligned that a book like this may no longer need a chapter on it; indeed, this chapter differs from the following chapters in that it explains a method of criticism that most college students and other readers of this book will in many ways already know, even if they do not know that they know it. The later chapters, by contrast, will introduce methods of criticism that, perhaps with the partial exception of feminist criticism, are far less familiar to most readers. Because the new criticism now seems dated, I used to have a student or two in most critical theory classes suggest that we skip it to make more time for studying the later methods. Eventually I tried skipping it, and then many students complained that they missed it, because they saw how other methods defined themselves against the new criticism, and they believed—wisely, I think—that they would understand those later methods better if they also understood new criticism. As much as new criticism seems part of our past, therefore, it also has a way of hanging on and defining our present.

THE INTENTIONAL FALLACY
AND THE AFFECTIVE FALLACY

Two additional concepts from new criticism, **the intentional fallacy** and **the affective fallacy**, attracted great interest, and both help us understand new critical assumptions. The critic William K. Wimsatt, a colleague of Brooks and Warren at Yale University, which became the hotbed of new criticism, and the philosopher of art Monroe C. Beardsley introduced these concepts in articles reprinted in Wimsatt's book *The Verbal Icon* (1954), a term that, like "the well-wrought urn," perfectly expresses the new critics' sense of the literary text or any other object of art as a self-sustaining artifact almost complete unto itself.

A fallacy is a mistaken (fallacious, false) idea or belief or an error in reasoning. (If it helps, you can translate *fallacy* simply as "mistake.") The idea, once widely advertised, that smoking is good for our health is a fallacy, and it is fallacious to believe that if Jean is intelligent and good-looking and Terry is also good-looking, therefore Terry must also be intelligent. (Terry might be intelligent, but we would need something else to prove it.) *Affect* refers to emotions. (The word *affect* should not be confused with the word *effect*.) Wimsatt and Beardsley coined the term *affective fallacy* to refer to what they saw as a logical error or mistaken belief about how we determine literary meaning. They argued that critics should not let their claims for the meaning of a literary text or other artistic object be determined by their emotions. As intrinsic critics, they believed that a text's meaning lies within the text itself, not in our response to it.

This is the opposite of the later approach sometimes called *reader-response criticism*, which assumes that we know a text only through our response to it. (See Chapter 11.) Whether or not a text exists apart from our response to it (a separate philosophical question), we never experience the text as an intrinsic object independent of our response to it. Emotions (affects) are inevitably part of our response. For that reason, later critics usually reject the idea that an affect- or emotion-influenced response must be fallacious. They do not believe that we can respond to literature without including emotions in our response.

While the concept of the affective fallacy receives little if any support today, the concept of the intentional fallacy continues to wield a vast influence, but it remains controversial. Like most contemporary critics who feel a deep skepticism about the new critics, I nevertheless agree with them about the intentional fallacy. But for many students it remains a confusing idea, and so it will merit extended consideration here. Traditionally, critics simply took it for granted that one route to interpretation was to determine what the author of a text intended, and they took it for granted that there was a perfectly reciprocal link between the author's intention and the best interpretation. If we knew the best interpretation, then we could say that it expressed what the author intended. If we knew what the author intended, then we knew the best interpretation. Nobody questioned it, not even the early new critics.

But Wimsatt and Beardsley, drawing out the implications of the new critics' belief in the text as a verbal icon, and thus seeking an intrinsic criticism that relied on the text by itself, argued that it was fallacious to suppose that the author's intention and a good interpretation of the text are necessarily the same. While they did not object to critics considering what the author may have intended, as a way to raise possible interpretations that the critics might not have thought of themselves, they still believed that any argument for an interpretation must come from the text itself.

Though individual critics have never reached a complete consensus about the intentional fallacy (that is to say, about whether it is even a fallacy), the predominant movements in critical theory after the new criticism all agree, from their various perspectives, on the principle of the intentional fallacy. To put it in a nutshell, they agree that what we think the author intended should not govern our interpretation of a literary text.

Putting the principle that way allows a certain nuance. It allows us to consider what we think the author intended as an aid to interpretation but not as a determinant of interpretation. It also hedges a key issue by saying "what we think the author intended," as opposed to saying, simply, "what the author intended," and that is because we can never truly know what the author intended.

That argument leads us to some brief glimpses ahead to methods of criticism addressed in the later chapters of this book. While the methods described later in this book differ in a great variety of ways, they do not reach different conclusions about the intentional fallacy, even though they have a wide variety of reasons for continuing to believe that what we might think an author intended should not govern our interpretation. The structuralists turned away from the traditional interest in individual authors and called for us to pay more attention to broader structures of language and culture, which have patterns and directions but do not have "intentions." The deconstructionists, with their focus on multiplicity, would not grant the idea that an author has one particular intention, free of internal contradictions that might undermine any one intention with competing impulses in multiple directions. Like the new critics, the structuralists and deconstructionists advocate a formalism that calls for us to interpret the text itself, not the biography of its author. Psychoanalytic criticism, with its belief in what it calls *the unconscious*, would suggest that a great many forces swirl through any given mind, including the mind of an author, including unconscious intentions that may differ dramatically from conscious intentions. In that context, what an author says or writes or even believes about his or her intention may not be the most powerful intention directing the author's actions. And especially as psychoanalytic critics begin to combine psychoanalytic thinking with deconstruction, they may come to believe that intentions are often too multiple and contradictory to allow us to say, convincingly, that the author's intention was any one particular thing, let alone something conscious and visible to literary critics. Feminist, queer studies, and Marxist critics as well as historical and cultural studies critics may point out ways that cultural assumptions influence a writer's ideas independent of or even against what writers suppose they intend. For all these methods, then, we often do not know what a writer intends, and it often oversimplifies things to believe that writers even have specific and complete intentions for every question we might ask about the texts they write.

Sometimes it seems clear enough. We can probably agree that Emily Dickinson's intentions did not include flying to the moon. We can probably agree (though not everyone does) that she intended to write poems. We can probably agree that she sometimes intended to write emotionally intense poems, and funny poems, and philosophical poems, as well as poems in ballad form (lines in iambic tetrameter followed by lines in iambic trimeter), like the hymns that she grew up with. But sometimes it is not clear at all. It is much harder to say, with assurance, that she wrote "Further in summer than the birds" to teach her readers a reverence for nature. We might argue more successfully that the poem itself teaches such reverence, based on the new critical principle of evidence from the words on the page, with or without using later methods of criticism, as opposed to supposing that we can tell what Dickinson was thinking outside the poem, that those thoughts equal her intentions for the poem, and that the poem succeeds in realizing those intentions. Criticism based on what we suppose the author intended can end up looking more like biography than like literary criticism. Biography has its own value, and it can overlap with literary criticism, but it is not literary criticism.

Nevertheless, the cultural habit of supposing that we can know, and usually do know, what authors intend and that their intentions should govern our interpretation of their writing is so strong, has come to seem so intuitive, that the concept of the intentional fallacy usually takes a lot of getting used to. And the truth is that it takes a lot of getting used to for professional critics as well as for students. Many professional critics slide easily into the habit of the intentional fallacy, even when they do not mean to. Even the early new critics, before Wimsatt and Beardsley, routinely referred to the author's intention, without thinking about it or realizing that such references might undermine their notion of concentrating on the text itself. Every time we say something like "Hemingway simplifies his language to" do this or that, the phrase "to . . ." suggests that we know his intention and that his intention can determine our interpretation.

Let me give an example from my own teaching that can help illustrate ways to think about authorial intention. One morning, I was teaching Walt Whitman's "Beat! Beat! Drums!" for a survey class in early American literature. I knew my stuff—or so I thought. I knew the poem, the history around it, the biography around it. I knew that Whitman wrote it in 1861 at the beginning of the Civil War as a call to arms. In today's lingo, we might call it a pro-war poem. Here is how the poem begins (and it continues on in the same vein):

> Beat! beat! drums!—blow! bugles! blow!
> Through the windows—through doors—burst like a ruthless force,
> Into the solemn church, and scatter the congregation,
> Into the school where the scholar is studying;
> Leave not the bridegroom quiet—no happiness must he have
>   now with his bride,

Nor the peaceful farmer any peace, ploughing his field or gathering
   his grain,
So fierce you whirr and pound you drums—so shrill you bugles blow.
                                                          (Whitman 419)

One of the students started discussing the poem as an antiwar
poem. I knew it was not an antiwar poem. I knew that in 1861
Whitman fervently supported the war, and so I knew that the student
was wrong. I didn't want to say, "You are wrong," fearing that that
would hurt the student and frighten the other students, so I asked,
"What do other people think?" I was confident that another student
would have the right answer and correct the first student. The next
student chimed in with enthusiasm, but to my astonishment the
second student agreed with the first student, and then a third student,
and then a fourth. By this point, I knew I was in trouble, especially
because each student, having learned the lessons of new critical close
reading, with evidence from the text, that I had worked hard to
ingrain in the class from the beginning, came up with great, specific
evidence from the poem itself. Look at all the terrible things that the
war is doing in the poem, they noted. It bursts. It is ruthless and
forceful. It disrupts the church and the congregants. It disrupts the
school and robs happiness from a new marriage, and so on. All these
were terrible things, the students argued, with perfect plausibility,
and so the poem must be protesting the war. To my mind, the students' post-Vietnam way of thinking kept them from seeing that
Whitman was saying that all these seemingly terrible things were
actually good because they gave us a noble and needed war that he
thought the Union would win in a few glorious weeks. I found myself
wanting to tell the students that they were wrong and that I knew
they were wrong because I knew what Whitman intended, but I also
knew that that was a feeble argument against the excellent evidence
that students had offered. I didn't know what to do, and to tell the
truth I cannot remember what I did. But whatever it was, it went
badly, and I let the students down.
   Since then, I have thought a lot about that bad day in the
classroom, and the picture has grown more complicated and interesting than a mere story of shoddy teaching. Whitman first published
this poem by itself, in an 1861 newspaper. Later, as the war continued, he kept writing war poems, and they changed a great deal in
mood and manner as the war's brutality deepened and dragged on
and as Whitman saw the war's devastation up close, working inti-

mately to nurse the wounded and dying. After the war, he gathered his war poems together into a volume called *Drum-Taps*, and he put "Beat! Beat! Drums!," his first war poem, written as a pro-war poem, near the beginning of the volume. "Beat! Beat! Drums!" can thus challenge any confidence in the traditional idea that we can say what an author intended and use that intention to govern our interpretation of a text. For it seems that Whitman published the poem in 1861 with one intention and then published it again in 1865 with another, opposite intention. After the horrors of the Civil War, which his poems evoke so movingly, the textual details that my students called attention to take on a different meaning from the one that I had seen in the poem or that Whitman seems to have seen in 1861. It seems that in 1861, his poem anticipated possibilities for the meaning of its language beyond those meanings he seems to have been conscious of. In short, Whitman seems to have had more than one intention for "Beat! Beat! Drums!" He not only had different intentions at different times, in some sense he seems also to have had different intentions at the same time, including latent antiwar impulses in 1861 and a willingness in 1865 to look back at his pro-war intentions and expose them to the scrutiny of his later understanding.

In this way, Whitman's poem, my students' insights, and my sorry effort to teach the poem can suggest the oversimplification inherent in the usual confidence that we can identify a particular authorial intention and then use that intention to determine our interpretation of a literary text. Intentions often come in such multiple and self-contradictory ways that they give the lie to any one overall notion of "authorial intention," and they may or may not match what a text actually produces, which is likely to be as multiple and as susceptible to contradictory readings as the intentions that may or may not lie behind them. As it turns out, most of the time when critics slip into reasoning from authorial intention, they simply take an interpretation they like, suppose that it matches what the author intended, and then use the supposition about intention as evidence to back up the interpretation. That slippery series of suppositions can deter them from coming up with actual evidence for their interpretation.

When students first encounter the critique of basing interpretations on authorial intentions, they often feel at a loss. What is literature about, if it is not about determining what the author intended? How can we find evidence, if the author's intentions do not qualify as evidence? Those questions are not so hard to answer, once we think about them. Literature may relate to its writer's personal history, but it is not the same as the personal history. So the evidence must come from the literature. Perhaps it need not come from the literature all by itself. It may come from the literature in relation to the writer's life story (as we have seen with Whitman) and in relation to many of the other things that we will study later in this book (gender, history, economics, and so on), but the evidence still needs to come from the literature if it is to back up a claim about the literature.

It can help if we shift one of the usual questions that students ask (and that critics and teachers ask). The question often goes like this: What was she or he (the author) trying to do? For example, what was William Faulkner trying to do by telling the beginning of *The Sound and the Fury* through the mind of a so-called idiot, an adult whose intelligence has not grown beyond that of a small child? Or what was Gertrude Stein trying to do by repeating the same phrases so many times? Or why did e. e. cummings splatter his lines of poetry in fragments across the page? When students ask what the author was trying to do, they usually hit a wall. They feel stumped, or they leap to claims that they cannot back up, and then they feel defeated. I propose that instead of asking why the author did this or that, we ask *what the effect is* of this or that. Students who feel defeated by the question about intentions usually come up with a flood of insight, interpretation, and evidence as soon as we shift the question from what the author was trying to do to what the effect is of what the author (or text) actually does.

The debate over the intentional fallacy has exerted considerable influence in areas outside literary studies. Legal theorists often ask what the writers of the United States Constitution, or the writers of a particular piece of legislation, intended. They debate whether we can know that intention and whether what we suppose we know about their intention should influence how we interpret the laws they wrote. Should we confine ourselves to the meanings the Constitution had in 1789, when in most states only propertied white men could vote, or should their words carry different meanings in the changed world we read them from today? If the meaning can change, then how do we determine the changing meaning? Similarly, we often ask how we can interpret each other's actions. If someone hurts someone else but we believe that that person did not intend to hurt anyone, then should we still condemn, either legally or ethically, the person

Common Misunderstandings

It is often said that the new critics believed that literary criticism should not address history, culture, politics, and so on. But the new critics never said that and resented being criticized for saying it. They were deeply knowledgeable about and interested in history, culture, and politics, and they often addressed such topics as part of the background for literary criticism, but they did not believe that such topics should be a focus for literary criticism.

It is sometimes said that the new critics wrote mostly about poetry and took little interest in fiction or drama. While most of the early new critical writing focused on poetry and often on the close study of language that we associate with studies of poetry, the new criticism grew so standard that it came to dominate the criticism of fiction and drama as well, though new critics were less likely to use language-focused terms like *paradox* and *tension* when they wrote about fiction and drama and more likely to write about patterns of character.

It is often said that the new critics believed there is only one correct interpretation. While, like other critics, they worked hard to back up their own interpretations and believed that their method of interpretation was the right method, they did not banish other views of individual works of literature, and indeed their method's focus on ambiguity can invite other interpretations of individual literary works.

who hurt someone else? Should we forgive? Should we blame? The study of critical theory can help us ask these difficult questions and think through our answers, even when we disagree.

HOW TO INTERPRET: A NEW CRITICAL EXAMPLE

Let us look at a more extended example of how new critics might read. A new critic would likely see an abundance of paradox,

ambiguity, tension, and possibly irony in Wallace Stevens' "Anecdote of the Jar" (1919):

> I placed a jar in Tennessee,
> And round it was, upon a hill.
> It made the slovenly wilderness
> Surround that hill.
>
> The wilderness rose up to it,
> And sprawled around, no longer wild.
> The jar was round upon the ground
> And tall and of a port in air.
>
> It took dominion everywhere.
> The jar was grey and bare.
> It did not give of bird or bush,
> Like nothing else in Tennessee.
>
> (Stevens 76)

A new critic might ponder the ambiguity of "in Tennessee." Typically, we place a jar on a table, but "in Tennessee" seems almost
paradoxically too broad and unspecified a space for an act as concrete,
mundane, and small as placing a jar. The jar emerges as a symbol. It
changes the world around it, imposing order on the "wild" and
"slovenly wilderness." It seems crafted. As a synthetic object, then, it
can symbolize art. The ambiguous little jar grows into something
paradoxically, even ironically, grand, perhaps so grand that it is "like
nothing else in Tennessee," a state not terribly associated with the
history and lore of the fine arts. Ringing with the echoing sound of
extended, lengthy syllables in "round," "surround," and "ground," the
jar looms "tall and"—in a strangely exalted locution—"of a port in
air," so much that "It took dominion everywhere." Yet as a mundane
object, "grey and bare" in "the wilderness," this out-of-place synthetic
intruder can also suggest something more ordinary. Even the line that
speaks of it as "grey and bare" enacts the spareness that it describes by
squeezing its thoughts into one-syllable words (like only two other
lines in the poem) and ending abruptly, metrically after only three
iambic feet, when all but one of the other lines have four feet. On the
one hand, then, the jar symbolizes the exalted grandeur of art, and on
the other hand it suggests trash, even litter. As litter, it cannot "give
of," or seems frighteningly dissociated from yet still in the midst of,
the surrounding natural world of "bird or bush." A sustained tension
between these two opposite possibilities suspends the poem in a lyri-

cally balanced evocation of opposite poles in the human imagination, perhaps suggesting or even symbolizing the vulnerability of art and the potential beauty and grandeur of ordinary things.

In proposing such a reading, I have not asked what we think Stevens might have intended. Nor have I gone much into history, apart from noticing, at the risk of snobbery, a little about the reputation of Tennessee. I certainly have not crossed the line into seeing the suggestion of litter as leading the poem into environmentalist critique. Nor have I rolled the jar, or the anecdote, around looking for cracks in the poem's unity. I did not risk suggesting, for example, that the poem's sometimes oddly exalted language seems evocatively out of place with its setting or its ironic reveling in bric-a-brac. Instead, our sample new critical reading concentrates on how the form of the poem relates to its meaning and expresses an attitude toward art itself.

      *   *   *   *   *

The new criticism was a brilliant innovation in the history of reading, understanding, interpreting, and enjoying literature. It gave critics a concrete set of goals, and gradually, in the 1950s, it grew into the dominant way of reading literature both in published criticism and in college and, eventually, often in high school classrooms. New criticism grew dominant in part because it offered a concrete method for teaching English classes and publishing literary criticism. If students could read and interpret literature based on close reading, on the words on the page more than on historical knowledge, that gave teachers and students a concrete goal for what to accomplish in the classroom, and in many people's eyes it made the classroom more democratic. The teachers' greater knowledge of history no longer gave them such an advantage over their students. If all the students could have the text in front of them at the same time, then the students who had a better previous education and the students who had read more or who knew more history or literature had less advantage over other students who had the same words in front of them. After World War II, when American college classrooms grew crowded with students on the federal G.I. Bill, which funded college educations for students who often would not have gone to college in earlier times, a more democratic classroom method held great appeal for American English professors looking for a new way to teach a changed population of students.

Meanwhile, the new criticism also changed English professors' research. English research, as we have noted, was typically historical. But with the new criticism, instead of publishing historical research about literature (which took time and library resources that many professors did not have), they could publish interpretations of literature, which did not necessarily take much more research than went into reading the words on the page or perhaps the words on the page and other works by the same writer or the writer's friends. Gradually, the pace of publication for literary criticism accelerated. In the past, literary research was usually too time-consuming for professors to do much of it while teaching their classes, and they could not usually make much use of their arcane historical research in the undergraduate classroom. But once new criticism came on the scene, professors realized that they could publish the interpretations they developed for their classes. Suddenly, they could compete with the publication records of scientists. In research universities, the new criticism gave English professors a way to meet the emerging expectation that they "publish or perish," that is, publish research or lose their jobs. A vast apparatus grew up to turn the publishing of literary criticism into a full-scale industry, and for research universities and some colleges, publishing literary criticism came partly to define what was expected from English professors. Propelled by the rapidly expanding economy of the 1950s and 1960s, new books and journals of literary criticism sprouted like dandelions.

The enormous commitment to research had consequences for teaching. Many college English teachers cared more about their research (usually consisting of interpretation, whether it involved much actual research or not) than about their teaching, and their teaching suffered. On the other hand, many teachers found that their research inspired their teaching. It certainly changed what they taught, because as the new critical focus on teaching interpretation changed criticism, so, in return, criticism's focus on interpretation changed teaching, in an accelerating cycle. The hyped-up spiral of critical interpretation, combined with the increasing professionalization of the culture at large, ignited an entire institution of modern "English," with parallel planets in the various departments of modern languages.

But eventually, the very systematicity of the new criticism that gave it such power also started to undermine it from within, because it grew formulaic and predictable. Experienced critics and teachers got to the point where they could crank out uninspired interpretations that drained the pleasure out of reading instead of generating the excitement that many readers felt when the new criticism really was new. They could also predict what other critics might say about a text, before they even read what other critics actually said. Graduate students looking for something new and professors exhausted with the old sought out alternatives to new criticism and developed a distance from new criticism that enabled them to look at it skeptically, with the same intense scrutiny that they had grown accustomed to bringing to literary texts. It took time for alternatives to the new criticism to coalesce, but new developments in linguistics, anthropology, and philosophy began to reach literary criticism, and in the 1970s literary critics began to transform those developments into new visions of literature and literary criticism. That is the story told in the later chapters of this book.

As readers move through the later chapters of this book, the new criticism may continue to present a challenge, even if it seems like a dated challenge, for new criticism retains enormous power. In many ways, it has come to define criticism itself, sometimes making it hard to get beyond new criticism even if we want to. If we work with more recent methods of criticism, many readers, still under the sway of new criticism, will see only the new critical dimensions of the criticism we write. I myself would almost never use such terms as *paradox, ambiguity*, and *tension* in my own criticism, because they would suggest new criticism, even if I used them in a non–new critical way. And just as readers tend to project new criticism onto other, more recent styles of criticism, contemporary students and critics sometimes slide into new criticism even when they set out to do something different. Without realizing it, they repeat new critical strategies and assumptions, merely dressing them up in the vocabulary of more recent ideas. We might ask ourselves, as we attempt to draw on post–new critical methods of literary and cultural criticism, how much we want to go beyond the new criticism, whether we want to bring any of the new criticism with us, and whether it is possible to hold onto certain features of new criticism and still reject others. Do we continue to believe in close reading? Do we continue to believe in evidence from the text? How much weight should we put on the unity of a literary text? Can we cherry-pick from the array of new critical ideas, continuing such practices as close reading, without continuing the new critical politics that most readers of later generations find disturbing? These are questions that I encourage readers to keep asking as we move through the remainder of this book.

❧ 3 ❧

Structuralism

Structuralism was the first wave in the flood of change that revolutionized literary criticism, beginning in the 1970s, in reaction against the earlier and, by then, seemingly dated revolution of new criticism. While hardly any critics call themselves structuralists any more, so that structuralism, like new criticism, can seem out of date, even so, as the first wave in a torrent, it set up the model for future methods. Those future methods frequently respond to and draw on structuralism's most provocative ideas, making a familiarity with structuralism crucial for understanding what comes after it. Indeed, it is often hard to tell where structuralism ends and many of the later methods begin. For that reason, in introducing structuralism we will also begin to introduce the later methods of critical thinking that both changed structuralism and absorbed it. Because of those changes over time, we cannot say that structuralism is any one thing, but we can summarize its history, describe its general principles and many of its practical strategies, and take into account how it evolved from what I will call early or classical structuralism into structuralism as later methods of thinking reshaped it and made it their own.

If we boil structuralism down to one idea, it is about understanding concepts through their relation to other concepts, rather than understanding them as intrinsic, in isolation from each other. Already that tells how structuralism differs from new criticism, which sought to interpret literary texts as intrinsic objects apart from the world around them. In that sense, structuralism is always comparative. For structuralists, we understand everything by seeing its **difference** from something else. We interpret the world by juxtaposing different concepts against each other in what structuralists call **binary oppositions**.

For example, we understand hot and cold in relation to each other, by their difference from each other, in binary opposition to each other. We cannot see meaning in either hot or cold except through such comparisons. To structuralists, hot versus cold is only one of an infinite number of oppositions that structure our perception and thought, including north vs. south, left vs. right, up vs. down, inside vs. outside, on vs. off, and so on endlessly.

The principle of binary oppositions comes from the Swiss linguist Ferdinand de Saussure, the founder of structuralist linguistics, as part of his broader description of the overall system of language. Saussure died in 1913 without publishing the ideas that would later make him famous. His colleagues, however, drew on students' notes to publish a version of his lectures, uninspiringly titled *Course in General Linguistics* (1916). When the French Jewish anthropologist Claude Lévi-Strauss fled the Nazi occupation of France in World War II, he escaped to New York City, where Roman Jakobson (pronounced Yockobson), an influential Russian formalist and linguist who would emerge as a key figure for structuralism, introduced him to Saussure's ideas. Lévi-Strauss then used Saussurean linguistics to shape his studies of Brazilian Indians and of kinship structures, inaugurating what came to be known as *structuralist anthropology*. The French writer Roland Barthes then developed an interest in Saussure's ideas through reading Lévi-Strauss, and together the writings of Lévi-Strauss and Barthes, along with eastern European émigré linguists led by Jakobson, propelled the broader intellectual movement that came to be known as structuralism, which had enormous influence in linguistics, anthropology, and literary and cultural criticism.

Instead of describing particular languages or particular uses of language, like previous linguists, Saussure set out to describe the overall system of language. He drew a binary opposition between **langue**, French for "language," and **parole**, French for "speech." For Saussure, *langue* refers to the overall system of language, such as the rules of grammar, while *parole* refers to an individual instance of language, such as a sentence, a news bulletin, or a poem. Since structuralists, sometimes under the rubric of what they called *semiology*, would take Saussure's theory of language as a general model for understanding the overall system of culture, I will draw on examples that go beyond language in the narrow sense of the term. (The terms *structuralism* and *semiology* have different histories, but they are sometimes used interchangeably. **Semiology**, or **semiotics**, tends to refer to the structuralist study of culture apart from linguistics or literature.) The rules of chess or football or dating, for example, are the *langue* of chess or football or dating, but any given move or game of chess, football, or dating is an example of *parole*. In setting out to describe the overall system of language, the *langue*, Saussure began a model of systematic study that, as we will see, came to define structuralism. (The term *structural* can refer to any structure, such as an engineer's design or a bridge, but the term *structuralist* refers to the tradition of study that emerged from Saussurean linguistics, as described in this chapter.)

For Saussure, language is not, as we usually suppose, a list of words applied to objects. Instead, he saw language as a system of signs, with each **sign** consisting of a sound-image, which he called a **signifier**, and a concept that the sound-image represents, which he called a **signified**. For example, the signifier *cat* represents the concept of a cat. (The signified is the concept of a cat. It is not the physical cat,

Ferdinand de Saussure
(1857–1913).

which Saussure calls the *referent*. Saussure's lack of concern for the referent may seem difficult to understand at first, and readers do not necessarily need to worry about it, but the explanation is that he describes language as a process in the human mind, which generates sound-images and concepts but does not generate referents, physical objects like cats, dogs, or trees.) Saussure saw a firm link between the signifier and the signified, so that any given sign is not merely the concept it represents (the signified) or its representation (the signifier), but the two bonded together like two sides of a coin or a piece of paper.

The link between the signified and the signifier is **arbitrary**. We can notice the arbitrariness when we observe that different languages have different signifiers for the same signified. In English, the signifier *c-a-t* has grown so familiar that we overlook its arbitrariness and tend to suppose that it inherently evokes the signified concept of cat. But it only seems to do so because we have naturalized the convention of attaching the signifier *cat* to its signified. To signify the concept of cat, English speakers could just as well have chosen the signifier *dog*. Or we could have called it *pizza;* if we had, then over time the convention of referring to the signified cat with the signifier *pizza* would have become so naturalized that we would lose our awareness of its arbitrariness, and *pizza* would evoke catness as *cat* does now. But the structure of the sign would still depend on an arbitrary, conventional bond (represented in Saussure's drawing by a bar) between the signified and the signifier, rather than on an inherent, natural connection. (Onomatopoeia is a partial exception to the notion that the link between the signifier and the signified is arbitrary, but even for onomatopoeia different languages use different words to represent the same concept. While a rooster crows

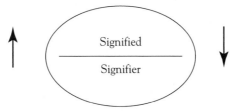

Saussure's model of the sign (signified and signifier).

cockadoodledoo in English, in Spanish it crows *kikiriki*, and in Japanese it greets the rising sun with *kokikoko*.)

We only recognize a signifier, such as *cat*, Saussure continued, by
processing its **difference** from other, potentially similar signifiers. We
recognize the word *cat* because it is different from *bat* and *cut* and *cab*
and so on, not because it has an inherent connection to the particular
signified that convention has attached it to. Each language has a
limited set of sounds, which linguists call **phonemes**, that its speakers
(people who know its *langue*) hear as marking meaningful differences.
English has about forty phonemes, linguists tell us, varying with the
speaker and dialect, but speakers of English have grown so accustomed to those phonemes that they are not conscious of them. It
could have worked out differently, such that we did not hear a
meaningful difference between the sound *cat* and the sound *cut* or
between *cat* and *cad* or *kit*. We apprehend the difference between
signifiers, then, by a conventional distribution of phonemes that
could have turned out differently and that to some extent has turned
out differently in different versions of English. Some English speakers
(such as Shakespearean actors) roll an *r* sound, but that causes no
confusion because we recognize two notably different sounds, the
rolled and the unrolled *r*, as the same phoneme. But in another
language, they could represent different phonemes, making a word
with a rolled *r* signify something different from an otherwise-identical
sound without a rolled *r*. Writing, Saussure notes, works the same way.
Two people may not write the letter *r* exactly the same way, but if we
recognize it as the letter *r*, then they both write it within the range of
possibilities that readers of English conventionally recognize as signifying the same concept. The writing system could have been constructed differently, such that the differing ways that two different
people write *r* could have signified two different letters. We thus come
to recognize signifiers, not because of an inherent quality within them,
but by their position in a system of differences from other signifiers.

To Saussure, then, **difference**—a system of comparisons and relations—produces meaning. Meaning is not inherent in the signifier.
On the contrary, it comes from an arbitrary system of conventions
that distributes the differences among signifiers. "In language," for
Saussure, "there are only differences," so that "language is a form and
not a substance" (*Course in General Linguistics* 120, 122).

Building on Saussure's linguistic model, structuralists contend
that we understand something by comparing it to other things, by its
difference from other things in a system of structures like the system

of language, as opposed to understanding things as essences sufficient unto themselves. Therefore, for structuralists, language itself, in a broad sense of the term that includes all systems of representation and not just words, constructs the things that we use it to describe. Language is not merely layered on top of something more important, like frosting on a cake or the cover on a book. Structuralists thus see reality as **constructed**, not as made up of underlying **essences** that language merely coats over or labels. This concept can take getting used to, because it can seem counterintuitive, since most of us are trained culturally to believe in an underlying reality, an essence, a pure signified independent of and separate from any signifier, independent of and separate from language.

In structuralist thinking, the world is not something that we discover. It is something that we produce, that we construct, through language. That is why in learning a new language we also learn a new way of seeing and understanding. The structures we apprehend in the world depend on the way the human mind imposes structure. To Lévi-Strauss, people across all cultures and times share a set of conceptual patterns or structures that guide human understanding of kinship, of "myth" or storytelling, and of all human culture. Each culture's kinship relations (who it calls an aunt or uncle or cousin, for example, or who it calls by a kinship term that may have no close analogue in English) or myths (stories) represent a **surface structure**, or *parole*, or individual instance of a broader **deep structure**, an overall *langue* or system of kinship relations or stories that all cultures share, and those structures are organized like language through a system of differences and binary oppositions.

Lévi-Strauss's ideas were vastly influential, but structuralism has changed a good deal since Lévi-Strauss. Rarely do structuralist-influenced thinkers continue to say that all people share a common, underlying human consciousness. Over the years, the interest in structure and difference that Saussure and Lévi-Strauss proposed gradually took on so much momentum that it overwhelmed the sense of a universal human deep structure in favor of a continually multiplying array of differences. Eventually, the sense of proliferating differences began to undermine the sense of stable systems at the base of structuralism. As the systems wobbled and then toppled in favor of more and more interest in differences, partly in response to the social disruptions of the late 1960s and early 1970s (the student and worker strikes in France in 1968, the war in Vietnam), structuralism evolved into deconstruction, the topic of the next chapter. The sometimes-blurry line between structuralism and deconstruction can confuse people new to these topics, because deconstruction, though it reacted against structuralism, nevertheless continued to use many of its concepts and terms. In a nutshell, structuralists believe in systems structured by difference, and deconstructionists believe in multiplicity, believe that the differences multiply so vastly that the systems unravel and leave only differences, without any systems left to preserve order. It would be easy enough to continue to describe structuralism without peeking ahead to deconstruction, but by glancing at what follows structuralism, we can better understand structuralism's limits and how it developed, and we can prepare to follow its momentum into deconstruction.

People who do not "get" structuralism sometimes suppose that the structuralist notion that the human mind produces the world we see means that for structuralism there is no reality. On the contrary, the structuralist idea is that reality is linguistic and structured, not that there is no reality but that we construct it, so that there is no reality independent of the language, the **discourse** that we use to construct it. Here *language*, or *discourse*, refers not only to words and grammars but also, more broadly, to all structures of perception, which, to a structuralist, we represent through words and grammars, through systems of representation. For structuralists, everything is **discursive**; everything is constructed. If you believe in a reality independent of and prior to language, then you believe in a **prediscursive** essence (which makes you an **essentialist**). You cannot back up that belief by offering an example, because as soon as you offer an example, you are using language and discourse. As we have suggested, it is not that there is a set of objects, a reality, and then language comes along afterwards and is spread on top like frosting on a cake. It is that reality is *always* linguistic, or, as the expression often goes, to get at basic assumptions of this sort, that everything is **always already** discursive, always already constructed and **mediated** by language.

Because this notion differs radically from the usual way most people think, students often have difficulty appreciating its implications unless they question it vigorously. Readers may choose not to accept this notion of language and discourse, but I suspect that they cannot disprove it. Some people dodge the debate about whether there is or is not a prediscursive reality by suggesting that if we cannot give an example of it, then it does not matter whether it is there or not. Regardless, it matters a great deal if everything is always linguistic and language is organized by a system of differences (or, as deconstructionists might say, more disruptively, by a play of differ-ences). How it matters will come across in a great variety of ways over the remainder of this book, with each later method following through the implications of this basic structuralist argument in dif-ferent but often complementary ways.

For the time being, we can start to glimpse how it matters if we think about different ways that people use language to describe what might otherwise seem like the same thing and how the different language makes that "same" thing come out differently. For exam-ple, if I say that when a reader interprets a poem, he pays close attention to the words, many people would think that my use of the masculine pronoun *he* to refer to all readers has social consequences, that it pays more respect to male readers than to female readers. A similar principle would apply if I use an expression such as "CEOs and their wives" or say that it is time for men to recognize that we need to resolve international disputes through peaceful negotiation. When one teacher explains an abstruse idea to students in language they understand and another teacher, across the hall, explains the same idea by using Latin expressions, phrases like "as you know," and a vocabulary that students do not understand, the different styles of teaching influence students' understanding of the ideas. That has social consequences if one style does more to reinforce a social sys-tem divided between those in the know and those not in the know. The different language for the same ideas has such different effects that the ideas are not finally the same. In short, language not only describes our world; it also produces the world it describes.

STRUCTURALISM IN CULTURAL AND LITERARY STUDIES

We are now ready to look at the implications of structuralism for cultural and literary studies. While structuralist literary critics paid close attention to literary form, leading some skeptics who knew little about structuralism to say that they were not so different from new critics, in fact they proposed a sharply different set of goals from the new critics, so different that the critical world, accustomed to new critical assumptions, had a tough time recognizing and processing the radical shift of structuralist thinking.

For new critics, the goal is to interpret the individual text. For structuralists, by contrast, the goal is to describe or interpret the larger system. They may simply describe the system, or at their most ambitious they propose a theory of the system and interpret the system. Indeed, though the founding new critics wrote a good deal of literary theory, structuralist theorists popularized the movement from literary criticism and literary interpretation to literary theory, a dramatically different enterprise from the usual new critical "reading" of an individual text.

To understand what it means to describe or propose a theory of the system, it can help to return to Saussure's binary opposition between the *langue* and the *parole*. A chart (structuralists love charts and graphs) may help us follow a series of terms for roughly the same binary opposition. Perhaps the clearest synonyms in English for Saussure's *langue* and *parole* are the *system* and the *instance*. Linguistically, a parallel pair of terms is the *grammar* and the *sentence* (where *grammar* refers, as linguists say, to the rules that allow speakers of a given language to make sentences that other speakers of that language can understand). Drawing on the terminology of the linguist Noam Chomsky, Jonathan Culler—whose *Structuralist Poetics* (1974) was the most thorough and influential account of structuralism for English-language literary critics—added the terms *competence* and *performance*, where *competence* describes the ability to process or produce language and *performance* describes the particular language we produce, such as a speech or a poem. Similarly, structuralists such as Tzvetan Todorov

Table 3.1. *langue* vs. *parole*

LANGUE[a]	PAROLE[a]
language[b]	speech[b]
system	instance
competence[c]	performance[c]
deep structure[c]	surface structure[c]
grammar (of language)	individual sentence
grammar (of literature)	individual text
poetics	poem (or other individual text)
theory of texts and textuality	interpretation of individual text

[a]Saussure's terms, in French.
[b]Saussure's terms, in English.
[c]Chomsky's terms.

have described the structuralist critic's task as uncovering a *grammar of literature*, as opposed to the new critic's task of interpreting an *individual text*, or as uncovering a *poetics* of literature, where *poetics* refers not necessarily to poetry itself but to a general theory, a theory of literature or of any other system. At the broadest level, then, structuralists can propose a theory of texts and of textuality itself.

But they do not always or even usually work at that broad a level, for they also take an interest in subsets of literature and in a vast range of cultural practices. For example, they might write about the grammar (or poetics or system, etc.) of poetry rather than of literature at large. Or they might study or write about other categories, smaller than or just different from "literature" or "poetry," such as sonnets, novels, comic books, wedding ceremonies, Gothic novels, buddy movies, chick lit, high school movies, horror novels or movies, slasher movies, Shakespearean comedies or tragedies, clothing styles, advertisements, zombie movies, political speeches, detective novels or movies, reality TV shows, baseball games, Halloween costumes, screwball comedies, professional wrestling matches, villanelles, restaurant menus, local newscasts, instant messages, haiku, romance novels, film noir, first dates, teen magazines, epic poems, college English classes, and so on through endless possibilities across culture. Whatever genre they study, they will try to reveal its grammar, or, as structuralists often say, its codes and conventions. And as structuralism increasingly takes on the broader task of interpreting culture at large, they may often think of those codes and conventions as cultural codes and conventions.

To take one example, let us look at TV shows. Admittedly, I am not up to date on TV shows and have no intention of getting up to date, but most of my students have seen reruns of the TV shows that I grew up with, so they can follow my examples. Readers who have not seen the shows I use as examples can fill in other shows and still follow the argument, since, after all, the point is that TV shows, like other cultural categories, follow a system that repeats itself. Let us begin with sitcoms ("situation comedies"). The genre has added a host of variations in recent decades (or so I'm told), and some shows, notably *The Simpsons*, routinely spoof the form, which requires knowledge of the form—of its poetics. The preeminent classic sitcom is *I Love Lucy*, which ran in 180 shows from 1951 to 1957, an era of sanitized feel-good family TV. *I Love Lucy* was so popular and such a staple of reruns that even these many years later, most of this book's readers may know its poetics intimately, whether they stop to realize it or not. We can uncover that knowledge, with its codes and conventions, and start to generate a poetics of the classic sitcom by teasing at the edges of the genre. Suppose that a long-lost episode of *I Love Lucy* was just discovered. We start to watch it, full of suspense, and then, at the thirteen-minute mark, Lucy gets lost. What will happen next? The answer is easy. She'll get found, or she'll find her way back. In short, each episode stages a problem before the midpoint commercial and then resolves the problem before the half hour ends. We know the form so well that we do not have to think about it, but thinking about it might help us come to know it better.

Now let's vary the scenario. In this version, we hit the thirteen-minute mark, and then—suddenly—Lucy dies. When I say that in the classroom, students typically react with a burst of uneasy surprise and a murmur of nervous chuckles. They have an adept competence as readers of the sitcom form, and so they know that Lucy cannot die. It's not in the form. It's not part of the poetics. If she did die, of course, then it would turn out that she had not really died, that she was only playing dead, or that some other character had made a terrible mistake, but the poetics, the conventions of the form, will not allow even that much. Playing with possibilities around the edge of the system helps uncover a poetics and set of conventions that we did not know we knew.

Or let's say that we hit the thirteen-minute mark, and then—Lucy has an abortion. Not possible, my students insist. Not imaginable— this is TV in the Eisenhower 1950s. Of course, women had abortions in the Eisenhower 1950s, but not TV characters, not national idol TV characters, and certainly not national idol TV sitcom characters, not Lucy. The form's conventions dictate that certain things can happen in a classic sitcom and certain things cannot happen. For one thing, no problem can arise that cannot be resolved at the end of the half hour. For another, there are unspoken rules or codes of social decorum or censorship. If we were to try listing those rules, we could learn a good deal about the sitcom form and the culture that it both represses and expresses. Later sitcoms, then, beginning with *All in the Family* (1971–1979), defined themselves by including what the earlier, classic sitcoms excluded. Each new wave of sitcoms, then, defines itself in relation to the previous wave. After *All in the Family*, things that were unimaginable in *I Love Lucy*—many of the same crises of social, political, and cultural strife that fill the daily news— shape the routine plots of many sitcoms while still speaking back to a recognized form inherited from *I Love Lucy* and its descendants. The dialogue between earlier and later sitcoms (structuralists might call it **intertextuality**, which simply means understanding one text by comparing it to another) allows us to distinguish, for example, between two different subsets or poetics of sitcoms, between shows that must resolve their problems in a half-hour frame and never refer back to the same problems in a later episode and other shows that continue to worry the same crises across multiple episodes or seasons.

Similarly, if we go a little outside the sitcom to, for example, the original *Star Trek* or, later, to *Magnum, P.I.*, what will happen if Captain Kirk or Magnum falls in love? Even viewers who have never seen the episode before but have seen other episodes in the series or other series like these will know the system and its conventions well enough to anticipate that the "love interest" (itself a structuralist category) will get killed off or sent away, because a rule in the poetics of the genre says that the hero has to stay single. In the same way, if Captain Kirk is captured by evil aliens, viewers know that somehow he will escape, and the episode plays off their knowledge of the genre to structure its suspense. They know that he will escape, but still they want to know how he will escape.

Several principles stand out from these examples. Students often ask how we can study the system without studying the instances, like a new critic. Actually, even a structuralist has to study the instances to study the system. Here we can draw on a classic philosophical principle called the **hermeneutic circle**, which says that to understand the part, we have to understand the whole, and to understand the whole, we have to understand the part. To describe the poetics of sonnets, for example, we need to consider individual sonnets, but to understand individual sonnets, we will also need to consider sonnets in general. Some critics will choose to study instances more, and others will choose to study the system more. We can turn structuralism to something like new critical purposes, if we want, by harnessing our study of the overall system (of sonnets or first dates or film noir or whatever) to the goal of interpreting the individual instance. And, as it turns out, that is exactly the more traditional option that many literary critics have chosen, retaining the fascination with readings of individual texts that the new critics provoked. On the other hand, the more we make the goal an interpretation of the larger system, the more structuralist our project and the farther we can get beyond new criticism. In this way, structuralism provides an alternative to new criticism or an expansion of new criticism, depending on how we work with the structuralism.

Students often ask how a structuralist can know whether a given instance fits into the system at all. If we find a long-lost episode where Lucy dies or has an abortion, then is it still really part of the *I Love Lucy* show, and is it still really a sitcom? And if we can't tell, students often wonder, then could that defeat the concept of a structuralist poetics? Rather than feeling defeated by the problem of odd or borderline examples, however, structuralists relish them, because the odd examples help us figure out the system's structure and boundaries. When we find an odd example, then we can enlarge the circumference of the system to include the anomalous case, or we can draw a boundary that defines the system by determining what conventions fit into it and what conventions do not fit into it.

In a sense, structuralists might say, the conventions, not the author, write the work. One episode of *I Love Lucy* is pretty much like another episode of *I Love Lucy*. The structuralist provocateur Roland Barthes (who gradually evolved into a poststructuralist) went so far as to write an article famously titled "The Death of the Author" (1968), playing off Friedrich Nietzsche's famous phrase "the death of god" and arguing that we would do better not to romanticize individual authorship. For Barthes (who, skeptics note, signed his article with his name), literature is written by the overall system of writing, not by individual authors. While many humorless authors were not amused, and while some critics would credit Barthes with exaggeration to make his point, the point bears taking seriously.

No writers make up, all by themselves, the system of writing—or of novels, plays, poems, or sitcoms. They inherit a repertoire of vocabulary, grammar, syntax, genre, and convention, and we might say that they do little more than rearrange the materials that they find around them. But as Barthes puts it: "The image of literature to be found in ordinary culture is tyrannically centered on the author, his person, his life, his tastes, his passions, while criticism still consists for the most part in saying that Baudelaire's work is the failure of Baudelaire the man, Van Gogh's his madness, Tchaikovsky's his vice. The *explanation* of a work is always sought in the man or woman who produced it, as if it were always in the end, through the more or less transparent allegory of the fiction, the voice of a single person, the *author* 'confiding' in us" (Barthes 143). We romanticize authorship partly to conceal from ourselves how repetitive it is, as part of our larger romanticization of individuality. But for Barthes, once the words are written, they take on a momentum of their own and trump the now irrelevant author. "Writing," Barthes says, "is the destruction of every voice, of every point of origin. Writing is that neutral, composite, oblique space where our subject [that is, the author] slips away, the negative where all identity is lost, starting with the very identity of the body writing" (Barthes 142). Drawing on Marxism as well as structuralism, Barthes saw the fascination with individual agents as a way of concealing the overall economic system's powerful way of reproducing itself. In the wake of Barthes's argument, criticism has often focused less on individual authors—or, to put it less romantically, on individual writers—and more on the social forces engaged in many writers' production of literature.

Readers who dismiss Barthes's notion of the death of the author might look at it differently if they think about how students in class discussions often refer to the author, not by name or as *she* or *he*, but as *they*. The habit of referring to the author as *they* can irk teachers. Since teachers often know more than students about the author's life and writings, teachers usually have more sense of who the author was than students have. But students who refer to the author as *they* are on to something nevertheless. They sense that authors do not write by themselves, that the production of literature is collaborative and social. In that way, a work of literature represents not only a single personality but also a cultural world.

I like to invite students—and here I will invite readers—into one more extended example: the detective novel. Before you read past this paragraph, I invite you to pretend that you have just read a hundred detective novels. Then, based on your (imaginary) sample, jot down a few characteristics you would find in more or less all one hundred novels (or detective TV shows or movies). Do not worry about odd or uncharacteristic examples, which we will get to later.

First (now that you have jotted down your list of characteristics), let us complicate the task by drawing on another structuralist binary to organize our poetics, or grammar, of the detective novel. Following a binary opposition described by Saussure, structuralists distinguish between the **synchronic** and the **diachronic**. Technically, a synchronic approach considers a language, or some other system, at one time (as suggested by the combination of "syn" and "chronic"), whereas a diachronic approach works chronologically and so considers how a language, or some other system, changes over time. In effect, however, I find it more useful to think of a synchronic approach, more radically, as proceeding without regard to time, vs. a diachronic approach, which works chronologically and so depends on time. For example, if I say, "I eat too much candy and junk food," then I am providing a synchronic description, because I am not addressing when I eat it or in what sequence of events I do the eating. But if I say, "Yesterday I had a couple candy bars before dinner and then crunched down a bag of potato chips before I went to sleep, but today the only thing I've eaten between meals is fresh fruit," then I have offered a diachronic description. In the same way, we might describe a novel synchronically by saying that it has three major characters from three different walks of life, with witty dialogue and lyrical description, whereas we might describe the same novel diachronically by saying that it begins with a romantic courtship that then gets broken up by a secretive stranger, who later turns out to be the long-lost mother of the heroine, but after the stranger is forced to leave, the heroine returns to her earlier love, only to find . . . , and so on. Our poetics of the detective novel can help sharpen the distinction between synchronic and diachronic. You might try sorting your list of characteristics of the detective novel into synchronic characteristics and diachronic characteristics.

Let us begin with the synchronic, with features of the detective novel that are not related to time. Of course, we need a detective. We also need a dead body (or at least a crime, but in a detective novel the typical crime is a murder, which produces a dead body). We also need suspects, a murderer, false leads (also called *feints* or *unreliable clues*), a motive, and a weapon. (Think of the board game "Clue.") If your list includes a femme fatale, then you were thinking of hard-boiled detective novels, a classic American genre; if it included a country house, then you were thinking of classic British detective novels. Each of those categories then becomes a subset within the larger category of detective novels. The same applies if you said that the detective novel has a Watson figure (after Dr. Watson, who recounts the adventures of his friend Sherlock Holmes). Some detective novels have a Watson figure, but most don't, so again we could see Watson-narrated novels as a subset of detective novels at large, which pretty much always have the items on our list. Already, as we sort what belongs on the list and what does not belong on it, we are refining and expanding our poetics, drawing circles within circles and producing a series of branches in the tree of possibilities. On the other hand, if you said that we discover the murderer at the end, then by saying *when* we discover the murderer you have introduced a diachronic feature.

For a single novel, it is easy enough to say, diachronically, that this happens and then that happens later. But for an entire genre of novels, describing the diachronic features gets more complicated. We might hypothesize that we find the body before we resolve who the murderer is, with the term *before* bringing in diachrony. If readers object to this hypothesis by noting that in a few novels we learn who the murderer is before we find the body, then I will grant those exceptions, but note, again, that we will hold off on uncharacteristic examples until later. Having made the initial observation, however, that we ordinarily find the victim before we find the perp, we are ready to move on to exceptions, which will show why quirky examples, instead of frustrating the project, as beginners often suspect, can advance the project by helping us elaborate our poetics. Since our interest in a novel that reveals the murderer before it reveals the murder comes partly through the way that it plays off the standard expectation, we can see that part of the interest in reading a detective novel depends on our competence in the poetics, conscious or not, which intensifies the interest in making that poetics, or grammar, explicit. Novels that reveal the murderer before they reveal the murderee, then, form a secondary subset of the poetics, like novels with a femme fatale, a country house, or a Watson-model narrator. Pursuing the diachronic characteristics further, we can suggest that if we get the murderer earlier, then we typically get the methods of murder later, whereas, reciprocally, if we learn the methods earlier, then we typically learn the murderer later. Either way, the reciprocal ratio between fingering the murderer and fingering the methods of murder allows a novel to draw out its mystery and continue the suspense.

Then suppose that we read a 101st novel, and it violates the grammar. That leaves us a choice. We can decide that it is not a detective novel, or we can revise our grammar of the detective novel. Perhaps, in the 101st novel, we never learn who the murderer is or never learn for certain. Or suddenly the victim stands up and talks, proving that he or she was not a dead body after all, but only seemed dead, like Falstaff in Shakespeare's *Henry IV*. Then we can refine our grammar. We might even say that instead of requiring a dead body, a detective novel needs a seemingly dead body. Then we can write a branch in the grammar, distinguishing between seemingly dead bodies that stay dead and seemingly dead bodies that pop back up and turn out to be alive. The popper-uppers themselves might branch into different categories, such as fakers vs. sleepers. Each branch has the potential to define the distinguishing characteristics of a particular novel or subset of novels and to provoke additional novels that talk back to it intertextually.

But if we reach a point where the branch takes so abrupt a twist that it no longer seems to belong to the same tree, then it has at least helped us decide where to draw the borders of the genre. Perhaps it takes us outside the detective novel, the whodunit, and to one of its cousins, the crime novel or the thriller. Or perhaps it turns out so differently that we end up placing it among more distant relatives, such as science fiction novels or historical novels or so-called literary fiction. Or it may take us to that kind of novel that works in more than one genre at the same time. For all these reasons, when we chart a poetics we often take special interest in borderline examples. They help tell us what defines the categories on each side of the border; and because they speak back to the genre and its poetics with intertextual gumption, we enjoy them. When a detective novelist came up with a narrator who turned out, at the end, to be the murderer, there was an uproar. (I won't name the novel, because I don't want to spoil it for people who haven't read it.) While some readers felt cheated, others realized that the novelist had talked back to the genre and revealed something about it that readers had not realized that they knew, namely, that the grammar that calls for a detective novel to have a murderer or the grammar that says that a subset of detective novels have a character-narrator should actually say a murderer who is not the narrator and a character-narrator who is not the murderer. The exception reveals the rule, and so, rather than toppling the system, exceptions hold special interest for the way they reveal the system.

While many readers find a poetics like this fun, thought-provoking, and illuminating about the detective novel and about the structure of novels and of literature in general, many readers—including some of the same people—find such structuralist descriptions limited for their lack of address to social concerns. Like the new critics, the structuralists have attracted criticism for a formalism that can seem isolated from the social world. But the history of structuralism is far more complicated, and Barthes's work, especially, often had much to say about the social world and popular culture. As anthropologists, Lévi-Strauss and his followers wrote directly about the social world on a large scale. The early literary structuralists, nevertheless, with their charts and graphs and neomathematical formulas, often produced work that many readers found arid and sterile. Binary oppositions like north vs. south, left vs. right, up vs. down, inside vs. outside do not seem to matter much to the problems and pleasures that energize our daily lives. Even so, the dry literary structuralism that did little to address the social world was a brief phase confined mainly to a few innovators and their followers in the late 1960s and early 1970s, a phase that we might call *classical* structuralism. As structuralism evolved, however, it usually merged with the methods discussed later in this book. When later cultural and literary critics think of binaries, for example, they more often choose culturally loaded examples, sometimes including binaries that change over time, or that we might want to change, or binaries that we disagree over how to interpret, such as feminine and masculine, wealthy and poor, more powerful and less powerful, queer and straight, and colonizer and colonized. In that light, such binaries as inside versus outside, north versus south, or east versus west no longer refer merely to abstract structures of opposition. Inside versus outside can carry suggestions about gender, while north versus south or east versus west can evoke geographical and cultural conflicts. Binaries no longer look simply like abstract facts. Instead, they are loaded cultural codes that people contest and seek to stabilize or change.

The poetics of the detective novel would shift if we asked a different set of questions from those that structuralists asked or if we combined structuralist questions with questions driven by social or psychological inquiries. To start thinking about alternative questions—even without having much space here to answer them—we might ask, for example, are the typical murder victims in detective novels from the same walks of life as typical murder victims in the culture at large? In the United States, murder victims are disproportionately urban, poor, juveniles, and people of color. That hardly seems true of murder victims in American detective novels. Perhaps detective novels then, obsessed though they seem to be with uncovering facts, are also dedicated, without even realizing it, to covering up other facts. How might such a pattern have developed, and how has it changed or stayed the same over time as the demography of detective novel writers and readers has changed? Detective novels seem preoccupied with guilt, law, transgression, punishment, escape, and curiosity. They also seem preoccupied with the value of individual life and the blame of individual murderers, for in detective novels the victims are individuals, not the broad swathes of the population killed by tobacco, by drunken driving, by unequal access to health care, by pollution or war, and the blame falls on individual murderers, as opposed to seeing the murderers themselves as victims of a social process. What do these preoccupations tell us? (What list of preoccupations might you come up with for another genre that interests you, such as science fiction, romance novels, or slasher or zombie films, and what would that list tell us?) As many readers have noticed, detective novels also seem obsessed with voyeurism, as in the very term *private eye*. Through that obsession, they release and, arguably, they constrain an abusive, antisocial desire, implying a likeness or connection between the impulses to look, to watch, and to kill. Through such mechanisms, a Marxist might argue that the detective novel fits snugly into capitalist ideology by condensing blame onto bad individuals instead of distributing it to social and economic causes.

In the same way that the early, classical structuralists were accused of slighting social meanings, they were also accused of slighting diachrony and history. In several respects, that accusation seems distorted. While Saussure's lectures focused on the synchronic rather than the diachronic and historical, his critics usually neglect that Saussure's colleagues never published his lectures on historical linguistics, which probably had more to say about diachrony. In any case, structuralism can work historically and diachronically as well as synchronically. We have already seen ways to gain insight into the structure of detective novels by noting their diachronic features, and we have seen how studying the conventions of the sitcom can show how later sitcoms speak back to earlier sitcoms intertextually, in the same way that later detective novels speak back to earlier detective novels. Similarly, the Russian formalists provided models for thinking in structuralist terms about history, and an active subset of structuralism has focused on studying narrative, which, by recounting an onward-moving series of events, has everything to do with diachrony.

Roughly, the Russian formalists offered an analogue to the Anglo-American new critics, in the limited sense that they shared an interest in formalist ways to read. But the new critics did not know about the formalists, who came to prominence two or three decades earlier and long remained little known beyond Russian-reading audiences. Sometimes, as well, the formalists took more interest than the new critics in bringing formalist ideas together with historicist ideas. Perhaps the most famous Russian formalist idea is Victor Shklovsky's notion of **defamiliarization** (*ostranenie* in Russian, sometimes translated more literally as "estrangement"). Defamiliarization refers to the way that literature, especially realist or satirical literature, can take familiar things and refresh our perspective on them. For example, when Emily Dickinson describes a bat as "a small Umbrella quaintly halved" (Dickinson 536), she helps us see something familiar in a fresh way that recovers a sense of its strangeness. Similarly, in Susan Glaspell's play *Trifles*, the male investigators see no meaning in the commonplace domestic details of Minnie Wright's life, but when women see the same details, they find them rife with meaning, defamiliarizing the disarray of Minnie's housekeeping to uncover the story of her marriage and her reasons for killing her husband. For Shklovsky, defamiliarization exposes the formalist technique of literature, "baring the device" (the form) and making us more aware of what the literature represents and of the literariness in literary writing. Later, the Russian formalists and their intellectual descendants helped bring Saussure and structuralism to a wider audience (as when Jakobson introduced Lévi-Strauss to Saussure).

Shklovsky proposed a formalist method for writing literary history. He argued that the system of literature changes over time by absorbing what may seem out of fashion and making it the new fashion. Shklovsky's model works from the classical structuralist notion that a structure is a closed system, changing by realigning its parts rather than by introducing something new from outside the system. In that sense, a structure works like a terrarium or, on a larger scale, an ecosystem. Jakobson later described a similar process as a "change of dominant," meaning that the going trend shifts from one dominant to another. The less dominant characteristics do not disappear but instead, as in Shklovsky's model, shift back and forth between times of increased dominance and times of decreased dominance. We might illustrate Shklovsky's hypothesis by the history of English-language poetic style and—to see more than one kind of text and system—by the history of women's hemlines.

Let us start with eighteenth-century neoclassical poetry, most famously represented by the poetry of Alexander Pope. Pope's language was elite, learned, conspicuously witty and ornate. Wordsworth, the great Romantic poet, famously reacted against the style that Pope typified, seeking instead a plain language of ordinary speech. Then the Victorians, such as Alfred, Lord Tennyson, and Dante Gabriel Rossetti, returned to an elite language, more lyrical and less witty than Pope's language but still, like Pope's, conspicuously ornate and poetic. Then the Imagists continued the pattern by reacting against what they saw as the falsity of poetic language by paring their poetry down to its barest bones. Soon after the Imagists, such high modernist poets as T. S. Eliot and the later Ezra Pound again made poetic language famously elaborate and arcane. And after modernism, in our postmodern time, the pendulum of history that

Shklovsky and Jakobson describe played out another variation, rejecting the by-then-predictable movement back and forth in favor of a postmodern eclecticism that courts all styles at once. The story of hemlines looks much the same. Over the twentieth century, they repeatedly bounced up and then down, and now they go every which way, at least when women wear skirts or dresses at all, as opposed to the hemlines of contemporary women's pants, which also vary.

Whether for poetry or skirts, the pendulum theory of how systems operate tells a good story and offers helpful historical insight. Even so, the formalist and structuralist model of history's swings back and forth has notable limits. No system is ever closed from the world or free to operate independently. Hemlines yo-yoed up and down not simply because of a law requiring them to reverse the dominant. They rose during World Wars I and II because so much cloth went into uniforms that there wasn't as much for skirts. Historically, then, the structuralist sense of an isolated system responding to internal, merely formalist laws can help describe the system but is not sufficient to describe it, for the social world has a way of cracking the boundaries of the system. This does not mean that we have to throw out the structuralist model, but it complicates the model. At the least, we need to enlarge the system to accommodate social history, which may prove much harder to describe by a predictably repeating set of rules. Similarly, the neat story of changing poetic diction over the centuries, taught to generations of students and regularly updated as the generations march onward, tells a reasonably accurate story of canonical, men's poetry but not so accurate a story of poetry at large. Now that critics are rewriting literary history to include the poetry of women and nonelite, working-class poets, the old story no longer holds up for so broad a field as the history of English-language poetry, where multiple styles have always coexisted, long before the

---

History of English-Language Poetic Style

Pope ⟶ Wordsworth ⟶ Tennyson, Rossetti ⟶ Imagism ⟶ Eliot ⟶ postmodernism

neoclassical ⟶ Romantic ⟶ Victorian ⟶ Imagist ⟶ high modernist ⟶ postmodernist self-conscious eclecticism of postmodernism. Structuralism can help us historicize, then, but in the process we need to make the structuralism flexible, need to make it as hard to predict as history itself.

THE STRUCTURALIST STUDY OF NARRATIVE: NARRATOLOGY

The structuralist study of narrative is called **narratology**. While narratology can lead to insight into individual narratives, and we may choose to use it that way, most narratologists, as structuralists, concentrate their attention on producing broader descriptions of a system. They describe the ways that narratives work in general or the ways that certain kinds of narratives work (the detective novel, for instance). They have two particular focuses: (1) what I will call **the tale and the telling** and (2) what is often called **narration**.

The tale is the sequence of events in the order they take place, and the telling is the sequence of events in the order they are told. In a story, the telling often follows a different sequence from the tale, because storytellers do not always begin at the beginning or end at the end. Instead, a telling flashes back and flashes forward. The tale includes all the events, but a telling must leave some things out, producing gaps (also called *ellipses* or *lacunae*). Wherever we can find a difference between the tale and the telling, we can ask what difference it makes to the story, to its art and its meaning, that the telling follows its own sequence instead of the sequence of the tale or some other sequence, a question that can give us a powerful way to interpret a story. In any story, the sequence of the telling is loaded with cultural codes and assumptions.

Jane Austen's novel *Pride and Prejudice* begins with a sentence pronouncing "It is a truth universally acknowledged, that a single man in possession of a good fortune, must be in want of a wife" and then swiftly moves to dialogue: "'My dear Mr. Bennet,' said his lady to him one day, 'have you heard that Netherfield Park is let at last?'" (Austen). Each of these sentences is rife with suggestiveness for structuralist and narratological interpretation. In some ways, the novel begins at the beginning, for after we have read the novel, we could say that the letting (renting) of Netherfield Park sets the story in motion. But the beginning launches an armada of questions. What effect does it have that the novel's telling begins there, as opposed,

A Tale of Terms

Different critics often choose different terms for what I am calling the tale and the telling, and the differences lead to confusion. Most readers will not need to know the other terms, but some readers, especially those who may continue to read structuralist criticism and theory, will come across the other terms, so for those readers it may be worth mentioning, briefly, the best-known variations. Like many structuralist ideas, the binary opposition between the tale and the telling takes its inspiration from the Russian formalists. Shklovsky and Boris Tomashevsky proposed a distinction between what they called, in Russian, the *fabula* and the *sjuzet*, terms that are sometimes used in English-language writing and that are rendered in English as *story* and *plot*. Those terms cause confusion, however, since story and plot seem similar. The linguist Émile Benveniste, and later the narratologist Seymour Chatman, proposed the much easier-to-follow terms *story* and *discourse*, while the eminent narratologist Gérard Genette called the same ideas *story* and *narrative*. I propose the terms *tale* and *telling* because they flow more easily across an English-speaking tongue and have a noticeable logic that makes them easier to remember.

perhaps, to beginning with a history of the Bennet family, or the birth of Elizabeth Bennet, or an exposition on the condition of lesser gentry, or an exposition on the range and limits of opportunities for women of the gentry class, or the history of Mr. Darcy (which the novel ekes out one bit at a time in an irregular and consequential sequence that turns out to be crucial to the plot and its suspense), or the story of Mr. Bingley, and so on? No narratological twist has to take the turns that it ends up taking. Instead, it represents a choice from an endless menu of narratological and cultural possibilities, a choice saturated with meaning and consequence.

The famous opening sentence of *Pride and Prejudice* did not have to come first, and it did not have to be in the novel at all. We could follow the story equally well without it. Had the novel begun with Mrs. Bennet's leading question, which starts the suspense going by telling us that someone new is about to arrive in the neighborhood, nothing would look amiss. But the first sentence suggests another kind of beginning besides the beginning of the plot proper that starts a moment later with Mrs. Bennet's question. The first sentence places the novel into a set of cultural codes, on the one hand with the forthrightness of raw announcement, and on the other hand with a directness so arch that it not only announces the code but also begins to tease it, potentially even to laugh at it. It also hints at a potentially tragic distinction between how such a code might play out for women, whom the code positions as objects, compared to how it plays out for men, its vaunted subjects. In almost sarcastically parroting the code's placement of women as objects and men as subjects, the arch tone has a way of making us think about the consequences of its gendered grammar (all the more so from the perspective of reading farther into the novel and then remembering or rereading the opening sentence). Such thoughts can resubjectify women and thus put under scrutiny the whole business of dividing genders into subject positions and object positions in the first place and also put under scrutiny the idea that such a code with its assumptions about marriage and desire, is a beginning that frames everything that follows.

This little example could be multiplied endlessly through many more interpretations and through every conceivable variation between the telling and the tale, or between multiple tellings in the same story (perhaps from the perspectives of different characters), or between any actual telling and another potential alternative telling of the same tale. The point, therefore, is that the seemingly simple rubric of the tale versus the telling offers an endless array of possibilities for interpretation, more than sufficient to carry a literature student through all the years of undergraduate and graduate study. And narratologists, ever hungry for variations and technical terminology, have charted a vast repertoire of variations in how stories play with the differences between the tale and the telling. The method carries suggestiveness not only for such obviously ripe examples as the novels of William Faulkner and the movie *Pulp Fiction*, which flag shifts in the sequence of the telling as part of their explicit method, but also for other novels and stories, films, reporting, conversation, and any other place where we find narrative.

Under the rubric of narration, we will look at four frequently discussed categories: focalization; direct, indirect, and free indirect discourse; narrative embedding; and narrative reliability. Let us start with the categories that are easiest to explain, recognize, and interpret: embedding and reliability.

Narrative **embedding**, or **nesting**, refers to what are also called **stories within stories**, cases where the narrative has a framing story and another story within the frame. Such nesting will also play high jinks with the relation of the tale to the telling. At the simplest level of description, a reader might simply observe that a given part of a narrative is embedded, but as with any wrinkles in the relation between the tale and the telling, readers looking to interpret the text can also ask what is the effect of the embedding. The frame or outside story, for example, might make us look at the inside story more skeptically, or the inside story might make us look more skeptically at the outside story. And if either wobbles, it can make the other wobble with it, sometimes setting off questions about narrative reliability.

The question of **narrative reliability** had already received a good deal of attention before narratology came on the scene, most notably in a classic of Anglo-American criticism, Wayne Booth's *The Rhetoric of Fiction* (first edition, 1961). Many high school and college students have faced questions about **reliable narrators** versus **unreliable narrators** (a binary opposition) without ever hearing of narratology, perhaps most famously with Mark Twain's novel *Adventures of Huckleberry Finn*. There, the white Huck decides that he will rescue his black friend Jim from slavery, even though rescuing Jim will mean, Huck believes, that Huck will "go to hell." Having been taught that slavery is acceptable and that helping a slave escape is stealing property, Huck believes that rescuing Jim from slavery is wrong, even worthy of damnation (literally going to hell). Readers, who presumably see that it is good to rescue Jim, need to understand Huck's world and his plight in different ways from how Huck understands them himself, even though Huck, who tells the story, is our only source. That makes Huck an unreliable narrator. In that sense he is typical of child narrators. When the narrator is a child, readers depend on the child's narration, yet in some ways readers usually understand the child's world better than the child understands it. Even adult narrators can turn out to be conspicuously unreliable, as in Ford Madox Ford's *The Good Soldier*, Albert Camus's *The Stranger*, and the many narrators, young and old, of Choderlos de Laclos' *The Dangerous Liaisons*. Critics often debate whether a narrator is reliable or unreliable, such as for Ishmael in Herman Melville's *Moby-Dick*, Nick Carraway in F. Scott Fitzgerald's *The Great Gatsby*, or Jake Barnes in Ernest Hemingway's *The Sun Also Rises*. In other cases, key pleasures or insights depend on understanding characters and events differently from how the narrator understands them, as in many of Dorothy Parker's stories or Edgar Allan Poe's "The Tell-Tale Heart" or Marlowe's tale in Joseph Conrad's *Heart of Darkness*. If we step forward from structuralism and peek ahead to deconstruction, however, we might draw on the deconstructionist sense of pervasive instability (discussed in Chapter 4) to suggest that there is no such thing as a reliable narrator. There will always be a way that some readers may choose to interpret a story differently from a narrator's way of interpreting it. Contemporary readers, for example, will often see race, gender, and class in sharply different ways from narrators of an earlier generation—or even of their own generation. And differences at so broad a level mediate different approaches to a narrative, both for melodramatic events and for mundane, barely noticeable turns of phrase and nuance, especially when we depend on a narrator to choose which events matter and how they matter.

In the same way as we question the concept of a reliable narrator, we might also question the common idea of an omniscient narrator. Many readers think of an exterior narrator (so-called "third-person" perspective, sometimes casually supposed to be the same as the author's perspective) on the model of an all-knowing, or omniscient, god. But just as we can question the reliability of any narrator, we can always find something that an exterior narrator does not know, can always find ways that we do not trust an exterior narrator's knowledge or understanding. Stories would be much simpler and easier to interpret if their narrators knew everything. Sometimes narrators act as if they know everything, and they may even attract our trust, more or less, but they cannot know everything and sometimes our trust can even lead us astray. For that reason, rather than calling more or less reliable and knowing exterior or third-person narrators omniscient, we might call them *seemingly* omniscient.

Questions about narrators and their reliability or omniscience lead to the related category of **focalization**, the narratological term for what was traditionally called *point of view* or *perspective*. Traditionally, when critics mention point of view or perspective they refer to the first-person voice of a character who narrates the story, as in the novels and stories just mentioned or in Charlotte Brontë's *Jane Eyre*, Charles Dickens's *Great Expectations*, William Faulkner's *As I Lay Dying*, Ralph Ellison's *Invisible Man*, and so on. Narratologists renamed the concept with the awkward term *focalization* partly to signal its difference from the traditional notion of point of view. Critics typically use *perspective* or *point of view* to signal whose voice narrates a story, but narratologists noticed that a character's perspective does not always come in the character's voice. Often, an exterior, third-person narrative voice recounts events by describing the perspective of an interior character, as in Henry James's *What Maisie Knew*, Gertrude Stein's *Three Lives*, Virginia Woolf's *Mrs. Dalloway*, and Leslie Marmon Silko's *Ceremony*. Whether an **internal focalizer** comes in first-person or third-person narration, the point to calling the character a focalizer is that the angle of mind comes through the character. Therefore, when we ask who is the focalizer, we cannot find the answer by checking whether the narrative comes in the first person or the third person. Instead of answering the question by checking whose words are used, we can answer it by checking whose *eyes or mind* the narration looks or thinks through.

Thus, to see how focalization works, we can ask *who is the **focalizer***. The focalizer might be a character (an internal focalizer), or it might be an exterior narrator. We might also ask who (or what) is the ***focalized***, the object of the focalizer's attention. Then we can ask what we can learn as an interpreter of that particular narrative by observing who is the focalizer and, perhaps, who is the focalized. What does that show about the relation between the focalizer and the focalized, and what does it say about the narrative? Is the focalizer consistent through the narrative, or does it shift? If it shifts, does it shift frequently or rarely, and how might that matter? What is the effect of the shifts? How can we tell a shift when we see it? When the focalizer is a character and the focalized is another character (as opposed to, say, a focalized object or idea), does the focalized character return the attention by looking back or thinking about the focalizer?

In some ways, every internal focalizer, also called a *character-focalizer*, is also the focalized of an exterior narrator-focalizer. It works that way even if, as in a first-person narrative, the exterior narrator-focalizer is never explicit and is only implied. In some ways, as well, every focalizer also thinks about herself or himself and is thus partly her or his own focalized. In any narrative that catches our interest, we can consider who or what are the focalizers and the focalized and what their relation to each other can suggest, perhaps in connection to whatever issues we especially care about in that narrative.

Let us return to Walt Whitman for another example, this time from section 11 of his long poem "Song of Myself":

Twenty-eight young men bathe by the shore,
Twenty-eight young men and all so friendly;
Twenty-eight years of womanly life and all so lonesome.

She owns the fine house by the rise of the bank,
She hides handsome and richly drest aft the blinds of the window.

Which of the young men does she like the best?
Ah the homeliest of them is beautiful to her.

Where are you off to, lady? for I see you,
You splash in the water there, yet stay stock still in your room.

Dancing and laughing along the beach came the twenty-ninth bather,
The rest did not see her, but she saw them and loved them.

The beards of the young men glisten'd with wet, it ran from their long
      hair,
Little streams pass'd all over their bodies.

An unseen hand also pass'd over their bodies,
It descended tremblingly from their temples and ribs.

The young men float on their backs, their white bellies bulge to the sun,
      they do not ask who seizes fast to them,
They do not know who puffs and declines with pendant and bending arch,
They do not think whom they souse with spray.
                                             (Whitman 197–98)

Here we might ordinarily—and reliably—say that the "lady," also
referred to as "she" and then as the "twenty-ninth bather," is the
focalizer. We could stop there and work with that idea interpre-
tively, or we could elaborate. We might note that the "twenty-eight
young men" are the focalized. We could also go on to note the first-
person narration as it shows up in the words "I see you," and we could
see the "I" as a focalizer with the "lady" as its focalized.

While readers might suppose that the "I" represents the exterior
narrator, the last concentric circle of narration, every narrative also
has an implicit exterior narrator, yet more exterior than the explicit
first-person "I." (Of course, many narratives do not have a first person "I.") Readers usually ignore or oversimplify the implicit exterior
narrator by thinking of it as "the author," not recognizing that the
exterior narrator may pursue ways of thinking that differ from what

historical evidence indicates the author may have thought. Most interpretations ignore the exterior narrator, but if we choose to pay attention to it, then we could say that the exterior narrator is yet another focalizer. The focalized of the exterior narrator's focalizing would be the "I" focalizing the lady who focalizes the young men. For every character-focalizer, as already noted, is also the focalized of a yet more exterior narrator-focalizer.

We could stop there. Or we might also observe that the lady implicitly thinks about herself thinking about the young men, for, as we have also noted, every character is partly her or his own focalized,

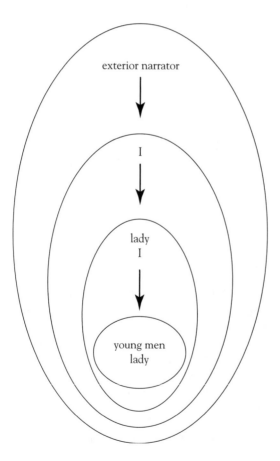

Synchronic Chart
of Section 11 from
"Song of Myself."

suggesting that the lady herself is another focalized of her own focalizing. Implicitly, the "I" also focalizes itself, but that remains far more distantly implicit than the lady's more visible gaze at her own thoughts as a focalized of her own focalizing.

Such a structure can be illustrated in the accompanying chart. This chart is synchronic. It does not show a chronological sequence. Potentially the "I" was looking at the lady before she looked at the men, for example, but that would be a diachronic feature not expressed in the chart. While classical structuralists would probably stop after completing the chart, later structuralists might consider its cultural meaning. The chart appears to sustain a cultural expectation that certain people look while other people are looked at. But perhaps it also rewrites or critiques the pattern. How does it matter, for example, that a woman looks here at men? Does that reverse a culturally expected pattern? What if we think of queer as well as heterosexual relations mediating and mediated by this structure? Is there evidence for heterosexual or queer identifications for any of these focalizing perspectives and focalized bodies? What difference might it make if we suppose a potentially queer angle for the exterior narrator, compared to a heterosexual angle? Or for the lady, or for the young men, or for some of the young men? For many readers, much of the interest in studying structures will magnify when we bring structuralist questions into dialogue with the methods described later in this book.

Focalization often has a close analogue in the way that film uses a camera and editing to encourage an audience to look as if through the eyes of a character, especially in the pattern of editing known as **shot/reverse shot**. A shot/reverse shot is a film sequence that alternates between a character and an object, implying that the character is looking at the object. Often, the object is another character, perhaps during dialogue, implying that the two characters look at each other while they talk with each other. A wider shot that directly shows the two characters looking at each other often sets up or punctuates the scene. The editing and camera work in effect funnel the viewer's eye into looking as if through the eye of the character or characters. In the same way, a verbal narration may set up a focalizer as a character whose view or thinking readers are invited to identify with (for better or worse, depending on the character).

Uncertain, flickering focalization often works through **free indirect discourse**, a style of narration that different critics call by different terms, including *free indirect style*, or, in French, *style indirect* *libre*. We can recognize free indirect discourse (FID) through its relation to its cousins **indirect discourse** (ID) and **direct discourse** (DD). Here, the term *discourse* refers to representations of speech or thought. DD is straightforward. It represents speech or thought directly, often in quotation marks, as in He said: "I love her." It can come without quotation marks, though in such cases the quotation marks are implied, as in He said: I love her, or He thought, I love her. DD can use the first person (I or we), though it does not always use the first person, because people do not always use "I" or "we" when they speak or think. ID is less straightforward but not terribly mysterious. It uses the third person (she, he, or they) to represent speech or thought through summary. The pivot word *that*, together with the third person, often (but not always) signal ID, as in He thought that he loved her. Free indirect discourse is trickier and more mysterious, which is why it has attracted critics' interest. Like ID, FID uses the third person, but it blurs the boundary between a narrator's language and a character's language, as in He was walking down the street thinking. He loved her. He really did. This time he was sure. He crossed the street, lost in his thoughts.

The great interest of FID comes because we cannot pinpoint the exact boundary between ID and FID. That interest might seem to reflect a sterile obsession with drawing lines. But in practice it can lead to provocative interpretation, because it requires readers to interpret the difference between, on one hand, the character's patterns of thought and speech and, on the other hand, the narrator's patterns. In the preceding example, the skeptical "This time" carries a different meaning according to whether we attribute it to the narrator or to the character. If we attribute it to the narrator, then the narrator can come across as knowing and the character as deluded. If we attribute it to the character, then the character can come across as wryly self-questioning, if still romantically enthusiastic. If the phrase read, "This time, confound it," or "This time, damn it," then we would know it came from the character, and the additional phrases would do more to fill out the character. But without those phrases, we measure the words against our surrounding experience of the character and the narrator, intensifying our interpretation of both of them. Such interpretation requires an alertness to a vast array of often-fluctuating and -contested cultural codes and conventions, such as codes that might tell us that certain vocabularies or turns of thought—including many that we might object to—are characteristic of a particular gender, age, region, education, race, mood, time period, prejudice, and so on. But those codes and conventions could come from either the narrator or the character, and either the narrator or the character (but especially the narrator) can also indulge in those codes mockingly. Readers find themselves hypothesizing interpretive patterns, supposing that a given character or narrator typically thinks in this way or that way and therefore that certain features of narration in FID hail from the character while others come from the narrator. The slippery boundary between ID and FID provokes interpretation even from casual readers who do not know about FID, though knowing about it can redouble the provocation. Indeed, in FID the boundary between structuralist categories gets so slippery that the study of FID slides structuralism into the deconstruction that we will look at more in the next chapter.

> Students often confuse focalization with direct, indirect, and free indirect discourse. We can use direct, indirect, and free indirect discourse to describe how focalization works, and we can use focalization to describe how free indirect discourse dips into and out of an internal focalizer's speech or thought, but speech or thought representation through direct, indirect, and free indirect discourse is not the same thing as focalization.

NARRATIVE SYNTAX, METAPHOR, AND METONYMY

The influential structuralists A. J. Greimas and Tzvetan Todorov, drawing on *Morphology of the Folktale* (1928), by the Russian formalist V. Propp, sought to describe narrative as like a sentence. Loosely summarizing this one part of their work, we can say that a sentence is a small narrative. It has a subject, predicate (verb), and object, and larger narratives also have subjects, predicates, and objects. The characters are subjects; the things the characters do are predicates; and the results (sought or achieved) are objects. Subjects can be divided among different kinds of characters, such as protagonists, antagonists, and helpers. Predicates can include such variations as going on a journey, learning, conquering, going on a quest, and transmitting a gift. Objects can include gifts, rewards, happiness, marriage, wealth, death. As the relation among subject, predicate,

Example of Narrative Syntax

1A Jane	1B interprets	1C the book	1D brilliantly.
2A John	2B eats	2C the sandwich	2D eagerly.
3A The dog	3B fetches	3C the stick	3D quickly.

and object shapes the syntax of a sentence, so a narrative also has syntax. This insight enabled structuralists to draw on Saussure's distinction between what is variously called the **syntagmatic**, or **horizontal, axis** on the one hand and the **paradigmatic**, or **vertical, axis** on the other hand.

Let us illustrate through a sample of three sentences (1, 2, and 3) with three sets of subjects (A), predicates (B), objects (C), and modifiers (D). We could substitute one subject for another from our pool of subjects (Jane, John, and the dog) and produce a sentence with the same structure, the same syntax, but a different meaning. Similarly, we could substitute one predicate for another, one object for another, and one modifier for another. Such movement within categories proceeds along the paradigmatic, or vertical, axis, whereas the movement from subject to predicate to object and, potentially, to modifier proceeds along the syntagmatic, or horizontal, axis (see Table 3.2).

The vertical describes a choice among elements (individual items) in the narrative or the sentence. John, for example, can interpret or eat or fetch. The horizontal produces the narrative: what

Table 3.2. Terms for the Vertical and Horizontal Axes

VERTICAL AXIS	HORIZONTAL AXIS
paradigmatic	syntagmatic
vertical	horizontal, sequential
analogy, similarity	contiguity, adjacency
substitution	combination
selective, associative	combinative
metaphor	metonymy

an object does to a subject and—if we use the modifier, D—how it does that. In this sense, we can keep one horizontal structure (one syntax of the sentence or narrative) while changing the vertical vocabulary, shifting, for example, from "The dog fetches the stick quickly" to "The dog eats the book quickly." Alternatively, we can retain the same vertical vocabulary while changing the horizontal structure, as in shifting from "Jane interprets the book brilliantly" to "The book brilliantly interprets Jane."

Roman Jakobson drew on the relation between syntagmatic and paradigmatic structures in his famous discussion of metonymy and metaphor, based both on abstract linguistics and on studies of brain-damaged patients who retain an ability to use either metaphor or metonymy but not both. Metaphors and metonymies are rhetorical figures. A **metaphor** describes one thing by something else that is not connected to it. A **metonymy** describes one thing by something else that is connected to it or part of it. In the classroom, I like to give examples and see if students can tell which are metaphors and which are metonymies. I might pick out a student and say that, in our class discussions, she is a real *spark plug*. That is a metaphor, because the student is not connected to or part of an engine. I hold up an 800-plus-page copy of George Eliot's *Middlemarch*, one of the great achievements of British fiction, and call it a *whale* of a book. Students recognize *whale* as a metaphor, because they can see that the novel in my hand is not connected to or part of a whale. I pick out another student and say, "I want to go out tonight but my car is down, so can I borrow your *wheels*?" That is a metonymy, because the wheels are part of the car. When pundits or bloggers calls for *heads to roll* at the White House, *heads* is a metonymy, because the heads are connected to, and part of, the people whom the pundits or bloggers want fired. But—to try a trickier example—we might say that *roll* is a metaphor, since heads are not connected to anything that will literally roll down the avenues of Washington like bowling balls. Even the expression White House could be a metonymy here, because most employees of the executive branch do not actually work in the White House, but some of them do, so that the phrase "the White House" has come, metonymically, to represent the administration overall.

Jakobson claimed that metaphor dominates in surrealist painting, and metonymy dominates in cubist painting; that metaphor dominates in romanticism and symbolism, while metonymy dominates in realism; and that metaphor dominates in poetry, while metonymy dominates in prose. For example, realism typically tends more toward prose fiction than toward poetry. If we were to write a realistic description of someone, such as the description in a novel, we might describe his or her bedroom or living space and use it as a metonymy that figures (figuratively represents) the person we are describing. A messy room suggests one thing about a personality, a sunny room another thing, and a meticulous room something else. We might also use clothing as a metonymy to represent the person metonymically, or we might characterize a particular body part to make it represent the person, such as brooding, suspicious, or cheerful eyes, a square or receding chin, twitching hands or a firm or feeble handshake.

The system is far from perfect. For one thing, a person with a messy room or sloppy clothes might have an organized mind, or someone with a receding chin might be more confident and assertive than someone else, who has a square chin. Such forms of represen-

---

Some Common Confusions

Confusion can arise because the use of the term *metaphor* as popularized by Jakobson's notion of a binary between metaphor and metonymy refers to a subcategory of the more familiar use of the term *metaphor*. In that sense, a metonymy is also a kind of *metaphor*, in the usual sense of the term *metaphor*, meaning a figurative use of one thing to represent another thing. Thus Jakobson's distinction between metaphor and metonymy distinguishes between two kinds of metaphor.

Confusion can also arise because many people already know the term *synecdoche*, referring to a figure that uses a part to represent a whole, and they often wonder about its relation to metonymy. A synecdoche is always a metonymy, but not all metonymies are synecdoches. When Christopher Marlowe, in *Doctor Faustus*, calls Helen of Troy "the face that launch'd a thousand ships," *face* is a synecdoche, and therefore it is also a metonymy. By contrast, when reporters write, "The White House announced today," the *White House* is a metonymy, because, as we have seen, it is connected to the president and the president's staff but is not part of them, so it is not a synecdoche.

tation may tell more about cultural codes and prejudices than about actual people. But that too is revealing, and it does not keep the prejudices from working figuratively in rhetoric, even in rhetoric that teases or mocks the prejudices. Having held up *Middlemarch* before my students and heard them agree that to call it a whale of a book is to use a metaphor, I then like to hold up *Moby-Dick* so that they can realize that calling *Moby-Dick* a whale of a book instead of *Middlemarch* changes the metaphor to a metonymy, because even students who have not had the pleasure of reading Herman Melville's behemoth know that it has, to say the least, a connection to a whale. Similarly, the lively student in my class may be a spark plug, and spark plug may be a metaphor, because she is not connected to or part of an engine. But what if my student is a robot? Then "spark plug" turns into a metonymy.

As the context changes and metaphors become metonymies or metonymies become metaphors, the structuralist confidence in categories may seem to unravel (especially to a deconstructionist). We might then ask why we should care about the opposition between metaphor and metonymy. While structuralists may have exaggerated the value of the distinction between metaphor and metonymy, recognizing it will allow us, at the least, to follow other people's references to it. A little more ambitiously, we can follow and appreciate the uses that other critical methods bring to the distinction, especially psychoanalysis. Along the way, a familiarity with the distinction between metaphor and metonymy will help us notice previously unsuspected turns and twists of figurative language in literature and elsewhere. (And for better or worse, referring to metonymies will allow us to describe what we notice in a cool and sophisticated-sounding way.)

*   *   *   *   *

By now, as readers approach the end of this chapter on structuralism, they may feel overwhelmed with terms and categories and wonder how they can remember them all, let alone use them. While this chapter confines itself to the basic structuralist terms and concepts and those most likely to be useful, the words can seem like a blizzard when they all are new. No one would expect students to use every concept in this chapter in a course paper or a test essay, whether in a definition of structuralism or in the interpretation of a literary text or of another cultural text or genre. But readers can start to acquaint themselves with the general principles (construction, binary oppositions, systems, and so on) and then choose from among the specific tasks and strategies. The survey of structuralism here can equip readers with the key questions and approaches that structuralists have brought to literary and cultural criticism and equip readers to follow how later methods continue to draw on those questions and approaches. Students of literature, who have sometimes chosen to study literature in part because they see it as less hard-and-fast than other fields, as more alert to the blurriness of emotions and art, sometimes find the rigor of structuralism a refreshingly systematic approach to literary study. But sometimes they take offense at it and see the obsession with systems as a desecration or a falsifying of literary and cultural values. Out of a similar mixture of interest in structuralism and suspicion of its impulse to systematize grew the way of thinking and reading discussed in the next chapter, on deconstruction.

✤ 4 ✤

Deconstruction

Deconstruction, in and of itself, is almost dead, but it retains enormous influence on current critical thinking. While deconstruction itself peaked in the late 1970s, an evolving version of deconstruction has been absorbed by later thinking and often remains crucial to, and even taken for granted by, contemporary cultural and literary criticism.

The founding figure and the intellectual force behind deconstruction was Jacques Derrida. His first widely influential book, *Of Grammatology*, appeared in French in 1967, and many of his later writings recast or extend the ideas of *Of Grammatology* for other contexts and issues. Advocates and popularizers saw his ideas as so revolutionary that they put him in the same light as Copernicus, Newton, Einstein, and Freud. His influence in literary studies grew so strong that many students supposed he was a literary critic or theorist. Still, while Derrida sometimes wrote about literature, he was primarily a philosopher, not a literary critic, even though, at least outside France, his work had little impact on philosophy until after its shock wave hit literary studies. Deconstruction has since carried its influence far beyond literary studies, not only to philosophy but also to all of the humanities and often to the social sciences, and debates still rage over its relevance for the so-called hard sciences.

As I risked summarizing structuralism in one concept, relatedness, so I will risk summarizing deconstruction in one concept, multiplicity. Deconstructionists believe in multiple meanings. They take Saussure's structuralist formula defining the sign as the signified

Jacques Derrida (1930–2004).

bonded together with the signifier, and they widen the gap between the signified and the signifier, focusing on what they call *free-floating signifiers*, or the free play of signifiers. That is to say, in deconstruction, seemingly singular or stable meanings give way to a ceaseless play of language that multiplies meanings. Because they use structuralism but go beyond it, deconstructionists are often called *poststructuralists*, although poststructuralism can also refer more generally to modes of criticism that came after structuralism, or to criticism that draws on deconstruction, even if it blends deconstruction with other methods, such as those discussed later in this book.

Let us clear up, early on, some common misunderstandings. People who misunderstand deconstruction often think that it says there is no meaning. Occasionally, carried away with their zeal, early deconstructionists said or implied that; but it is not representative of deconstruction. On the contrary, and most characteristically, deconstruction actually multiplies meaning. In a related misconception, people who know little about deconstruction often suppose that it simply means destruction. But deconstruction is not destruction. It can change the way we view things, but it does not destroy anything. It offers more, not less. In deconstruction, there is always more, a surplus of meaning and rhetoric that Derrida calls a *supplement*.

Poststructuralism and Postmodernism

These related terms have caused confusion, because some people use both terms to refer to the intellectual movement spearheaded by deconstruction, while most people (myself included) use *postmodernism* to refer to contemporary developments in architecture, literature, and popular culture, retaining the term *poststructuralism* for the intellectual movement. It seems to me that we can better characterize the movement in aesthetic style by its placement in a time period (after modernism) and its reaction to a previous age (modernism) and that we can better characterize the intellectual movement by the shape of its ideas (a response to and development from structuralism), though in many ways the shape of its ideas can also represent its time period.

With so sprawling a proliferation of meanings, deconstructionists often turn their attention to what they call *decentering*. If readers find a center, then they can see how the center organizes the things around it into a secure, stable, unified system. In a novel or a play, for example, traditional critics might pick out a particular feature—such as a pivotal scene, word, or character—and describe it as central to the overall work (whether or not they actually use the term *central* or *center*). They might argue that the scene, word, character, or other central feature helps shape the rest of the play or novel, puts other scenes, words, or characters in a meaningful light that leads to a particular interpretation. Any reader will recognize that way of thinking, because it is a routine way to understand any phenomenon, cultural or literary.

But deconstructionists do not believe that systems can be secure or unified or that we can capture cultural objects with single explanations. To a deconstructionist, everything is multiple, unstable, and without unity. In this view, we cannot tie language down; we cannot tie the signified tightly to the signifier. Without the tight bond between the signified and the signifier that Saussure imagined, the signifiers start to float freely, even playfully away from any particular signifieds. Deconstructionists focus intensely on those signifiers. That is, they focus on language itself, which they see as constructed out of free-floating signifiers. With their intense interest in language, they see everything as figurative, as dense with rhetoric and textuality. For deconstructionists, then, rhetorical, figurative meanings—the play of signifiers—proliferate so much that they displace literal meanings. For literal meaning, the signified and the signifier would have to be bound tightly together, limiting the play and the meaning of language. But because the signifiers inevitably drift away from any one signified, the meaning of language, rhetoric, and textuality multiplies beyond the possibilities of literal language, beyond the possibilities of the carefully organized systems that structuralists charted.

What do you call it again—*deconstruction?*

This is *not* important, but only people who know hardly anything about deconstruction say "deconstruction*ism*" or "deconstruction*alism*." Perhaps they are thinking of analogies to words like "structur*alism*." The usual terms are *deconstruction, deconstructionist,* and *deconstructive.*

Though many deconstructionists, and occasionally even Derrida, use the verb *deconstruct* (and it has even entered the popular talk of the general public), I think that using the verb *deconstruct* and referring to deconstruction as an action misses a key point. Since deconstruction refers to a basic principle of all language, we cannot really deconstruct something. If critics want to think deconstructively, then, instead of deconstructing a text, they find the way that it is **always already** deconstructed. They don't do it to a text. Instead, they expose the way that it is already done, the way that a text has always already deconstructed itself.

Deconstructionist interpretation frequently follows what has come to be called a **double reading**, a two-stage reading. In the first stage, the critic identifies a confidently singular interpretation, free of multiplicity and deconstruction. Often, it is an interpretation that a structuralist critic might propose, such as an argument about the overall system or perhaps a binary opposition or center that organizes the text into a stable, coherent system. Then in the second stage, the critic finds things that undermine the structure, things

Table 4.1. Deconstructive Terms

FOR NONDECONSTRUCTIVE IDEAS	FOR DECONSTRUCTIVE IDEAS
truth, substance, essence	play, free play, undecidability, aporia
center	decentering
nature	culture
stability	instability
	différance, surplus of meaning, supplement
speech, voice, phonocentrism	writing, textuality
literalness, logocentrism	rhetoric
origin, authority, authenticity	suspicion of stabilizing ideas such as origin, authority, authenticity
metaphysics of presence	absence

that (in deconstructionist lingo) "break down the binary" or "explode the binary," or a moment of **undecidability** (sometimes pretentiously called an **aporia**), showing how the free play of the text's signifiers—its language—goes beyond the capacity of the system to confine it to one meaning or set of meanings.

It is not hard to do a double reading, because we can always find something that troubles or breaks up the system. But it is harder to do a double reading well, because to do it well we have to find something that troubles or breaks up the system in interesting ways. For that reason, if you want to set up a double reading, do not make your first reading so obviously unconvincing that it is easy to knock it down. The more plausible your first reading, the more interesting your interpretation will grow when your second reading knocks the first reading over. Sometimes, instead of asking your readers to buy into your first reading and then blaming them for trusting you, you can tell them ahead of time that the first reading is provisional, a target that you will soon reconsider from a more critical and deconstructionist perspective.

Table 4.1 can help readers understand double readings as well as, more broadly, the range of concepts that lead to double readings.

Deconstructionists did not design this chart, but I have put it to-gether to illustrate deconstructionist concepts and terms, including terms that we will get to later in this chapter, making the chart a reference point to return to as the chapter goes on.

The first column of the chart represents standard concepts familiar outside deconstruction, grouping them roughly into three related sets. Some of the terms are familiar, while some Derrida made up (metaphysics of presence, phonocentrism, logocentrism), but they all refer to standard concepts outside deconstruction. The second column assembles a parallel set of concepts. Again, some of them are familiar terms or concepts, while some of them are Derrida's own, but they are all deconstructive concepts that Derrida sets against the more familiar concepts in column 1.

Typically, in the first stage of a double reading, deconstruction-ist critics will pick out a supposedly secure interpretation or struc-ture and describe it with terms or concepts from column 1. Then in the second stage, they will say that the concepts in column 1 do not really work and that the concepts in column 2 work much better.

Newcomers to deconstruction often think they have discovered a fatal contradiction in Derrida's methods when they observe that Derrida and his followers use the very concepts (those in column 1 of the chart) that they object to. But Derrida anticipates that objection. Indeed, he is quick to say that even though he believes we should try to get beyond the concepts that I have listed in column 1 of the chart, we can never get beyond them entirely. He says that we can try to get beyond assuming secure meanings, but we cannot get beyond them. Even to criticize stable concepts and say that they are actually un-stable, we still need to use the ostensibly stable concepts. Occasion-ally, therefore, when Derrida uses a word that expresses a stable concept, he will write an X over the word to show that although he must use the term he does not mean to endorse it (a practice that Derrida picks up from the philosopher Martin Heidegger). In de-constructionist lingo, to cross words out that way, using them but marking the use as provisional, is called **bracketing** them or putting them **under erasure** (or in French, *sous rature*).

There are a variety of ways to pursue a deconstructionist interpre-tation, with or without a double reading. A double reading might give more or less equal time to the first reading and the second reading. Or it can condense the first reading into a brief gesture. Or the critic can dispense with the first reading altogether and go directly to a deconstructionist reading or integrate references to one or more potential first readings through the length of the deconstructionist reading.

Regardless, to produce a deconstructionist reading, critics typically pick out part of a text and study its language, rhetoric, and figuration with great intensity, searching out ways that the text unravels its own assumptions and produces more meaning than it can unify and more meaning than a simple structure can contain. Indeed, if you want a formula for how to read deconstructively, then reread the previous sentence, so long as you keep in mind the ironic qualification that the idea of a formula is itself antideconstructive, bracketed, under erasure. Deconstruction is thus like new criticism, in that both pursue a close attention to language, but deconstruction radically reverses new criticism through a fascination with disunity. Whereas new critics argued that the text fits together in organic balance and unity, deconstructionists might consider how a text can *seem* to fit together (the first stage of a double reading), but they end up showing (in the second stage) how it breaks apart.

Let us consider, for example, Ezra Pound's famous two-line poem "In a Station of the Metro" (1913):

> The apparition of these faces in the crowd;
> Petals on a wet, black bough.
>
> (Pound 35)

A new critic might seek out symbols in the apparition, faces, crowd, petals, bough, wetness, or blackness, perhaps finding a paradoxical, ambiguous tension between the abstractness of the first line and the concreteness of the second line and resolving the seeming conflict into a balance that unifies the poem. A structuralist could pursue a similar reading, finding a binary opposition between the opening abstraction and the concreteness that it gives way to. The first line can work as a signifier to the second line's signified.

A deconstructionist could ignore such interpretations and go immediately to something more multiple or begin with those interpretations and use them as a first reading to set up a double reading. If the first line's abstractness can work as a signifier to the concreteness of the second line's signified, then a deconstructionist can just as well flip that reading and see the second line as a signifier to the first line's signified. Perhaps that could still work within a structuralist reading, because even in mirror image it retains the same binary structure. But the possibility of turning the structuralist reading on its head suggests the potential for an instability that might lead us to doubt the stability implied in reading the poem as a binary or in seeing its signifiers as bound firmly to its signifieds. To continue a deconstructionist approach, then, we could take any number of possibilities, so long as we take more than one. We would likely pursue at least several angles and suggest how they also generate more possibilities, keeping the meanings circulating continuously. Often, to show how those meanings cannot settle into a stable structure, we would seek out **internal contradictions** or **internal differences** that frustrate any interpretation of the text as holding a singular, stable meaning. From a deconstructive perspective, everything has internal contradictions, if we allow ourselves to see them.

In a sense, as we have noted, the first line can seem more abstract, especially in the term *apparition*, and the second line can seem more concrete because of its reliance on touchable, specific objects. On the other hand, the petals float loose, grammatically, from any article or demonstrative pronoun. That is to say, no "the" or "these" precedes them and places them in a context. The lack of such terms sets the petals' would-be concreteness in a contradictory, framing abstractness. At the same time, in the first line the definite article *the* and the demonstrative pronoun *these* make the poem refer to a contradiction: a specific ghostliness, with specific but undescribed faces in a specific but undescribed crowd. Each line thus has contradictions built within it that multiply the permutations of its opposition to the other line.

In this famously short poem, the title works like a line unto itself, interrupting the potential binary opposition between lines 1 and 2. If we continue the figure of opposition, tracing the continually unraveling and reraveling opposition between the concrete and the abstract, then we might see the title as concretizing because of the way it places the poem in a specific place, the Metro, the Paris subway. Still, in the early twentieth century the Metro was abstractly a signifier of modernity at large and especially of mechanized modernity and the urban future. That future is both suggested and undermined in the lyrical petals of the second line. The petals can suggest nature, a quiet antithesis to the screeching metallic modernity of the Metro. At the same time, together with the poem's imitation of Japanese styles (such as haiku), the petals can suggest the role that Japanese understatement and Japanese ways of envisioning nature were coming to figure a new visual modernity in modern European art. Japan also promised a new modernity militarily and economically, as it shocked the world with its defeat of Russia in the

1904–1905 Russo-Japanese War. Meanwhile, the darkness of the Metro can match the darkness of the black bough, while the lights in the Metro's darkness can match the sheen of wet petals set against the blackness of the bough. The poem's semicolon (which in some drafts was a colon) thus evokes a flickering hesitation between continuity (which a colon would signal, like an equal sign) and discontinuity (which a period between lines would signal). For every flicker of continuity in this poem, as these brief ruminations begin to suggest (and one could write about this reverberating little poem at much greater length), has both within it and beside it a flicker of discontinuity, not a matching flicker that settles the contradictions into equilibrium or new critical balance and unity, but rather a continuously unequal, unbalanced disequilibrium, always more and less than what it contradicts.

Such a reading suggests how deconstructive literary interpretation can work. In deconstructive interpretation, the meanings never stabilize. Deconstruction does not destroy or remove meaning but instead multiplies meanings and continues to circulate those multiplying meanings and to defy any sense of a single or stable truth or essence. But it is not as if anything goes. Deconstruction offers many meanings but not any meanings. Suspicious though deconstructionists may be of systems, they still rely on evidence and argument to develop an interpretation. The logic of evidence and argument may in some sense lie under erasure, but as deconstructionists seek out internal contradictions in the objects they interpret, they also embrace deconstruction's own internal contradictions by continuing to rely on evidence and argument. That reliance makes a deconstructive reading more than an exercise in self-infatuation or anarchy. Instead, like more traditional interpreters, deconstructionists seek to communicate with and convince others.

WRITING, SPEECH, AND *DIFFÉRANCE*

It is time to look further at some of Derrida's specific ideas, already hinted at in Table 4.1 (deconstructive concepts). (Readers may find it helpful to refer back to Table 4.1 while reading this and the next paragraph.) Whether you concern yourself closely with the details or not, a review of these ideas can help you understand the larger pattern of Derrida's thinking. Perhaps in part to dramatize his thinking and to shock us into paying more attention, Derrida makes the counterintuitive claim that writing came before speech. Derrida thinks we put far too much emphasis on speech. He calls that emphasis *phonocentrism*, just as he coins the term *logocentrism* for the belief that signifiers, words, can contain the essence of their signifieds (*logos* is ancient Greek for "word"). That leads some deconstructionist feminists, along with Derrida, to refer to the patriarchal belief in stable meanings as *phallogocentrism*, combining the words *phallus* and *logocentrism*. Derrida thinks that Western culture is phonocentric. That is, he thinks that in Western cultures people usually take for granted that secure meanings and identities rest in the sound of the voice, as if the voice exposed a person's *essence*, revealing that person in some *essential* way. Against that notion of secure essences, against the notion of secure signifieds fastened tightly to their single signifiers, Derrida sets *writing* and the figuration or free play of language, because writing so advertises its status as the proliferation of signifiers that we cannot tie writing down to secure meanings. Thus, he tries to privilege writing over speech, and so he says that writing came first. But by *writing* he does not necessarily mean actual script. Instead of the actual script, he means the system of representation that Saussure outlines in the formula of the signified and the signifier, except that for Derrida the signifier is always floating freely away from the signified. In short, by *writing*, Derrida means systems of representation. We may imagine, he argues, that speech gets outside of representation and becomes the pure signified. But we can never get to the pure signified, he believes, apart from the representing signifiers. We can only keep adding and multiplying the signifiers. There is no origin and no endpoint. We can never get to the *presence* itself, what he calls the "metaphysics of presence," because, in Derrida's lingo, the free-floating signifiers guarantee that there is always an *absence* between the signifier and the signified.

In the same vein, Derrida coins the now famous term **différance**, which combines the French words for *defer* and *difference*. In making up this new word, he changes the second *e* to an *a* (which, in French, also leads to an accent mark on the first *e*), partly to make visible the difference between *différance* and *difference*, even though, in French, the two words sound the same. (In English, by contrast, we can hear the difference between *différance*, with an accent on the third syllable, and *difference*, with an accent on the first syllable.) Derrida's point is that there is always difference, always a gap between signifier and signified, so that the continuous play of signifiers, instead of taking us closer to the signified, always defers the signified. *Différ-*

Indeed, he advertises his refusal to begin at the beginning by starting off with the word *therefore*, which we might expect to find at the end. But that can remind us that in Derrida's way of thinking, there is no beginning, no origin and no ending, but instead a continuous circulation and deferral. In the same vein, having begun at what sounds like the end and thus undermined the idea of both beginning and ending, Derrida winks at us in the middle of the essay by saying such things as "I would say, first off, that *différance*, which is neither a word nor a concept," and "Let us start, since we are already there, from the problematic of the sign and of writing" (Derrida 7, 9). We might also notice, at the beginning, that when Derrida says that he will speak of *a* letter, the letter he speaks of is *a*. While such a pun fits perfectly into Derrida's style, the play works in English (which Derrida knew) but not in French. Regardless, each time Derrida says difference, he defers *différance* and calls attention to the difference between *différance* and difference, and each time he says *différance*, he defers difference and calls attention to the difference between the two words or concepts (or nonwords and nonconcepts) again, so that his language can never arrive at one term or the other but can only keep deferring them and signifying their endless play.

By writing in so slippery and playful a style, Derrida enacts his ideas, instead of just explaining them. He sees philosophical and critical writing as a process rife with multiple meanings in the same way that literary texts are rife with multiple meanings. He invites us to read his writing, and other philosophical and critical writing, in the same way that we might read the multiple, playful language of a witty, punning Shakespearean sonnet. Philosophical and critical writing, for Derrida, does not carry a truth function that sets it apart as a stable refuge from the instability of literary writing. In that sense, for Derrida, the two ostensibly different kinds of writing slide into each other and no longer seem so different. Any effort to draw a line that separates stable from unstable writing, informative writing from "creative writing," gives way to an endless *différance* that undermines what we may have supposed was a stable binary. While Derrida's detractors have seen such a view as a self-indulgent inflation of the literary value of philosophical and critical writing, including his own, other critics have seen it as an encouragement to expand our sense of the literary and to enlarge the range of what literary critics study. In that sense, deconstruction has contributed to a reluctance to draw a circle around poetry, drama, and fiction and say that only those things can be worthy of literary and critical study.

Today, influenced as well by the cultural studies movement (which we discuss in Chapter 9), literary critics study much more than poetry, drama, and fiction, as presumably this book has already made clear. Today, literary critics also study film, autobiography, critical and philosophical writing, and an enormous range of cultural and popular cultural practices, from popular music to comic books and from politics to identity theory.

DECONSTRUCTION BEYOND DERRIDA

By the mid- to late 1970s, deconstruction was the rage. Paul de Man, Geoffrey Hartman, and J. Hillis Miller, a group of established literary critics at Yale University, made themselves Derrida's disciples, adapting his philosophical writings to literary criticism. Famous as "the Yale School," they popularized deconstruction for Anglo-American literary studies. Deconstruction—as a word but not as a concept—entered the popular language, usually used by people who have no idea what it means and who suppose, to the dismay or amusement of philosophers and literary critics, that *deconstruct* is just a sophisticated way to say *destroy*. Traditionalists were horrified by deconstruction, and sometimes they dubbed the Yale School the Yale Mafia or even the hermeneutical Mafia. Enthusiasts made it seem as if no article or book of literary criticism, outside the most old-fashioned scholarship, could be taken seriously if it did not refer

The de Man Controversy

Soon after Paul de Man died in 1983, a researcher discovered that as a Belgian citizen in World War II, he had written antisemitic journalism and sympathized with the Nazis. Some people used de Man's sordid past as an argument against deconstruction. While I bow to no one in my abhorrence of the Nazis and of de Man's collaboration, and while I am ready (as we will soon see) to criticize the classical deconstruction that de Man represented, I do not think that de Man's foul journalism makes an argument against deconstruction. That kind of argument—a so-called *ad hominem* argument—is the

equivalent of saying "I disagree with you because you're ugly."
If we are to object to deconstruction, we will need to address its
arguments and practices. De Man's close friends Derrida and
Hartman, both Jews with profound experience of antisemitism,
while not in the least defending de Man's collaboration, insisted that the de Man they knew years later bore no resemblance to the earlier de Man who wrote those ugly articles.

to Derrida, de Man, Hartman, or Miller, and for a while they seemed
to represent the future of literary criticism.

But even faster than the Yale School came to monopolize the
landscape, they faded away before the force of feminism, Marxism
and historicism, queer studies, and postcolonial studies, so that now
deconstruction has survived not so much as a separate method but as
a way of thinking that blends with and helps shape those other
methods. Derrida and the Yale School came to represent what we
might think of as classical or high deconstruction, as opposed to the
way that deconstructive thinking took new shapes as it blended with
other methods, as we see later in this volume. If the early leaders of
deconstruction were mainly men, soon feminists such as Hélène
Cixous, Barbara Johnson, and Gayatri Chakravorty Spivak, who
translated Derrida's influential *Of Grammatology* into English, drew
on deconstruction for feminist criticism. (On Cixous see Chapter 6
on feminism, and on Spivak see Chapter 10 on postcolonial and race
studies.) Already, in my sample deconstructionist reading of Pound's
"In a Station of the Metro," I have gone beyond the limits of high
deconstruction, drawing on historicism to consider how Pound's
poem evokes the onset of mechanistic modernism and the new
Japanese ascendancy in modern art and politics.

When deconstruction's early opponents responded to it with horror,
their alarm set off a roiling scandal in English and other literature
departments across the world and in the popular press. To its outraged
critics, deconstruction threatened the end of literary studies.
It replaced the rigor of new criticism and structuralism with a mean-
ingless, anything-goes chaos that desecrated literary art in favor of
abstruse, in-group philosophy and sybaritic navel gazing. But many
other critics of high deconstruction thought through its limits more
patiently, and sometimes more sympathetically, even when they rejected it strongly.

As a rough consensus emerged on the limits and problems with high deconstruction, two concerns stood out. First, if everything is about the free play of language, the free play of signifiers, the free-floating of signifiers, and so on, then all texts are alike. It seemed that every high deconstructionist interpretation reached the same con- clusion about every text, and experienced readers could predict the ending of a high deconstructionist interpretation while they were still reading the beginning or before they started to read it at all. Second, the repetitious insistence on the free play of meaning often grew so abstract that it seemed to treat texts as isolated language games cut off from the social and material world, where particular meanings make an enormous difference in people's lives. And so, to many critics, after the initial hoopla, high deconstruction—the deconstruction of Derrida, de Man, Hartman, Miller, and their followers—came to seem both predictable and irrelevant.

As it happens, Derrida intended for his writings to have social meaning, and later in his life, perhaps responding to his critics, he often made the social commitments in his writing more explicit. The comparative lack of social concern among the American decon- structionists, led by the Yale School, distorts Derrida's works, or at least it distorts his apparent intentions, even while many readers continue to believe that the work does not live up to those intentions. Derrida's writing and the writing of many of his followers can seem disconnected from the social world because his densely punning, mischievous, winking style of writing and thinking plays so exuber- antly with the signifiers that it can seem to lose track of the signifieds.

For literary or cultural interpretation, the solution to these prob- lems is surprisingly simple. If we make the deconstructive reading our conclusion, deciding at the end of our argument that the text is about the free play of signifiers and the endless meanings of language, then our interpretations will get tiresomely predictable. But if we begin with that and then ask what consequences the play of language has in a text and in its social world or in its readers' social world, then we have exciting new leads to follow, and then deconstruction can greatly help us interpret the text and its worlds. That is why de- construction continues to exert a strong influence on later critics, who look at what difference a particular deconstructive multiplic- ity might have in, for example, a feminist, queer, Marxist, or his- toricist context in relation to specific social issues. In that mode, deconstruction more often goes under the label of **poststructural- ism**, which allows critics to continue deconstruction's sense of multiplicity without continuing the sense of social disconnection that can characterize classical, high deconstruction. While deconstruction can seem like an irrelevant language game in the hands of its early advocates, in later hands it helps poststructuralist critics understand the issues they care about most, including political and social as well as aesthetic issues, because deconstructive multiplicity shapes the crises and pleasures that run through our daily lives. The mere fact (or claim) of multiple meanings is no longer the point. The point is how the multiple meanings work in particular historical and social settings. All this explains why almost no one does straight-out or high deconstruction any more. It can seem cut off from the world. And yet, because it can provoke so many interesting ways of thinking about the world, even while classical, high, or pure deconstruction is pretty much dead, deconstruction continues to wield enormous influence as people use it to think in ways that go beyond deconstruction itself but that still use deconstruction.

Returning briefly to our short deconstructionist reading of "In a Station of the Metro," we might say that a classical deconstructionist reading would concentrate on the disequilibrium and instability of the language as ends in themselves, making and drawing on more general claims about the continuously circulating figuration of literary signification. Such a reading often ended up by concluding that the figuration is vertiginous, dizzying. To later critics, such a conclusion often seems formulaic and disturbingly asocial. A later reading, from critics interested in the crises of and reshapings of modernity, might dwell on the poem's disequilibrium, not simply as an abstract linguistic vertigo, but rather in relation to modernist anxieties about mechanization, warfare, colonialism, and anticolonialism (the implications of Japan's defeat of Russia). They might contrast that sense of social crisis with the poem's status as an icon of understated aesthetic experimentation, seeing the urge to pare language down to minimal images as conflicting with the recurring desire to use those images to represent cultural crisis and cultural optimism.

DECONSTRUCTION, ESSENTIALISM, AND IDENTITY

Both the classical deconstructionists and the later poststructuralist thinking that draws on deconstruction look skeptically at the traditional confidence in stable literary meanings, which they see as essences. The belief in essences, in turn, has come to be called **essentialism**, and those who object to essentialism, both in and beyond literature, are called antiessentialists. The conflict between essentialism and **antiessentialism**, propelled by deconstruction but drawing as well on many other cultural motives, has animated a great deal of critical discussion and theorizing over the last two or three decades and shows little sign of diminishing. We have already begun to look at the notion of essentialism in the previous chapter, on structuralism, where we used the term *essence* to describe the idea of an underlying reality independent of linguistic representation, drawing an opposition between essences and constructions. In that sense, antiessentialists are also called *constructionists*.

Wait—A Deconstructionist and a Constructionist Would Both Object to Essentialism?

Yes, it is confusing, but the same ideas can be both deconstructionist and constructionist, without contradiction. The two terms have different histories that converge mainly by coincidence, but the point here is that deconstructionists object to essentialism, and construction is typically seen as the opposite of essentialism. Though the terms *construction* and *deconstruction* sound like opposites, they are not. Both refer to process as opposed to essence. Language sometimes works out in unexpected ways—which is exactly the deconstructionist and constructionist point.

Actually, most people whom other people call essentialists do not call themselves essentialists. Usually, the term *essentialist* is a term of abuse, and antiessentialists use it as a way to dismiss an argument. In response, their accused opponents often say some more sophisticated form of "Whoops, sorry, I didn't realize that I'd slipped into essentialism" or, more often, "No, I'm not making an essentialist argument," and then they try to explain how their argument is not essentialist. Occasionally, however, some critics take pride in explicitly calling themselves essentialists, although from my own antiessentialist perspective, or—to put it more modestly—from my nonessentialist perspective, those who explicitly call themselves essentialists usually have a poor grasp of the debate around essentialism and the implications of endorsing the term.

An essentialist believes that the issue at hand, whatever it may be, has an underlying essence, a basic and defining set of qualities that do not change across history and geography. To make the principle concrete through examples, we could discuss essentialism in a variety of contexts. For example, we could propose that there is an essential concept or signified for the signifier *cat,* the term we discussed in the previous chapter's review of structuralist linguistics. An essentialist would say that the signifier *cat* is unambiguous, because all cats share a set of characteristics that only cats have and that do not vary across time and place or from one cat to another. An antiessentialist might say, on the contrary, that *cat* can refer to the familiar domestic feline or to a hugely inconsistent range of felines, domestic and wild, living and extinct. It can also refer to a bulldozer, a stylish man, any of several different colleges of advanced technology, the act of masculine philandering (catting around), a backbiting woman, a catfish, a CAT scan, a catalytic converter, and so on through a long and continuously evolving list of other meanings. For antiessentialists, that list of examples may seem to prove the point that language has no essence and instead circulates continuously through chains of unstable signifiers. But in such an argument the debate can seem like an abstruse scrimmage over abstract linguistic theory. In practice, by contrast, and especially since the heyday of high deconstruction, the greatest controversies around essentialism have raged around questions of human identity.

Who are you?

And what do you think about the question *Who are you?* Most of us feel a pressure to answer that question in oversimplified ways, and many of us resent the question, yet we repeatedly ask it—if only in our own minds—about ourselves and about others, and we repeatedly have to answer it, not only in our own minds, but also in social introductions and on official forms. Sometimes the question comes in revealingly blunter form: *What* are you? We feel that someone asking that question wants one kind of answer, but there is more than one thing that defines who and what we are. If I answer that question by saying that I am a Baptist, or an English major, or a lesbian, or a New Yorker, or a basketball fan, then my answer seems to slight the way that I am also more than one thing, and my answer can seem to reduce the many things that I am to one or merely several qualities. Moreover, it can imply that if I define myself as an English major or a lesbian, and if that characteristic defines me, then all lesbians or English majors must be alike. And in some ways, most people believe, at least some of the time and for certain criteria, that they are alike. We attribute at least some meaning to the signifier *lesbian* or *basketball fan*, suggesting at least a degree of commonality across all the people we might describe with those signifiers. And yet, at the same time, we know well that lesbians and basketball fans are not all alike, that they vary enormously, that each group is rife with internal differences. Every description of a group of people, therefore, sets off a potential tug-of-war between the impulse to describe them by things they have in common and the impulse to describe them in ways that call attention to, or at least acknowledge, differences within the group.

Essentialists believe that they can define the essence of a person's identity. That is, they believe that people have a fixed identity, that their race, ethnicity, or gender (to name only the most frequent examples) expresses that identity, and that members of a racial, ethnic, or gender group will all act and think in a shared set of patterns. Some essentialists also believe that to understand a group one must be a member of that group. For example, an essentialist might say, "Because I am a woman, I understand sexism better than men understand it." It is easy to criticize essentialism, because it can often deteriorate into plain prejudice. The person who believes that all blacks love to dance and sing is an essentialist, as well as a racist, and that kind of essentialism helps give essentialism a bad name. But it is not always so simple. Many people believe that a woman necessarily understands sexism better than a man or that a brown-skinned Briton or American necessarily understands racism better than a white-skinned Briton or American. Indeed, the historical pattern has much to back up such beliefs, since men as a group have a tawdry history of sexism, and American and British whites as a group have a tawdry history of racism. The difficulty comes in how we extend generalizations about a group to predicting everything about the group, for every member of the group, across all times and places. An antiessentialist might say that most women understand sexism in most ways better than most men but that to make such claims about men and women overall is unfair to both groups. When sexism is so dominant, for example, it can distort women's thinking as well as men's thinking. Such an argument can get tricky, for it can easily deteriorate into an embarrassingly defensive propping up of the people who, given the differentials of power, may need propping up the least, and a slighting of racist and sexist history. And so the debates over essentialism take on tindery proportions and may look different from different angles and for different issues.

The complications multiply and the sparks often fly when it comes to sorting out the difference between an essentialist generalization and an antiessentialist generalization. It would be an essentialist generalization to say that Chinese Americans are inherently or innately better at math than other Americans. Some might argue that it would not be an essentialist generalization to say that Chinese American families focus on math in the schools more often than most other American families. A lot is at stake in the difference between those two statements. In the same vein, while it would be essentialist and racist to say that all blacks love to sing and dance (or, speaking to more likely conditions, to *imply* that all blacks love to sing and dance), that should not remove the value of studying or admiring black musical traditions. The problem comes, and I would say that the disrespect for African American or Chinese American intellect and culture comes, in reading the accomplishments of African American musicians or Chinese American math students as essentialist, biological, and inevitable, as in their blood rather than in their hard work and imagination. The mass media, for example, which routinely turns representations of African Americans to sports and music and neglects African American intellectual life, fosters an essentialist set of expectations from the general populace, both African American and non–African American. And the model minority myth fosters an essentialist set of expectations about Chinese Americans, such as when, for example, Chinese American English majors, who may not care any more about math than most other English majors, discover with surprise that other students in their dorm ask them for help with math. Similarly, we can see a tragically essentialist set of expectations when African American high school students tell other African American high school students not to hit the books so hard, because that is "white" or, more simply, when media-saturated clichés about African Americans make students fear that other students *might think* they are "acting white."

By contrast, antiessentialists or nonessentialists (my own more modest term) typically keep at least one eye on the ways that people in any given group differ from each other and on the many different identities that any one person may express. One person, for example, might identify as a man, an Illinoisian, a math lover, a Chicano, a heterosexual, a Chicagoan, a Republican, and so on. Someone else might share some of those identifications, and so feel a common bond, but not share all of them. In one context, at a Young Republicans meeting or on a date, one identification might stand out; but in another context, perhaps a debate over global warming or a drive along Lake Michigan, another identification might stand out. People are so multiple that no one identification and no predictable group of identifications can adequately define the person for all contexts.

And yet antiessentialist arguments that focus on people's multiplicity can make many of us uncomfortable, because we often want to focus on our likeness with other people, not on our difference from them or not *only* on our difference. People who do not get the point think that deconstruction takes meaning away from identity. But that is to mistake deconstruction as a process that removes meaning, when instead it multiplies meanings. That is where generalization comes in, and the challenge is to find ways to generalize about groups of people that do not demean people by essentializing them. It is not really such a tough challenge, but the cultural habit of essentializing thought and language, of reducing people to only one or two of their many identities, can make it seem tough.

It can help to keep in mind that people have reasons for essentializing. People take pride, for example, in women's identity or Puerto Rican identity or many other identities. But these are historical and cultural processes and constructions, not essentialist absolutes, as we can see when we think how different the connotations are if we talked about pride in white identity. Deconstruction and poststructuralism can help us find ways to generalize about identity that see it as a historical and cultural process rather than as a stable essence.

We can find a helpful model in the cultural studies scholar Stuart Hall's discussion of cultural identity. Born and raised in Jamaica, Hall has lived his adult life in Britain and written about both Jamaican and black British identities. He notes that some people have described Jamaican identity as African, others as European, and others as American. Rather than allowing any one of these influences to characterize Jamaican identity by itself, Hall chooses all three, so that he reads each history in multiple ways. He triangulates the three histories to describe Jamaican identity, not as an essence, but as a process. "Perhaps," writes Hall, "instead of thinking of identity as an already accomplished historical fact, . . . we should think, instead, of identity as a 'production,' which is never complete, always in process,

---

Frequently Asked Question

Students often wonder how they can offer a deconstructive reading of a film or work of literature that obviously proclaims its own deconstruction. They worry, for example, that to point out that Gertrude Stein's poem "Tender Buttons," James Joyce's novel *Finnegans Wake*, Borges's stories, or films like *Being John Malkovich, Memento,* and *Primer* can be read deconstructively is only to point out what any reader or viewer already knows. But even when a work is not self-evidently deconstructive, it takes no great insight to point out that it is deconstructive after all. Because if deconstruction is a principle inherent to all representation, then it is a routine rather than a distinguishing quality of any particular representation. And therefore, whether the work is obviously self-deconstructive or not, the goal is not to point out that it is deconstructive. Instead, the goal is to point out what difference its deconstruction makes for something that you care about in the work—its approach to gender, art, religion, or whatever most stirs your interest and imagination.

---

and always constituted within, not outside, representation" (Hall 68). In this view, identity is not a stable signified that a single signifier passively represents. It is a continuous process of multiple signifiers and signifieds circulating through each other, *producing* identities, not merely labeling identities that are already statically there. In addition to applying Hall's model to Jamaican identity, we could choose a similar structure, with different particulars, for any other identity we might want to describe. What, you might ask, are the multiple components of your identity or one of your identities or the identity of someone else whom you know?

HOW TO INTERPRET: MORE DECONSTRUCTIVE EXAMPLES

Let us take two more examples. In the United States, most people, over the years, have thought of the American populace through the lens of a black/white binary, as if all Americans were white or black (and certainly not white and black). Americans often essentialize black and white so thoroughly that they do not realize that the American schema of black and white, or black versus white, does not hold for much of the rest of the world, which often sees itself in other terms. In Great Britain, to take one example, the term *black* includes people of African and south Asian ancestry, while in the United States it includes only people of Sub-Saharan African ancestry. Americans tend to think of race as an essence, rather than as a construction, but as we will see in Chapter 10 (on postcolonial and race studies), the study of race, partly influenced by deconstruction, has increasingly come to see race as a changing idea constructed by culture rather than as a biological essence. Americans—with and without the influence of deconstruction—are gradually recognizing that the black/white binary vastly oversimplifies American and global culture and demography. But the cultural pressure driving (and constructing) the black/white binary remains forceful, such as in opinion polls that purport to tell us that whites think this and blacks think that, which can pressure members who identify with either group to think the way that they are told their group thinks, producing a self-fulfilling prophecy. From a deconstructive perspective concentrating on the figurative force of language, the terms *black* and *white* thus carry a figurative force in the American setting in excess of their truth value. That figurative force generates a truth effect, characterizing white and black as essences and as opposites, misrepresenting both whites and blacks and, in the process, misrepresenting the millions of Americans who do not identify as white or black. The black/white binary is thus a falsely totalizing polarity, magnetizing a wide range of variables into two opposite poles. Along the way, as it cuts out of the calculus the millions who are neither black nor white, it also oversimplifies both whites and blacks by characterizing each group as if all its members were all alike, as if there were no internal differences within the group, making each race look like an essence and denying its multiplicity.

For a final example, imagine a magazine advertisement with a picture of a gorgeous car. Think of the car as a signifier. Can we tie it to a secure signified? Can we say what is its essential meaning? If we chase after the signifier and catch it, will we arrive at the signified? Presumably not. Presumably we will never reach satisfaction (as the Rolling Stones told us), because there is always a gap between the signifier and the signified. Once we get the car (if we get it), the

5

Psychoanalysis

The profile of psychoanalysis in literary and cultural criticism has zigged and zagged over the years since psychoanalysis first attracted wide interest early in the twentieth century. The early popularizers of psychoanalytic criticism attracted as much derision as interest for their confidence that readers could reduce art to biography and make writers' early childhoods and a few phallic symbols explain everything about their writing. Beginners may still think that is what psychoanalytic criticism is, but as you read this chapter, I hope you will discover something far more mysterious and challenging.

Later in the twentieth century, as structuralism and poststructuralism emerged in literary, film, and cultural criticism, critics found a model in the psychoanalytic narrative of gender. They built on the structuralist and poststructuralist rereading of Freud by the French psychoanalyst Jacques Lacan, and they also built on feminist critics' rethinking of gender. In these ways, during the 1970s and 1980s, psychoanalytic criticism reinvented itself in poststructuralist and often in feminist clothing. While many feminists looked at psychoanalysis with all the enthusiasm of a cat for a dog, other feminists saw it as offering a potentially feminist description of entrenched patriarchy. Meanwhile, the growth of socially focused criticism, under the flags of Marxism, historicism, and cultural studies, brought yet another challenge. Some socially focused critics saw a chance to build on the new excitement about psychoanalytic criticism; others saw a conflict between the psychoanalytic interest in individual minds and the Marxist, historicist, or cultural studies interest in broader social structures. For a while, the sparks cast by these conflicts kept psychoanalytic inquiry at the trendier cutting edges of literary, film, and cultural criticism. But in recent years the ascendancy of socially focused criticism (as discussed in the remaining chapters of this book), combined with a sense from some critics that psychoanalysis describes white European and Euroamerican thinking better than it describes the rest of the world, moderated the influence of psychoanalysis in contemporary criticism. That has not deterred psychoanalytic critics, however. While their ways of thinking have less widespread influence than in recent years, psychoanalytic critics continue to develop and intensify their ideas.

$$* \qquad * \qquad * \qquad * \qquad *$$

Since psychoanalytic criticism developed in response to psychoanalysis, and psychoanalysis is a clinical practice, psychoanalytic criticism has origins of a different kind from the other critical methods discussed in this book. That is to say, Sigmund Freud, the founder of psychoanalysis, developed his ideas through the observation and treatment of patients, which plays no role in the history of the other critical methods that this book discusses. While some contemporary critics overlook the continuing influence of psychoanalysis's history in clinical practice, a brief (and necessarily selective) review of clinical psychoanalysis can help introduce psychoanalytic thinking, clarify popular misconceptions, and ground psychoanalytic criticism in its history.

Psychoanalytic critics (with rare exceptions) are not psychoanalysts, in part because it takes a long apprenticeship to become a psychoanalyst. Ten years of preparation and study are not unusual—and that is ten years *after* a doctorate (either an M.D. or a Ph.D.). To become a psychoanalyst, you also have to be psychoanalyzed.

Contrary to common misconceptions, psychoanalysis is not ordinarily for psychotics. That is, it is not for the seriously insane. Freud believed that psychotics might be beyond the help of psychoanalysis. Instead, he saw psychoanalysis as something for ordinary neurotics, including, we might say, many of the people who will typically read this book.

Let us clear up some additional common confusions early on. Psychology, psychiatry, and psychoanalysis are not the same thing. Psychology is the umbrella term, but there are many forms of psychology, and psychiatry and psychoanalysis represent two of those forms. Psychiatry is medical psychology. To be a psychiatrist, you need an M.D. Psychiatrists can prescribe drugs, which for many years have played an increasing role in psychological treatment. Psychologists who do not have an M.D. cannot prescribe drugs, though they sometimes work with psychiatrists to integrate drugs into treatment. Psychoanalysis is the branch of psychology that works in the tradition founded by Sigmund Freud, and, if measured by the number of clinical practitioners, it is a small branch. If students of the humanities cross the campus green to go, for example, from the English, French, comparative literature, or history department to the psychology department, they will find little or no teaching or research in psychoanalysis. The psychology professors might even laugh or sneer at the very idea of psychoanalysis. They might tell students that if you want that, you had better go to the English department. But even in the humanities, where there may be psychoanalytic critics, there almost never are actual psychoanalysts. The academic home of psychoanalysis lies not in colleges and universities but rather in psychoanalytic institutes (which sometimes are affiliated with universities). Psychoanalytic institutes themselves vary widely, depending on how closely they hold to Freud or identify with any of the various post-Freudian directions that have emerged since late in Freud's career.

Clinical psychologists can provide therapy. The therapy they provide comes in many varieties and usually has little to do with psychoanalysis. Only psychoanalysts can provide psychoanalysis, a relatively rare practice that differs from the many other varieties of therapy. To be psychoanalysis, the process must work in accord with the psychoanalytic understanding of the human mind, which we will soon describe. The analyst and the analysand (the patient) must also meet frequently. For some years, five or six days a week was the norm, but practicalities have gradually eroded that dogma. For many years, four days a week was the minimum, but now three days a week is acceptable. Regardless, the frequent meetings indicate the intensity of the process, and so does the duration. Psychoanalysis often takes years. One year would be relatively quick. The analysand lies on a couch (we will soon see why), comical as that may seem to the unfamiliar eye. Some psychologists and psychoanalysts also offer therapy that works in accord with psychoanalytic thinking but is less intense, might not take as long or require as frequent meetings, and might not use a couch. That would be psychoanalytically oriented psychotherapy but not psychoanalysis.

THE PSYCHOANALYTIC UNDERSTANDING OF THE MIND

What, then, is the psychoanalytic understanding of the human mind? Let us start with three key principles. They can provide a context and overview that will help us go on to develop the picture in more detail, and then we can see what happens when psychoanalysis leads to psychoanalytic criticism. While Freud's model changed over the years, for our purposes we will focus less on the trees and more on the forest—less, that is, on the changing story of his developing ideas and more on the general pattern, especially as it has gone on to influence recent cultural and literary criticism.

1. The **unconscious.** Do not confuse Freud's term *the unconscious* with its pop derivative, the *subconscious.* No one who is knowledgeable about psychoanalysis talks about the *subconscious.* *Sub-* suggests something underneath but still fairly accessible if we just dig a layer or two down. *Un-* suggests something more radical, something not just underneath awareness but utterly without awareness. (*Unconscious* means not conscious, unaware, but it does not refer to *conscience,* which is another term altogether.)

2. Repression, drives (instincts), and **defenses.** When we feel threatened by our drives, we often defend against them and repress them. That generates the unconscious, which consists of repressed drives. Freud famously argued that excess repression of psychological drives leads to neurosis. But contrary to many common misunderstandings, Freud did not see repression as inevitably a bad thing. If not for repression, we would all be having sex with each other and killing each other. Therefore, we need repression. While some repressions can hurt us psychically, in many ways we also thrive on repression. We **sublimate** repressed drives, meaning that we redirect them to other activities, which is how we build culture and civilization.

3. The **clinical method of psychoanalysis,** which we have already begun to review, calls for the analysand to talk to the analyst, so that psychoanalysis is sometimes called "the talking cure." The analysand is asked to **free associate**—to say anything and everything that comes to mind, no matter how randomly. The analyst listens. Contrary to popular misconceptions, the analyst says little. Certainly the analyst does not give advice, at least not ordinarily. The analyst might give advice and go well beyond listening if that could deter a suicide or might give advice far along into the analysis (perhaps after years).

Also contrary to popular misconceptions, the analyst says little or nothing to interpret the analysand, at least not until far into the analysis. Mainly, the analyst listens, sometimes responding with the simplest of remarks or questions. For example, an analyst might say something like "How does that feel?" or "What do you think about that?" or might respond with a slow, contemplative "hmmmm." Such minimal but mysteriously suggestive responses from the analyst return the process to the analysand's thinking. And such responses, especially if they come at the right time and in the right way, can encourage an analysand to think more deeply (in the sense of thinking through feelings), more questioningly, and—gradually— more honestly.

Meanwhile, the analysis is shaped by what psychoanalysts call **transference**. During psychoanalysis, analysands, preoccupied with their own concerns, can transfer onto the analyst emotions that apply to someone else, typically another authority figure, such as the analysands' mother or father. We might think that transference would interfere with an analysis, cluttering it with an obstacle course of troubled emotions. But since those emotions likely have much to do with what the analysis is about, analysts who understand transference can take advantage of it to help analysands work through their neuroses. At the same time, however, analysts run the risk of not understanding transference, because they themselves can mask their perception of analysands by what psychoanalysts call *counter-transference*. That is, just as analysands transfer emotions from their earlier life onto the exchange with analysts, so analysts transfer emotions from their earlier life onto the exchange with analysands. Analysts, for example, might see their analysands as versions of the analysts' children or siblings. Again, that threatens to undermine the analysis but will not undermine it if the analyst understands the process. And to understand their own entanglements in counter-transference, psychoanalysts believe, they need to have been analyzed themselves, which is why someone has to have completed psychoanalysis before becoming a psychoanalyst. Transference also explains the couch. By lying down in a relaxed position without facing the analyst, the analysand's thoughts can associate freely without the transference overwhelming the free association.

While practicing psychoanalysts typically pay far more attention to transference than literary and cultural critics do, transference has attracted the interest of critics, who propose that it can describe the way that readers or audiences respond to a literary text or any other cultural text—a film, a song, a pop star, or a cultural crisis such as war, terrorism, disaster, or political controversy. We read and interpret cultural issues and objects much as analysts and analysands read and interpret each other, transferring our own concerns onto cultural events in ways that shape our response to those events. That is partly why different individuals and to some extent different groups (different classes, age groups, races, religions, genders, regions, and so on) interpret the same events in different ways.

Transference and other features of our emotional architecture also influence our understanding of and response to psychoanalysis itself and to psychoanalytic criticism. Psychoanalytic thinking takes it for granted that our encounter with psychoanalysis will provoke resistance, because psychoanalysis studies the unconscious, and we have a psychic stake in keeping the unconscious unconscious. That makes the study of psychoanalysis different from the other ways of thinking discussed in this book. While we can learn to itemize the features of psychoanalytic thinking more or less as easily as we can itemize the other ways of thinking in this book, psychoanalysis takes longer to absorb. Typically, it takes years, because it is an emotional as well as an intellectual perspective. Indeed, psychoanalysts see "intellectualization" as a **defense**, a means of repressing threatening emotions. While psychoanalysis is harder to absorb than more specifically intellectual patterns of thought, we can still begin that process here. And whether readers are interested in absorbing it into their own thinking or not, we can introduce psychoanalytic thinking and, at the least, equip readers to follow other people's use of it.

Psychoanalytic criticism, however, can provoke derision from actual psychoanalysts. The idea that someone who has not been analyzed can truly think psychoanalytically strikes some analysts as amusing, but not all analysts look at it that skeptically. There is, nevertheless, a cultural divide between actual analysts and literary critics. Literary critics relish detail and often take pride in elaborate and clever interpretation. Analysts often see detail, elaboration, and cleverness as defenses against simpler and more basic emotions. Where the literary critic says, in effect, "Aha!" or "Look at me!" or speaks in arid, stuffy jargon ("The constituent components of transference adumbrate a bifurcated utilization of possibly negative experiential impacts that . . ."), the psychoanalyst says, "Hmmmm."

Indeed, Freud's goal was far more limited than the popular understanding of Freud recognizes. He did not usually set out to cure people. Instead he sought, much more modestly, to transform neurotic suffering into ordinary unhappiness.

As you read this chapter and think about the questions it raises, I recommend that you do not try to disprove psychoanalysis. Psychoanalysis has an irritating, frustrating response to efforts to disprove it: It sees them as a defense against psychoanalysis and thus as evidence for what they seek to refute. In that sense, psychoanalysis is a closed system that, at least from the perspective of that closed system, we cannot disprove. We can disagree with it, or with parts of it (and psychoanalysts and psychoanalytically influenced thinkers disagree among themselves about many things), and we can decline to accept it, but we cannot disprove it. I recommend that rather than trying to prove or disprove psychoanalysis, to see it as true or untrue, right or wrong, you simply try to get used to it and look at it as a way of thinking, in the broadest sense of thinking, which includes emotion.

SIGMUND FREUD

Let us approach an introductory overview of Freud's ideas, especially as they have influenced contemporary literary and cultural criticism, by describing Freud's account of gender as literary and cultural critics have come to understand it. Practicing psychoanalysts sometimes focus on the patterns that gender hardens into, using language that can seem essentialist to cultural and literary critics. Cultural and literary critics, by contrast, draw on the deconstructive critique of essentialism and the sense of culture as a process, an ongoing construction. In that way, they call attention to the antiessentialist implications in Freud's narrative of gender. From their perspective, Freud's account undermines the routinely taken-for-granted stereotypes that see gender as an essence, that suppose one stable and correct way to be feminine and one stable and correct way to be masculine. The focus on the psychoanalytic narrative of gender as a construction also draws on and feeds back into the dialogue between psychoanalytic criticism and criticism that comes out of feminism and queer studies.

Freud's interpretation of the construction of gender tells a story. People are born, according to Freud's story, in **polymorphous perversity**. *Polymorphous* means "many forms," and *perverse* means "turning upside down or overturning." Thus Freud means that people are born without any particular sexual or gender identity. Instead, infants begin with sexual drives that toss and turn randomly in any and all directions. Typically, then, the process of growing up narrows human identity and desire. In Freud's model, the child typically moves through a series of stages, from polymorphous perversity to desires that focus on the oral (as infants approach the world through their mouths), then on the anal (as they take pride in learning to control their bowels), and then on the phallic, finally leading, for most people, to the adult, heterosexual, genitally focused sexuality that Freud saw as the goal of healthy sexuality. Within this model, all humans have homosexual and heterosexual desires as part of their polymorphous perversity, but some of those drives remain unconscious, while other, more conscious drives go on to define a person's adult sexuality. (For a critique of the term *homosexuality*, see Chapter 7.)

Many contemporary cultural critics reject Freud's story. They see it as naturalizing masculinity and heterosexuality, as if those were a norm and everything else, including femininity and queerness, were a deviation from the norm. Yet many contemporary cultural critics, including many feminist and queer studies critics, find Freud's narrative an illuminating description of how gender often works, even though it does not always end up at the heterosexual masculinity that Freud took as a goal and a norm. Such critics may object to how gender often works, but, in part because they object to it, they find Freud's description revealing.

Freud's story takes one path for infant boys and another for infant girls. Writing from the sexist presumptions shared by most men in his time and place, Freud took his story of boys as the foundation of his thinking. He turned to the ancient Greek story of Oedipus, familiar to many readers through Sophocles' play *Oedipus Rex,* to describe the path of gendering for boys. Through a fateful series of events, Oedipus—without realizing what he is doing—kills his father and marries his mother. In Freud's model, the infant boy feels an attraction to his mother. That much might be no surprise. But Freud extended the story from there. He saw the boy as beginning to look at the father as a rival for the mother and thus as feeling an unconscious desire to kill the father, so as to have the mother to himself. Moreover, the boy observes that the mother has no penis, and he supposes (still unconsciously) that the mother has been castrated. He fears, therefore, that he too might be castrated, and more specifically he fears that the father might castrate him for desiring the mother. That is what Freud called **castration anxiety**. Meanwhile, the erotic desire for the mother, the desire to kill the father, and castration anxiety all represent forbidden emotions that must be repressed. In repressed form, these forbidden desires stay alive, but only in the unconscious. The father's threat of castration, Freud believed, produces what Freud called the *superego*, which we can describe as conscience, authority, and law. (Again, you will not want to make the common beginner's mistake of confusing the words *conscious* and *conscience*.)

Typically, the boy seeks to win his mother's love by identifying with his father. Identifying with his father helps the boy defend against the desire to kill his father, because it denies and represses such desire. Through identifying with his father, then, a typical boy grows into adulthood as a heterosexual. As an adult, he displaces his desire for his mother onto a gender-similar "object," a woman who is not his mother, and he lives his adulthood heterosexually. But if the boy fails to defend against his desire for the mother by identifying with the father, then he can identify with the mother and grow into adulthood as a homosexual.

Sigmund Freud
(1856–1939), 1907.

Working from this model, Freud sees adult neuroses as deriving from early childhood traumas that interfere with the child's psychic development. The child's development can stall at the oral, anal, or oedipal stage, or it can move on partly but still have trouble growing completely out of those stages. And in what Freud called the **return of the repressed**, repressed drives can pop back up in the form of neurotic symptoms, disguised representations of unconscious desires. Indeed, he observed, neurotics repeat the same symptoms over and over, a pattern that Freud called the **repetition compulsion**. Through analysis, he believed, people could "work through" their neuroses, coming to a more comfortable sense, or at least a less uncomfortable sense, of how to live with emotions that may have taken a troubling form but that at their root are ordinary and do not need to offer an obstacle to well-adjusted adulthood.

Frequently Asked Questions

When first exposed to Freud's ideas, many people wonder how his model can work for infants who never know their parents, since such infants do not necessarily turn out differently from infants who do know their parents. Psychoanalysts do not worry about that, however, because they see nonparental care-givers as filling more or less the same psychic role as parents in the construction of gender. They also see the general role of authority in the culture at large as filling the psychic role of parents, even when actual parents are not there.

Sometimes, people who do not know much about psycho-analysis say that Freud must be wrong because they know a son who adores and wants to be like his father or a son who despises his mother. Therefore, they suppose, sons do not necessarily hate their fathers and love their mothers, and so Freud must be wrong. But such thinking shows little understanding of Freud's ideas. To Freud, a son who unconsciously hates his father will often defend against the hate by identifying with his father, and a son who unconsciously desires his mother will often defend against his dangerous desire by turning away from his mother. In that sense, Freud wins either way. If the son despises his father, that proves Freud's point, and if the son loves his father, that also proves Freud's point. As we noted earlier, Freud's ideas offer a closed system. We can reject them, disagree with them, or object to some of their details, but we might find the overall system hard to disprove.

Beginners sometimes react with outrage to Freud's notion of childhood sexuality, believing that children do not have sexual desires. Such outrage usually underestimates how thoroughly Freud understands childhood sexual desires as unconscious. From within the closed system of psychoanalysis, the outrage at Freud's ideas looks like evidence of a wish to keep those desires unconscious. Outrage—as opposed to neutral disagreement—suggests an emotionally intense need to repress what Freud invites us to acknowledge.

Freud admitted, notoriously, that he was perplexed about the gendering of infant girls, and his story about girls has more twists and turns than his already intricate story about boys. It begins like the boys' story: The infant girl feels an attraction to her mother. Again, the desires that Freud describes for the infant girl are unconscious. Like the boy, the girl observes the mother's supposed castration, and she feels disillusioned by the mother's castration and by her own supposed castration. She thus renounces her love for her mother and turns her attraction to her father, but she senses that her attraction to the father is not allowed, and so she turns back to identifying with her mother. Identifying with the castrated mother, she suffers from what Freud calls *penis envy*, so that she desires a baby from her father as a substitute for her supposedly castrated penis. As an adult, she displaces her desire for her father onto a gender-similar object, a man who is not her father, and she lives her adulthood heterosexually. But if the girl remains fixated on her love for her mother, then she can grow into adulthood as a homosexual.

Critics and psychologists unsympathetic to psychoanalysis often reject Freud's account in its entirety, as we have noted. But many continue to believe in it or take the general outline with great seriousness, even if they reject some of the details (and there are more details than a short summary can include). Still others, as we will see, work within classical psychoanalysis (and here the term *classical* means Freudian) while continuing to develop it in new directions.

Notably, Freud's description of women as, in effect, failed men defined by their "lack" of a penis and suffering from penis envy has not appealed to all feminists, as you might imagine. And yet feminism is divided about Freudian psychoanalysis, for some feminists (encouraged by Juliet Mitchell's influential *Psychoanalysis and Feminism*, 1974) insist on its value as a description of how patriarchal culture works for women and men, a description of what feminists want to change. As you also might imagine, Freud's account of the construction of gender as ideally culminating in healthy heterosexuality has not appealed to critics who respect queer desire. Even so, many queer studies cultural critics find that psychoanalysis offers a valuable description of how heterosexist culture works, just as feminists sometimes value its description of patriarchal culture. In these ways queer studies and feminism also draw on each other.

Moreover, Freud's story of gender also holds value for queer studies critics who more or less accept the outline of the story without accepting Freud's sense that the story has a predetermined and preferred goal. While Freud took what he saw as healthy, adult, genitally focused heterosexuality as a goal, others look at the story he tells and note that, as Freud himself observed, it often turns in directions other than the direction that Freud preferred. Repression does not always narrow the polymorphous variety of possibilities for sexuality and gender into genitally focused heterosexuality. Freud's idea that everyone begins in polymorphous multiplicity and retains polymorphous desires, at least unconsciously, can help us understand how many people, and in some ways all people, reach adulthood driven by a wide range of desires outside the usual definitions of mainstream heterosexuality. In that sense, beyond what Freud had in mind, his model not only offers a logic for heterosexuality; it also offers a logic for queerness.

HOW TO INTERPRET: MODELS OF PSYCHOANALYTIC INTERPRETATION

Film, literary, and cultural critics, however, write about cultural practices. They are not psychoanalysts. Movies, magazines, poems, and pop songs, for example, do not lie on a couch, free associate, and hope to find a healthier way to live daily life. Critics thus try to draw on psychoanalysis as a way of thinking without actually doing psychoanalysis. And over the years a variety of strategies has emerged, beginning with strategies closer to actually doing psychoanalysis and then expanding from there. There are many ways to divide up the possible goals of psychoanalytic critical interpretation, but I will divide them into the following general categories. Psychoanalytic criticism can interpret authors. It can interpret characters. It can interpret the literary form itself. Or it can interpret audiences, that is, readers and their surrounding culture.

Critics can interpret an author psychoanalytically, almost as if they were psychoanalyzing the author. Interpreting the author often catches readers' interest. It has the fun of gossip and storytelling, but it has more to do with biography than with literary or cultural criticism. It can also risk treating authors as if they were the sole producers of the works they write, versus the structuralist sense that the overall system of writing produces a given piece of writing (as in the discussion of "the death of the author" in Chapter 3), and versus the Marxist sense that social practices, not just romantically isolated individuals, produce writing. The psychoanalytic description of authors will continue, but in these ways it seems limited as literary and cultural criticism.

Critics can also interpret characters psychoanalytically, such as characters in a play, movie, novel, or story. While that continues to hold appeal for many critics, its appeal has limits, because it treats characters as if they were people. The distinction between characters and people often proves challenging when readers first hear of it. Some readers respond by asking, why not treat characters as people? Isn't that what we read literature for, enticingly realistic characters? That is one reason we read, though one among many reasons, including the pleasure or interest we find in language, art, social interpretation, plot, structure, humor, philosophy, and so on. But characters are not people, and to pretend that they are can falsify their status as literary characters, as verbal and filmic artifacts. When I sit next to a stranger on the bus or joke with a friend, I assume that they have lives outside our bus ride or friendship, and that assumption influences how I think about them. But characters in a novel or film exist only in that film or on the pages of that novel. They do not have a life before, after, or outside the events of the novel or film. Some characters are more like people, such as characters in so-called realistic novels or movies, and some are less like people. But because we often take realism for granted, it is hard for many readers and viewers to recognize the frequency of characters who are less like people, unless we mention a wide range of examples, such as characters in cartoons, romances, horror stories, adventure tales, or satires, whether in novels, poems, plays, and stories or in movies and TV shows. In such cases, ranging from *The Spanish Tragedy*, *Pilgrim's Progress*, *Peter Pan*, *Six Characters in Search of an Author*, *Tobacco Road*, *The Sot-Weed Factor*, *Star Wars*, *The Lord of the Rings*, and the *Harry Potter* series to *Mission Impossible*, *Pirates of the Caribbean*, *As the World Turns*, *Buffy the Vampire Slayer*, and *Kill Bill*, to interpret the characters psychoanalytically, as if they were nonfictional people, would often misconstrue them grotesquely.

Psychoanalytic interpretation beyond the interpretation of authors and characters varies greatly and remains less standardized, agreed on, and familiar to most readers and even to many professional critics. Still, we can summarize a wide range of uncoalesced practices by saying that psychoanalytic critics can also interpret the form of a literary work or they can interpret the audience and culture that reads or views the work. For example, Catherine Belsey has proposed a psychoanalytic interpretation of the form of realist fiction. As we have noted, most readers take realism for granted. They do not even recognize it as a form, as a distinct set of conventions (as structuralists would say) that shape realist writing. In that sense, realist writing is not a reproduction of reality so much as a repetition of a form so familiar that we often suppose it reproduces the reality outside the fiction, even though it does not. We hold a realist novel, for example, in our hands. It fits on two-dimensional pages glued together between covers, unlike the world outside the book that we often suppose that a realist novel reproduces. Realist writing tries to tell a true and complete story. But to tell some parts of a story, it must always conceal other parts, for it can never tell everything. In that sense, even a realist text that presents itself as telling the whole story has an unconscious story that it represses. While a new critic might set out to describe a literary work as unified, a psychoanalytic critic might find conflicts between what a literary work proclaims or a film makes most visible and what at the same time they try to repress. Where a new critic looks to find how everything fits coherently together, a psychoanalytic critic, especially if influenced by deconstruction, might seek out internal contradictions, impulses that jar against each other and compete for control.

Reading a series of Arthur Conan Doyle's Sherlock Holmes stories, Belsey observes how the stories circle obsessively around women's sexuality and desire while at the same time keeping wom-

en's sexuality and desire invisible. In "The Adventure of Charles
Augustus Milverton" (easily available on the web, because the
copyright has expired), for example, Holmes and his sidekick
Dr. Watson come to the aid of "the Lady Eva Brackwell, the most
beautiful *débutante* of last season," who "is to be married in a fort-
night to the Earl of Dovercourt." But as Holmes explains to Watson,
the evil blackmailer Milverton "has several imprudent letters—
imprudent, Watson, nothing worse—which were written to an im-
pecunious young squire in the country. They would suffice to break
off the match" if Milverton shows the letters to the earl, unless
Holmes and Watson can steal the letters from Milverton. Holmes,
therefore, crafts a plan. Disguised as a "rakish" plumber, the invet-
erately single Holmes cozies up to and even proposes to Milverton's
maid to get the information he needs to burgle Milverton's house.
"But the girl, Holmes?" asks Watson, concerned about casting aside
the housemaid to save the Lady Eva. Holmes shrugs his shoulders and
responds that he has little choice, but that "I have a hated rival who
will certainly cut me out the instant that my back is turned"—and
then in the same breath he changes the subject by proclaiming
"What a splendid night it is!" (Doyle 159–63).

While Holmes calls the Lady Eva's letters merely imprudent,
describing them in the passive voice as letters "which were written,"
as if she did not write them but they wrote themselves, Milverton, by
contrast, calls them "sprightly—very sprightly." But the story never
quotes the letters or reveals what they say. By not telling us what the
letters say, Belsey implies, the story dances around and evades the
Lady Eva's sexual desire, just as it dismisses the housemaid's desire. If
readers knew what the letters said and found it salacious, they might
lose sympathy with the Lady Eva, which would take the point out of
Holmes's scheme to rescue her from Milverton's evil machinations.
On the other hand, if readers knew that the letters were innocuous,
then readers could lose sympathy with the desire to marry a man who
would reject the Lady Eva for something so trivial. Either way, the
story represses feminine sexuality while at the same time teasing us
with the continuing consequences of the feminine sexuality that it
represses. In deconstructive contradiction, the story depends on what
it also conceals.

And that, Belsey argues, is how realist literary form works. Even
the extreme realism of the Sherlock Holmes stories, which define
themselves by a compulsion to uncover and explain, depends at the
same time on a corresponding compulsion to hide and repress,

the unconscious other side of the realist coin. In that sense, we can read the realist and detective compulsion to uncover and explain partly as a symptom, as the return of the repressed, as a repetition compulsion that flamboyantly proclaims the feminine sexuality that it also represses. And so the Sherlock Holmes stories, in so many ways stories about masculine friendship—the intense friendship between Holmes and Watson—reveal as well an intricate dependence between public masculine friendship and the urge to keep feminine sexuality private.

Already, in this reading, we can see how a psychoanalytic interpretation of form can lead to an interpretation of the culture that helps produce the story. In writing the stories of Sherlock Holmes or the many other stories, including other detective stories, that circle around women's sexuality, writers do not produce these stories by themselves. The stories are partly a product of a culture that writes through them. (Here I am drawing again on the idea of "the death of the author," from Chapter 3.) In that sense, the culture helps produce the stories and helps produce audiences, readers, who want to read the stories and who therefore make stories like these and other realist detective stories into a cult phenomenon. An interpretation of stories like these can therefore offer a broader interpretation of a culture and its readers. It invites us to question the ways that the world we live in privileges men's sexuality and friendship over women's sexuality, yearning to acknowledge women's sexuality while yet respecting it so little that the culture props up an array of habits and teases, even in realist fiction, that reveal a compulsion to belittle and repress women's sexuality.

FROM THE INTERPRETATION OF DREAMS TO THE INTERPRETATION OF LITERATURE

Freud gave special attention to dreams, most famously in his book *The Interpretation of Dreams* (1900), because he believed that dreams offer a window to the unconscious. And Freud's ideas about the interpretation of dreams have interested literary critics because the interpretation of literature is like the interpretation of dreams.

Many people think that Freud believed that dreams represent wish fulfillments, but that is not exactly what Freud argued. In *The Interpretation of Dreams*, he proposed that "A dream is a (disguised) fulfillment of a (suppressed or repressed) wish" (Freud, Standard Edition IV, 160), a far more interesting and intricate idea than saying that dreams themselves directly represent wish fulfillments. In other words, a lot happens on the road between the unconscious and its representation in dreams. Sleep relaxes the defenses, allowing the impulses in the unconscious to try making their way out of the unconscious and into the dream. But a range of processes gets in the way, and Freud called those processes the **dream work**. The dream work gets in between the unconscious and the dream and then between the dream and our memory of the dream. In that way, the dream work mediates between the **latent content** of the unconscious and the **manifest content** of the dream.

While the manifest content of a dream, the dream itself, may be more open than the consciousness of waking life to impulses from the unconscious, the dream does not represent a wish fulfillment directly, because the unconscious repressed wishes still seem so threatening, even in a dream, that they can only appear after the dream work changes them. In that sense, the dream work comes between, mediates, the unconscious and the dream. The dream work operates through the overlapping mechanisms of **censorship**, which rejects threatening unconscious wishes, and **compromise**, which allows them to enter the dream only after they have changed into something less threatening. The dream itself, therefore, is a compromise between impulse and repression. Censorship and compromise themselves come in four forms, which Freud called **displacement**, **condensation**, secondary revision, and considerations of representation.

Displacement refers to the psychic process of representing one desire by another, less threatening and more acceptable desire. The wish to take revenge on the father, for example, might appear in a dream in the less threatening form of a joke about the father or a punch on a punching bag or a fantasy of outperforming the father at a particular task. More defensively, it could appear as a wish to identify with and be like the father, thus taking shape indirectly, in the form of denying the desire for revenge. The same censorships and compromises can shape the mind in waking life, but the censorships

latent content ⟶ dream work ⟶ manifest content

How Dream Work Operates
dream work ↑ censorship and compromise ↑ displacement, condensation, secondary revision, considerations of representation

and compromises in dreams often take more unexpected and perplexing forms than when we are awake.

Condensation refers to the psychic process of merging multiple wishes into fewer, less threatening, and more acceptable wishes. A memory of being punished for masturbation, for example, might combine with a memory of being teased for an interest in the arts and end up in a dream as a desire to destroy a sculpture or—depending on the dream and the degree of compromise and denial—to produce a sculpture. Worries about an overly protective mother might condense with less threatening worries about an overly protective teacher, leading to a dream about the teacher that also expresses, in disguised form, the anxieties about the mother, displacing the mother onto the teacher and condensing the two together.

We all know how hard it sometimes is to describe a dream or even to remember it, and our memories of the few dreams that we remember at all do not usually last long. When we try to recount a dream, the difficulty of recounting it makes us change the dream, sometimes knowingly, yet unable to help ourselves, and, Freud suggested, sometimes not knowingly, unconsciously. The same process of displacement and condensation that makes the dream work, mediating the unconscious impulses on their route to the dream, comes in again and mediates the retelling of a dream, which Freud called *secondary revision*. In that sense, the dream work takes place twice, making it still harder to identify the remembered, narrated dream in any direct way with the wish fulfillments and unconscious desires that lie at the beginning of its history.

Besides the interference from censorship, condensation, and secondary revision, the dreaming mind might not find acceptable words or objects that represent its impulses accurately, a problem that Freud calls *considerations of representation*. And so the dreaming mind chooses from what it finds available. It draws on recent, innocuous memories, what Freud called "the daily residue," such as memories from the previous day about ordinary people, objects, and events, the bric-a-brac and busyness of daily life—perhaps a lost hat, a bug in the bathtub, or an engrossing TV show. A fascination with incest, for example, might get displaced in a dream or in the secondary revision of a dream onto a more acceptable fascination with something from daily life that is not related but has a similar sound, such as insects. Or a fear of seeing a parent's forbidden genitalia, evocative of seemingly threatening sexual drives, might get displaced onto and condensed, in a dream, with a fear of something else that is hairy, such as a furry pet, or—circling back to condense with the previous example—a hairy-looking insect or a family member's hair in the bathtub. In these ways, displacement, condensation, secondary revision, and considerations of representation overlap and merge with each other. In that light, we might see secondary revision and considerations of representation as variants of displacement and condensation, thus simplifying the four categories into two categories. We might even see condensation itself as displacement, condensing the four categories into one.

Moreover—to return to rhetorical figures discussed in Chapter 3—Jacques Lacan proposed that we can see displacement as metonymy and condensation as metaphor. Indeed, the overall process of the dream work as a mediation between the latent content and the manifest content, that is, between impulse and dream, calls to mind the use of literary language and film technology as mediations between psychic impulses and art, between psychic impulses and a poem, film, novel, play, painting, or song. When we interpret film and literature, therefore, we look at their art as something like psychic dream work, as a mediation of impulses meaningful both for what they disguise and for what they do in the place of what they disguise.

For example, when Vardaman Bundren, the traumatized five-year-old boy of William Faulkner's novel *As I Lay Dying,* proclaims, in a famous passage, "My mother is a fish" (Faulkner, *As I Lay Dying* 84), he displaces his anxieties over the loss of his mother onto the loss of a recently caught fish. Like his mother, the fish has just died. But he finds it less traumatizing to process the death of a fish than the death of his mother, and displacing his fears over the death of his mother onto the death of a fish can help him process the death of his mother. Still more, it can help process the blow he has received all his life from the emotional loss of his mother, since she cares far more about some of her other children. For the young Vardaman, her death threatens to expose and intensify that earlier loss, because once she has died he can no longer deny the neglect he has suffered all his life. In response, Vardaman defensively grasps at the straw of the dead fish, condensing and displacing all these anxieties onto one less threatening object. We might even say that he poses the fish as a metonymy disguised as a metaphor. That is to say, in the fish Vardaman chooses an object that appears to have no connection to his mother, allowing him to pretend, psychically, that the displaced emotions he anguishes over through the fish have no (metonymic) connection to his mother but instead, have only a more safely distanced (metaphoric) capacity to figure his emotions over his mother.

In the same way, the little girl of Elizabeth Bishop's poem "First Death in Nova Scotia" pauses in perplexity, trying to understand the unexpected death of her little cousin Arthur. Unable to process his death, as she approaches his body at his wake, she displaces and condenses her emotions onto a stuffed loon in the same room. Like little Arthur, the loon is dead. But she finds it less traumatizing to ponder the mysterious death of a stuffed loon than the more threatening death of her cousin. By displacing her sense of her own vulnerability, exposed by the death of Arthur, onto the death of a bird, and onto the lifeless photographs of the royal family that loom over the stuffed bird, she can process Arthur's death and its foreboding of her own potential death or the death of others around her.

And yet Vardaman and the little unnamed girl of Bishop's poem are characters, words on paper, not people. As words, the character Vardaman and the character in Bishop's poem offer analogies to psychologizable people, but those analogies stop short of the three-dimensional range that might apply to a person. Structuralists and deconstructionists might say that a person, like a character, is still a text, still a set of representations. But even so, a person offers seemingly infinitely more text than a character offers.

To turn a psychoanalytic reading in more literary directions, then, directions that consider the literary form itself, we could say that Vardaman's desperate displacement and condensation dramatize an ongoing process of displacement and condensation across the novel and its literary modernist architecture. As Vardaman displaces his psychic energy from his mother to a fish, so *As I Lay Dying* keeps shifting from one focalizer to another with each of its many shifts between chapters. Flamboyantly, those shifts epitomize the modernist literary fascination with multiple perspectives. They expose the inadequacy of any one perspective, much as psychoanalysis recasts essentialist ideas of gender and personality into narratives that could have gone and could yet go in multiple directions. Any given telling of a story becomes one version, slanted to evoke a way of seeing that is only one among many competing ways of seeing.

The kaleidoscope of shifting displacements invites us to ask what other displacements they can represent. For example, we might think of the displacement of racial conflict in *As I Lay Dying*. Vardaman's name comes from James K. Vardaman, a notoriously racist white Mississippi politician. Racial conflict was pervasive across the world that Faulkner writes about, and yet, though Faulkner signifies it through Vardaman's name, racial conflict otherwise remains almost unmentioned in the novel. In effect, *As I Lay Dying* displaces racial conflict into the class conflict that overlaps with it. At the same time, it also displaces class conflict by condensing widespread and tragic poverty into one trivial family of buffoons, making it appear minor and dismissible. Such displacements risk allowing social criticism to degenerate into comic oddity. Evasive displacement is a form of denial, then, socially as well as psychically.

In Ernest Hemingway's short story "Cat in the Rain," we see another revealing series of psychic displacements. The story focuses on an American woman traveling in Italy and aching with a vague sense of dissatisfaction. Looking out a window, she sees a cat in the rain and hurries out to rescue the cat from the downpour, as if rescuing the cat can somehow reverse her dissatisfaction. But when she reaches the place where she saw the cat, it is gone, and she finds herself returned more forcefully to an aching emptiness. Maybe, she thinks, she should let her hair grow long again. "I want to pull my hair back tight and smooth and make a big knot at the back that I can feel. . . . I want to have a kitty to sit on my lap and purr when I stroke her." "Yeah?" her husband asks, unimpressed. "And I want to eat at a table with my own silver and I want candles. And I want it to be spring and I want to brush my hair out in front of a mirror and I want a kitty and I want some new clothes" (Hemingway 169–70). While a new critic might ask what the cat "symbolizes," we would oversimplify the emotional resonance of the cat's free-floating vagueness if we tried to reduce it to representing one desire, like the desire for a baby that some critics have imagined might explain the story. Part of the mystery lies in the inability of the cat or any other object to contain, to condense, the restless displacement of dissatisfaction. The many objects of desire in the woman's serially expanding list each evoke dissatisfaction with her condition as a woman. She complains that her hair is short, like a boy's. Staying in a hotel, far from home, she imagines that the accoutrements of middle-class American feminine domesticity—long hair, a kitty, a table, silver, candles, new clothes—might fill the emptiness that haunts her. But each time she names an object of desire, it cannot fill the needs that she asks it to fill, and so she must name another object and then another and another, in a chain of metonymic displacements that gradually unravels any expectation of satisfactory completion. Her choice of objects depends on clichés of femininity. She grasps after the clichés with so little hope that she ends up exposing the hollowness both of the clichés and of her restless desire, its inability to speak to the range of feminine possibility and fulfillment. Yet she continues to hunger for fulfillment, as if she does not know how to see or believe in other, less cliché models of feminine possibility. And so she is stuck between desire and an inability to pin down any satisfactory objects for her desire.

In this way, the psychic impasse of a character dramatizes a broader social impasse about women's desire and about the restless incapacity of literary language to express desire beyond a culture's entrenched patterns and clichés. Structuralists call those patterns and clichés *cultural codes and conventions*, and Marxists, as we will see in Chapter 8, call them *ideologies*, unconscious patterns of social assumptions. Deconstructionists might call the restless incapacity of literary language to express desire an instance of *différance*, of the incapacity of free-floating signifiers to produce stable expressions of signifieds. Thus a panoply of ways of thinking, from feminism and deconstruction to Marxism and psychoanalysis, can help critics converge on a set of closely related and overlapping questions.

Let us look to Shakespeare and turn once more to Faulkner for more traditionally psychoanalytic examples, though, as we will see, even a more traditionally psychoanalytic example can draw on a diversity of critical methods. Believing that the central problem in Shakespeare's *Hamlet* is explaining Hamlet's delay at killing his uncle Claudius, Freud argued that the Oedipus complex could explain Hamlet's delay. By killing Hamlet's father and marrying Gertrude, Hamlet's mother, Claudius lives out the oedipal fantasy that Freud supposed would shape Hamlet psychologically. For Hamlet to kill Claudius, therefore, would feel to Hamlet unconsciously like suicide, like killing a version of himself. But as soon as Hamlet's mother dies, Hamlet finally kills Claudius. Freud argued that Hamlet can kill Claudius once Gertrude dies because her death releases her son from the burden of seeing Claudius as living out Hamlet's unconscious fantasies. Freud's argument, expanded on by his follower Ernest Jones, has attracted skeptics as well as adherents. Skeptics reject the idea of unconscious oedipal anxieties altogether or find Freud's explanation too convoluted, or else they find that such an interpretation treats a dramatic character too much like a person. But we should be clear about one issue that often confuses beginners. It does not matter, for Freud's argument, that Shakespeare lived 300 years before Freud and could not have read or heard about Freud's ideas. Psychoanalytic interpretations of literary texts do not suppose that the author read or knew about Freud. The idea is that psychoanalysis describes patterns of thought and emotion that began long before Freud described them.

In Faulkner's novel *Light in August*, the oedipal anxieties stand out more explicitly than in Shakespeare's *Hamlet*. Joe Christmas never knows his biological parents, but he responds oedipally to his adoptive parents, Simon McEachern and "Mrs. McEachern" (we never learn her first name). Joe fears affection from Mrs. McEachern and prefers punishment from Simon (who is usually called just "McEachern"). Affection from his adoptive mother would threaten to make conscious his unconscious and dangerous love for her or at least for the possibility of feminine affection that she represents. In the same way, Joe defends against his unconscious desire to kill the brutal McEachern by identifying with him, posturing his body just like McEachern's, their "two backs in their rigid abnegation of all compromise more alike than actual blood could have made them" (Faulkner, *Light in August* 148). He continues that identification later in life, beating his partner, Lucas Burch, with the same rhythmic strokes of the hand that McEachern used to beat Joe. Finally, though, Joe gives in to his desire to kill the father. He smashes a chair onto McEachern's head and then runs off, for all he or anyone else knows having killed his adopted father. His immediate response, however, is not guilt but instead a burst of delight and desire, "exulting of having put behind now at once and for all the Shalt Not, of being free at last of honor and law," qualities that, from a psychoanalytic perspective, boys learn oedipally through identifying with the father and his threat of castration, the threat that originates concepts like honor and law. "He cried aloud, 'I have done it! I have done it!'" (207).

Then he instantly decides that his crime against his stepfather means that he should get married, as if, once he has killed his rival, he no longer needs to block his affection for the feminine, apart from the need to displace it from his mother or stepmother onto another woman (in Joe's case, a tellingly older and more experienced woman). In this sense, psychoanalysis has it both ways. Whether the son hates his father or loves his father, hates his mother or loves her, psychoanalysis reads the intense psychic investment through an oedipal lens that makes either hate or love a version of the same desire. It may come indirectly, in the form of a defense, or it may come directly, but either way, as the opposite of indifference it shows the deep psychic investment that Freud describes in oedipal terms.

Light in August also invites us to carry this interpretation beyond treating characters as if they were people. In pitiable imitation of his adoptive father's violence, Joe gets stuck in a repetition compulsion, adopting his father's violence as a way of cutting off affection from women. He beats and brutalizes women (arguably including rape and murder), trying to protect himself from the vulnerability he feels in the face of feminine affection and assertion. In a world where women have recently won the right to vote (1920) and, more largely, a world of changing gender assumptions that the right to vote can represent, self-pitying American masculinity often saw itself as threatened by women's increasing public and domestic power. Defending against that sense of shifting gender relations, men often seek to establish their own toughness. They code toughness as masculinity, but since such toughness is a reaction (what psychoanalysts call a *reaction formation*) rather than a stable truth of gender that has to be that way, it always lies under threat, both from women's toughness, which challenges the exclusiveness of a supposedly masculine domain, and from women's affection, which threatens to expose men as vulnerable to emotions outside the defensively contrived rhetorics of toughness.

Just as Joe beats and brutalizes women, therefore, he also beats and brutalizes men, especially men who threaten his stereotypically brutal masculinity by coming too close to him in masculine affection. When Joe and some neighboring white boys show off to each other by paying a black girl for sex, he reacts by furiously fighting with the other boys, without even knowing why. In one sense, he could identify with the black girl, for though at that point in the novel he lives as a white person, he believes that he may have black ancestry. But he also seems to sense that by taking turns with the abused girl, the boys express a relation with each other more than with the poor girl whom they otherwise do not know and whom they do not associate with as peers. At that point, by the frightened standards of a homophobic world, their male-to-male bond of friendship veers threateningly close to a sexual bond, and so Joe's explosion into violence against his male friends seems unconsciously to defend against the threat to his self-conception as heterosexual. Similarly, when he takes on a male roommate, he ends up beating his roommate, trying to protect himself from imagining the possibility or even the appearance of gay desire.

Joe's compulsively repeated rhetoric of stereotypically heterosexual masculine toughness in posture, gesture, language, and violence does more than just passively reflect these defensive cultural dynamics of gender that psychoanalysis can help us understand. As we will see in the discussion of new historicism in Chapter 9, literature is not simply a passive reflection of culture. It also actively participates in, even helps generate, the culture it reflects. In that sense, Faulkner's novel engages in the implied cultural debates about gender that it also depicts. Like Joe, it evokes a fear of changing masculinity. Changing femininity takes on its importance, in this masculine-centric story, not as much on its own terms as through its implications for changing masculinity. In the process, the repetitive shape of the narrative, dramatizing its own helplessly compulsive repetition of patterns of gender, also challenges the patterns that it portrays. For in one sense, these compulsions lock the novel in a cultural neurosis, but in another sense, they also portray the psychic prison of that neurosis and invite, even plead with, readers to look critically at troubled patterns of gender and to begin to change them.

Incest and Incest Anxiety in Literature and Literary Criticism

Freud's famous notion of the Oedipus complex supposes that men and women repress a desire to commit incest with their parents, and that healthy adult sexuality comes from displacing incestuous desire onto culturally more acceptable objects, that is, onto lovers who are not our parents. Drawing on Freud's ideas, literary critics routinely discuss incest anxiety in literature as if it were like any other literary motif, like a color pattern or an image pattern. I think it is important, however, for critics, teachers, and students to take a step back from that ordinary sense of literary motif and think about the risk of approaching incest anxiety or incest itself as a routine literary motif in a world where, as we have come to realize since Freud, actual and terribly abusive incest—as opposed to mere incest anxiety—is not as rare as Freud supposed.

Within psychoanalytic circles, there is heated debate about the role of actual incest as compared to the role of incest fantasies. Freud treated his patients'—especially women patients'—memories of incest as fantasies, but some more recent scholars, led by Jeffrey Moussaieff Masson, have argued that many of Freud's patients were actual incest victims.

Whether Freud or Masson is right about Freud's patients, in the classroom, when we discuss incest anxiety in a work of literature, I remind myself that there are likely to be incest victims in the classroom, just as there are likely to be incest victims reading this book. Treating incest as merely a literary motif can rebrutalize incest survivors by making light of their trouble. But silence about incest, even literary incest, can also make light of their trouble by sweeping it under a rug of denial. Thus I take a moment in the classroom to reflect explicitly, as I am doing here, on the seriousness of incest that, regardless of where we stand on the Freud–Masson debate, lies at the root of psychoanalysis. I ask us to take seriously the sad routine of abusive relations in many families. Perhaps then as we read and contemplate the abuses and anxieties portrayed in film and literature, we can go beyond passively reflecting the crisis and can help ourselves speak back to the trauma of child abuse.

JACQUES LACAN

As Freud's long career went on, his ideas evolved and changed, and his followers divided between those who held to classical, Freudian psychoanalysis and others who veered off in many different directions. Of the various offshoots of classical psychoanalysis, those that have most influenced literary and cultural studies include Jungian psychoanalysis, developed by Carl Jung, and, by far the most influential, the ideas of the French psychoanalyst Jacques Lacan.

Jung's notion of archetypes shared by different peoples in a "collective unconscious" attracted interest in literary criticism, especially in the 1950s and 1960s. Critics brought Jung's ideas together with those of anthropologist James G. Frazer, whose famous *The Golden Bough: A Study in Magic and Religion* (first edition, 1890) tracked myths that different cultures share, such as myths of death and rebirth. But just as anthropologists no longer take Frazer's work seriously, so Freud and most other psychoanalysts and psychologists have rejected Jung's ideas. Jung has had more influence in popular culture, impelled by the writings of Joseph Campbell, than in scholarship or psychology. Nevertheless, the study of myths and archetypes gradually won a modest profile in literary studies, leading to "myth criticism" or "archetypal criticism" and culminating in the sophisticated writings of the Canadian critic Northrop Frye. Frye's ideas, especially influential in the 1960s, still attract respect, especially in Canada, though their influence on contemporary literary criticism has diminished.

Lacan's writing is notoriously difficult to read, let alone summarize, the more so because, like Freud's, his ideas evolved and changed over many years. I will focus, therefore, less on a comprehensive description of Lacan's ideas for their own sake than on describing them as they have exerted the most influence on literary and cultural criticism. In that light, I will introduce Lacan's notion of the mirror stage and then summarize his ideas according to his triad of three related *orders*, the imaginary, the symbolic, and the real.

According to Lacan, at six—eighteen months infants go through what he called **the mirror stage**. In the mirror stage, the infant, before developing a sense of its own subjectivity, sees its reflected image and identifies with the reflection. The mirror image makes the seemingly fragmented bits and pieces of the infant's body seem to cohere for the first time, impelling a coherent image of *I* (that is, of ego, subjectivity, or self).

For Lacan, infants—responding to the seemingly coherent image of wholeness in the mirror stage—come to live their psychic lives in **the imaginary**. In the imaginary, there is no difference and no absence. Instead, there is fullness and immediacy. In the imaginary, therefore, there is no self versus other, no sense of distance or incompleteness. While Lacan and Jacques Derrida (on Derrida, see Chapter 4), rivals for the acclaim of French poststructuralism, usually remained silent about each other and, when they acknowledged each other, liked to make much of their differences, we might say that the imaginary is like what Derrida called the *metaphysics of presence*, full presence with no absence.

But the imaginary cannot last in unquestioned fullness. After all, it is imaginary. The Oedipus complex disrupts the imaginary through the threat of castration. Lacan redescribes the Oedipus complex. He calls the father's opposition to the son's desire for the mother **the Father's No**, or **the Law of the Father**, or **the Name of the Father**. The Father's No does not need to be explicit and does not depend on the presence of an actual, literal father. It is so woven into the culture that it will be perceived, regardless of whether the father is around or explicitly sets out to interrupt the infant's desire. The Law of the Father, the father's prohibition of incestuous desire, is the origin of ideas about propriety or right and wrong, the origin of rules and law. For Lacan, it is a patriarchal origin, sustained by passing the Name of the Father onto the next generation, as in the patriarchal privilege and control evoked by the custom of passing the father's— but not the mother's—family name onto the next generation. As you can see, Lacan was far from feminist. Yet many feminists value his ideas, as they value Freud's, for their description of the patriarchal cultural assumptions and patterns that feminists abhor.

When the Father's No interrupts the imaginary, it casts the infant out of the imaginary and into **the symbolic**, into language. While in the imaginary there is no difference and no absence, in the symbolic, difference and absence reign. Instead of the fullness and immediacy of the imaginary, in the symbolic there is incompleteness and distance, characteristics inherent to language and representation. Instead of sounding like the metaphysics of presence, the symbolic is like Derrida's description of writing and all language, fraught with an irreconcilable gap between signifiers and signifieds. In that way, the symbolic is like the difference, deferral, and absence that Derrida called *différance*. Any idea of the self or the subject, for example, depends on an idea of the loss of the self, because we cannot recognize selfhood unless we compare it to its absence. Presence, therefore, depends on absence, and absence depends on fullness.

Through most of Lacan's career, he paid little heed to **the real**, the underlying intransigent that resists definition. For that reason, as Lacan's influence gathered force in cultural and literary criticism, the imaginary and the symbolic received most of the attention. Later in his career, Lacan wrote more about the real, and some recent Lacanian critics, including the provocative Slovenian philosopher Slavoj Zizek, give it special attention. The real is a mysterious con-

Jacques Lacan (1901–1981).

cept that is not the same as reality. We can represent reality with signifiers, but we cannot represent the real. The language we would use to represent the real evokes our distance from the real. The real is the raw kernel over which the imaginary and the symbolic operate and compete. It cannot be explained or described, but only inferred, as when Zizek likens the real to the alien in the movie *Alien*. The real is the origin of hunger and the trauma of the indescribable that can never reach meaning. It is the in-between of competing explanations, shaping reality without being part of reality. While dedicated Lacanians like Zizek now often focus on the real, on what cannot be explained, most other critics continue to address the imaginary and the symbolic, with little concern about the real.

So goes a highly summary outline of Lacan's version of Freudian psychoanalysis. We can understand this outline better if we think of the symbolic as adding to, rather than utterly replacing, the imaginary. To make sense of that, it can help to expand our sense of what the imaginary can refer to. Drawing on the ideas of Marxist philosopher Louis Althusser and historian Benedict Anderson's book *Imagined Communities* (1983), which influentially expand from Lacan's idea of the imaginary, we can think of the imaginary as referring to social spaces where we focus more on identity than on difference. For example, it can refer to ethnic or national spaces where people identify with each other because they see themselves as sharing the same ethnicity or nationality. In this sense, the imaginary is ideological. Althusser defined ideology as an imaginary relation to real conditions. (For a fuller discussion of Althusser's view of ideology, see Chapter 8.) That is to say, the imaginary captures an emotional commitment and investment that may differ from the true picture of things. After all, it is imaginary.

In this sense, when we focus more on our likeness with others, we focus more on the imaginary, and when we focus more on our difference from others, we focus more on the symbolic. We never live in the imaginary alone or in the symbolic alone. The imaginary is like a comfort zone. When we feel a sense of oneness or merging with parents, family, friends, with people who share a religion, a homeland, a race, nationality, or set of political beliefs, with fellow sports or music fans (think of crowds cheering at a political rally, a sports event, or a concert), when we feel a sense of oneness or merging in love, in all such emotions of union and likeness, we dwell in the imaginary. That is what Anderson calls an **imagined community**. By contrast, when we feel a sense of difference or even conflict, sometimes in the same settings where at other times we might dwell in the imaginary, then we dwell instead, or at least dwell more, in the symbolic. We live in the symbolic when we confront hostile or strange ideas and beliefs or when we confront competitors, enemies, or strangers. But we can also feel that sense of difference among parents, family, or friends. People who share a religion or homeland, a race or nationality, a set of political beliefs, or even a love for the same team can still argue with each other, and lovers, of course, do not always see things the same way.

Mostly, then, we live in the symbolic. Life can hurt. It is not all or even mostly comfort. But while we live in the symbolic, we also spend much of our lives chasing after the imaginary. The symbolic and the endless deferral and difference that Derrida calls *différance* mostly keep us from reaching the imaginary. Desire has trouble getting to its object. Difference, deferral, and *différance* keep interfering. Instead of the signifier and the signified merging, the gap between them remains stubborn. When we wake up in the morning and look in the mirror, most of us, on most mornings, are at least partly questioning or critical. We do not relax into pure comfort. Instead, we see difference and absence. We think that we should wash or comb, cover over this or add to that.

And yet we do achieve the imaginary, relatively, more at some times and in some places. We even make choices between the imaginary and the symbolic. When we work for a political party or join with a religious, racial, national, or ethnic group, we choose to focus more on our likeness with the members of that group and less on our difference from them. Sometimes we even delude ourselves into forgetting the difference. If we essentialize a group of people, supposing that they are all alike (that all Jews or Chinese, all blacks or Muslims, all Christians or women or men are alike), we give way to the imaginary so much that we risk denying the symbolic. Still, we can focus on the imaginary without denying the symbolic, as when we form alliances with others that enable us to focus on what we have in common without denying the differences. Imagined communities can do good things or not-so-good things. They can abuse those who do not fit in or help those who do and those who do not fit in. It depends on what people make of the imagined communities.

Lacan and Lacanians often discuss what they refer to as **the phallus**, and they also discuss what they call **the gaze** or **the look**. Much as the distinction may make unfamiliar readers laugh, it is important to understand that the phallus is not the penis. For Lacanians, who—like Freudians—see women as psychically castrated versions of men, the phallus refers to patriarchal authority in general, not necessarily to the physical male organ signified by the word penis.

The gaze or the look refers to what Freud called "the scopic drive," the way that looking itself is steeped in the erotic. Looking plays a crucial role in literature, popular culture, art, and—not least—film. We might think of the gaze or the scopic drive as the symbolic visually pursuing the imaginary, trying to collapse the distance and difference between desire and the object of desire, for we stare at a film with desires that it appeals to, desires that it invites us to satisfy by looking, but that no film ever can satisfy. The look itself can be so hypnotizing that, as film theorist Christian Metz argued, film uses the look to erase what Marxists call its means of production. It can mesmerize us into seeing a film as if we were in the imaginary, as if the film were simply natural and not the product of elaborate editing, intricate technology, and the cooperation and struggles of an enormous crew of filmmakers, financiers, marketers, and traditions and conflicts among filmmakers and audiences.

Within a film, on a stage, or in the text of a play, novel, or poem, characters, actresses, and actors gaze at each other or at something else, while audiences and readers gaze at the characters, actresses, and actors gazing. When we gaze at the other, however, we do not see the other itself. Instead, we construct the other by projecting onto it what we wish to see, fear seeing, or know how to see. In Lacan's cryptic words, "When, in love, I solicit a look, what is profoundly unsatisfying and always missing is that—*you never look at me from the place from which I see you*" (Lacan, *Four* 103). We cannot see the other. In between the subject and the object comes the symbolic that interrupts the imaginary, the *différance* that interrupts the link between the signifier and the signified. When we look at each other, then, we see not the other itself but instead what our own desires project onto the space of the other. When we suppose that we see the other itself, we misread—as we often do—the symbolic as the imaginary, but sooner or later the symbolic will rear up and remind us that the other is not what we desire it to be. It is not the same. It is different.

Here it can help to look briefly at an example of Lacan's famously cryptic, knotted, and mischievous writing. Lacan's essay "The Agency of the Letter in the Unconscious or Reason Since Freud" (1957) has held particular interest for literary critics, perhaps in part because it draws directly on Saussurean linguistics and discusses figurative language, sometimes in a style that itself draws on the figurative play of literary writing, including Lacan's interest in surrealist poetry. This is the essay where Lacan connects Jakobson's description of metaphor and metonymy to Freud's description of dream work, aligning metaphor with condensation and metonymy with displacement. In the process, he reconsiders Saussure's model of the sign as a construct of the signified attached to a signifier. Lacan imagines the signified as two doors that look alike and the signifier as a word on each door. On one door, the signifier is "Ladies," and on the other door the signifier is "Gentlemen." Lacan insists that his example of "twin doors ... symbolizing ... the laws of urinary segregation" is not merely a "low blow," for it shows "how in fact the signifier enters the signified, namely, in a form which, not being immaterial, raises the question of its place in reality" (Lacan,

Ecrits 151). Thus signifiers segregate us, in this case by gender. In that way, signifiers produce differentiation and structure. For Lacan, then, drawing on Saussure, differentiation and structure model and define language, which, as Saussure argued (as we saw in Chapter 3), is a structure of differences, of signifiers differentiated from signifieds and of signifiers differentiated from each other. In short, for Lacan, signifiers and language are not "immaterial," not mere labels written onto reality after the fact, but instead are themselves reality, are themselves truth.

The differentiating truthfulness of language matters because, as Lacan proclaims in a famous, oft-repeated phrase that brings Saussure and structuralist linguistics to Freudian psychoanalysis, "the unconscious is structured like a language." That means, in part, that the unconscious is not a random hodgepodge of chaos. It has structure, for it speaks through recognizable patterns of figurative language, leaving us, as a poem leaves us, "at the mercy of a thread woven with allusions, quotations, puns, and equivocations" (Lacan, *Ecrits* 169–70).

> Who, then, is this other to whom I am more attached than to myself, since, at the heart of my assent to my own identity it is still he who agitates me?
>
> His presence can be understood only at a second degree of otherness, which already places him in the position of mediating between me and the double of myself, as it were with my counterpart.
>
> If I have said that the unconscious is the discourse of the Other (with a capital O), it is in order to indicate the beyond in which the recognition of desire is bound up with the desire for recognition.
>
> In other words this is the Other that even my lie invokes as a guarantor of the truth in which it subsists.
>
> By which we can also see that it is with the appearance of language the dimension of truth emerges. (Lacan, *Ecrits* 172)

Like a poem, then, the other that is the unconscious can be interpreted, but it cannot be erased into paraphrase. An interpretation of a poem can mediate a poem, can understand it at the distance of "a second degree," but even while it signifies the signified that is the poem, an interpretation cannot replace the poem. It cannot merge the signified and the signifier into one thing, for one still mediates the other. "In other words," as Lacan puts it to describe "the Other" of the unconscious, there is always mediation, always difference, always structure. For Lacan, as for Saussure, mediation, difference, and structure are language, which is the "truth" that Lacan uses to describe the ceaseless figuration of signifiers that express the unconscious through metaphor and metonymy.

Returning, then, to Hemingway's "Cat in the Rain," we might think of a moment when the American woman tries to appease her dissatisfaction by looking at her reflection. She is long past the mirror stage. "She went over and sat in front of the mirror of the dressing table looking at herself with the hand glass. She studied her profile, first one side and then the other. Then she studied the back of her head and her neck." She asks her husband, then, "Don't you think it would be a good idea if I let my hair grow out?" He answers that he likes "it the way it is," but she responds: "I get so tired of it. . . . I get so tired of looking like a boy" (169). When she looks in the mirror, she does not see anything comforting. She does not see an identity between herself and her desire. She sees only difference and deferral. She even looks at one mirror through another mirror, trying to see past difference, trying to escape the limits of her reflection, but seeing only more reflection, seeing the reflection of reflection, difference multiplying its own difference. She turns to her husband, hoping to find an identification with him, but he declines to identify with or reflect her dissatisfaction. Ironically, he identifies with the way she looks, but he cannot identify with her dissatisfied looking at the way she looks. She is so wrought up in difference that she feels difference in, and even feels thwarted by, his identification with her.

She supposes that she looks like a boy, and she would rather look and feel like what she supposes that a woman should look and feel like. But as we have seen before, the expectations for women, the codes of femininity, while culturally powerful, are yet so culturally unstable that despite her hopes she can muster no confidence that one or another signifier of femininity will close the gap between how she looks and her hunger for a way of looking and feeling that can transform her emotions into an imaginary stability of fullness and presence, free at last from the pangs of difference and dissatisfaction. When she looks in the mirror, therefore, she sees her femininity cut off. She sees her bobbed hair, what Lacanians might see as her psychic castration, the Father's No or the Law of the Father. Mired in the symbolic, she sees herself as a lack, not a presence. She gazes at her absence as if it were her only form of presence, and in that way she defines what she is by what she is not, by what she lacks and has cut off.

Such a reading can go beyond simply interpreting character. The conflicts it describes dramatize and join in a broader cultural debate, in the age of the bob-haired flapper and the newly acquired vote, about women's cultural and psychic future. The conflicts that such a reading describes ponder, in effect, whether women's kernel of desire must remain elusively in the real, escaping over the horizon like the cat, never describable but always almost there, half-threatening and half-inviting, or whether women can escape beyond the vision of femininity as a lack and find a way to assert an alternative future.

We could see such defining of women by what they supposedly lack as misogynist, and many feminist critics read Lacan and psychoanalysis that way. At the same time, as we have noted, many feminists see Freudian and Lacanian psychoanalysis as rooted in misogyny but still providing a revealing description of misogynist cultural assumptions, practices, and burdens, a description that offers a potentially feminist diagnosis of what feminists seek to change. Indeed, feminism and psychoanalysis came to the fore of criticism at roughly the same time, and so we move from psychoanalysis in this chapter to feminism in the next chapter.

✻ 6 ✻

Feminism

To this critic's thinking, at least, no movement in intellectual and cultural history has done more to change literary criticism than feminism. Though the word *feminism*, as a term for supporting women's rights, did not enter the English language until the 1890s, feminism can trace its history back to Mary Wollstonecraft's *A Vindication of the Rights of Women* (1792) and beyond. But feminist literary criticism, in some ways like feminism in general, gathered its force gradually, moving through such landmarks as Virginia Woolf's *A Room of One's Own* (1929), Mary Ellmann's less well-known *Thinking about Women* (1968), and Kate Millett's galvanizing *Sexual Politics* (1970) and then finally coalescing in the late 1970s and the 1980s.

For literary criticism, feminism is not a method in the sense that new criticism, structuralism, deconstruction, and psychoanalysis are methods. It does not zero in on codifying a set of operations that one might turn like a crank to produce a new epistemology or a new literary criticism, though it produces those things nevertheless. While feminist criticism certainly has method and has changed literary critical method in general, it is not so much a method in itself as an area of interest and even a commitment. In that sense, the shift to feminism marks a change in this book that will continue through queer studies, in some respects through Marxism (which may define itself more by its methods but which also defines itself by its commitment), and through postcolonial and race studies.

At its most fundamental level, feminism is a simple concept. It is about taking women seriously and respectfully. It sets out to reverse a pattern and history of not taking women seriously, a pattern so deeply ingrained that it can seem natural, like mere truth. Feminists sometimes call that habit of not taking women seriously, not respecting women, **misogyny**, and misogyny is part of the broader cultural history and practice of centering on men to the exclusion of women, which feminists dub **patriarchy**.

Like queer studies and in some ways postcolonial and race studies, feminism derives also from an identity category, and thus the principles that feminists have thought through often overlap with, feed into and feed off of similar issues in other identity-related studies, including African American studies, Latina/o studies, Asian American studies, and American Indian studies, to name only those that have the most visibly institutionalized space in contemporary American academia (where their position nevertheless often remains precarious). As feminists think through identity, they draw on and contribute to the debates about essentialism and identity that we have seen in the previous chapters on deconstruction and psychoanalysis. In a spirit that runs partly parallel with deconstruction and that partly intertwines with deconstruction (including feminist deconstruction), we can say that feminism sees women not as one thing but as many different things.

Feminist debates about identity take us to a rough historical outline that loosely tracks feminism through a series of three waves. **First-wave feminism**, beginning with Wollstonecraft's arguments for women's education, focused on establishing women's right to vote, officially recognized in the United Kingdom partly in 1918 and fully in 1928, and in the United States in 1920. **Second-wave feminism** defined itself along a broader cultural agenda, beginning in the 1960s. While in practical politics second-wave feminism often concentrated on achieving equal rights, like first-wave feminism, the theoretical movements most associated with second-wave feminism concentrated more on describing or even celebrating the distinctiveness and specialness of women, sometimes under such rubrics as *cultural feminism*, which claimed a women's culture that was kinder, gentler, and more peaceful than the dominant culture, or *difference feminism*, which was less interested in equal rights than in establishing women's difference and superiority. Second-wave feminism often focused on a sense of sisterhood and shared identity among all women, which by the late 1970s and early 1980s led many feminists to react against it, so that a **third-wave feminism** developed. Third-wave feminism objected to second-wave feminism as essentialist and

Postfeminism?

To my mind, we live, loosely speaking, in an extended age of third-wave feminism, but some people say that we are in an age of *postfeminism*. What is postfeminism? It is different things to different people. To antifeminists, the term offers a chance to make people believe that feminism has come and gone. To others, however, the *post-* suggests a dialogue between feminism and poststructuralism, including a reaction against second-wave feminism. But I would suggest that third-wave feminism already expresses that dialogue, while the prefix *post-* threatens to undermine the feminist side of the conversation, relegating feminism to the past. To yet others, including some poststructuralist feminists, the term *postfeminism* suggests an ongoing readiness to reimagine feminism for changing times. To my thinking, the idea that we are in an age of postfeminism is a lamentable form of cultural consumerism. It treats feminism like a consumer product, something to be used up and gotten rid of so that we can go on to use up another product that we will soon get rid of in the same way. It reduces feminism to a fashion of the moment. In that context, it is no surprise to hear people referring not only to postfeminism but also to postpostfeminism. I would rather that we get used to it and accept it: Feminism is here to stay.

sought instead to build a feminism that focused more on the variety of women, building coalitions across racial and national boundaries and often engaging with the antiessentialist impulses of deconstruction. In practice, most feminist critics and theorists today do not define themselves entirely through this or that wave but draw on all three waves to pursue nonessentialist, political, and cultural agendas.

While the division of feminism into a series of waves oversimplifies overlapping histories and dialogues, the movement from second- to third-wave feminism roughly parallels the history of feminist literary criticism. Early, groundbreaking feminist literary criticism had much to do with second-wave feminism. It revolutionized critical thinking and laid the ground for a dialogue with the poststructuralist, Marxist, queer, and historicist thinking that characterizes more recent movements in feminist criticism. The popular feminism that most people encounter in journalism, in the mass media, and in the caricatures from fearful antifeminists continues to rely on second-wave feminism to represent all feminism. Similarly, the ideas that drove early feminist literary criticism continue to dominate what most readers understand about what feminist literary criticism might be. For that reason, one of the goals of this chapter is to acquaint readers with the specific strategies of early feminist criticism so that readers can come to recognize them as distinct strategies, much as the chapter on new criticism sets out to help readers who took new criticism for granted come to recognize it as a specific set of strategies. In each case, the goal is also to pose alternatives, whether to new criticism or to the approaches of early feminist criticism, thus allowing readers, and perhaps even encouraging them, to critique those approaches. Then readers will be in a good position either to continue the practices of early feminist criticism more knowingly or to work to develop more recent and less publicized feminist alternatives.

EARLY FEMINIST CRITICISM

Early feminist literary criticism, as Toril Moi notes, focused on what came to be called **images of women** (after the title of a 1972 anthology of feminist criticism), at first primarily in male-authored works but eventually also in female-authored works. By now, many feminist critics see the focus on "images of women" as limiting and old-fashioned, because it tends to imply that women characters must be good "role models," which seems to confine literature to a narrow, predictable range of possibilities. For example, it excludes parody and much comedy, such as in feminist writing that makes fun of particular kinds of women or feminist writing that may set out to portray unrealistic characters. In feminist writing, as in most writing, characters can come in all kinds—good, bad, or too unrealistic to be either good or bad.

We have all been in classes or conversations where people say that they do not like this or that movie or book or play because a character is unrealistic, including times when they say they object to a work because it portrays an unrealistic stereotype, perhaps even a demeaning stereotype. In that sense, "images of women" criticism will always stay with us (unless sexism disappears from history), and it has close parallels in criticism that focuses on what we might call (coining some phrases) images of African Americans or images of American Indians or Catholics, immigrants, Muslims, or old people, and so on. In all these areas, images criticism plays a huge role, but to later feminist critics it came to seem that images criticism played far too large a role. Perhaps it comes down to this: When do the characters work as role models, inviting people to be like the characters and thus offending us if the characters seem demeaning, and when do they end up, far more, doing any of the many other things that literary characters can do, such as make us laugh or feel sad, dramatize a story, make us think about language or a social issue, probe our psychologies, or astound us with their unpsychological but entertaining difference from actual people. (If you try, you can probably plug a variety of books and movies into each of those categories.)

Moreover, feminist critics study many topics and issues besides character. A narrow focus on expecting realistic character can lead to **prescriptive criticism** or even **prescriptive realism**, which presumptuously tells writers how to write (prescribing how they should write rather than describing how they do write), telling writers that they must present "realistic" characters or characters that offer "positive role models." We can see why early feminist criticism would err in the direction of prescriptive criticism, because there was so dire a need to point out the powerfully misogynist traditions of cultural history, literary history, and literary criticism. There is no sign that that task will end, but given the success that feminist critics have had in that domain, they have grown more and more interested in doing other things as well.

Prescriptive realism is also sometimes referred to by the title of another early (1977) anthology of feminist criticism, *the authority of experience*. The problem there lies in the assumption that one kind of experience is authoritative, as in the statement "As a woman, I know what sexism means," whereas to many feminists, including poststructuralist feminists, experience varies, and so does the interpretation of any given experience. After all, another person could say, "As a woman, I appreciate it when men protect me from bothering my little head with working or going to college and having to read all those difficult books or managing money or voting." For poststructuralists, including Lacanians (as we saw in Chapters 4 and 5) and many poststructuralist feminists, experience is never stable. It is always mediated by culture, which shapes how people understand it. In the same way, as we will see in Chapter 11, on reader response, critics have debated whether, when different people read the same text or interpret the same experience, their different projections onto it mean that they end up seeing different texts and experiences rather than the same texts and experiences. Poststructuralist feminists might argue, therefore, that if we believe in the authority of experience, then we think that we can lock the signified onto one signifier and isolate that signified from other signifiers. But in poststructuralist criticism, both *authority* and *experience* have often become suspect words, especially *authority*. What looks like authority to one person may look like opinion to another. What one person says is an authoritative perspective on women's experience may look to another person like a misogynist perspective ("I'm so glad that men protect me"). To many feminists, authority seems like the target of feminist criticism, not the justification for it.

The word *experience*, however, continues to provoke debate. To many critics it seemed for a while that poststructuralists, including poststructuralist feminists, had put an end to appeals to experience, at least among critics who kept up with the debates in cultural criticism. But in recent years a number of critics have come to the defense of experience, especially critics of color, notably bell hooks, who fear that if we banish experience from critical thinking, then in many people's minds white experience will blot out the experience of people of color. While such critics realize that the concept of experience is open to abuse, because different people have different experiences, leaving no one experience authoritative, they also point out that all criticism depends on experience, even if different people have different experiences and interpret them in different ways. The point then becomes, not to do away with reasoning from experience, but, on the contrary, to reason in ways that take into account the multiplicity of experience.

Feminist criticism began by studying the often-disturbing images of women in literature written by men and opposing those images to the authority of women's experience, but the concentration on writing by men quickly came to seem limiting. Feminist critics turned increasingly to women's literary history, contributing to a massive movement beyond the standard set of literature that critics and teachers typically studied and taught, which came to be called the **canon**. In this respect, feminist critics of all colors and heritages worked to "expand the canon," joining together with critics of African American literature and then increasingly of Latina/o literature,

Asian American literature, American Indian literature, black British literature (such as works by British writers of Caribbean, South Asian, and African heritage), and literature from around the world, including English-language literature in English departments, and— beyond English departments—literatures in other languages. As part of this project, literary critics have dug into the archives to uncover forgotten works of literature, ranging from works once famous and then forgotten (a common category for women's writing) to works never published. For several decades now, these recovery efforts have dramatically enlarged the range of literature that critics, teachers, and students read and study.

In this context, feminist critics not only study "images of women" in works by men or even in works by women, but also bring all the wide-ranging resources of literary criticism to study women's literary history from all ages and of all kinds. Feminist literary criticism and history, therefore, are not about "celebrating" women's writing. While such celebration had its place in early feminist criticism, which had the uphill task of making it known that there was a great deal more women's writing, and a great deal more deeply admirable and appealing women's writing, than most readers realized, after a time such celebration starts to seem demeaning, starts to suggest that we doubt women's writing and need to compensate for our doubt by celebrating women's writing. But feminist literary criticism and women's writing overall have now come so far that we can accept the value of women's writing without needing to worry about such doubts. Now, instead of making feminist literary criticism about proving that women's writing is worth reading and studying, we can take that as a given and bring to it the full resources of our critical methods and energies. Indeed, the now-dated focus on the "celebration" of women's history and writing—and of the overlapping categories of history and writing from the variety of racial, ethnic, and national peoples who have left a literary legacy—has long since reached the point where it can turn counterproductive. It can play into the hands of reactionaries who protest that African American studies or feminist studies, for example, are not serious intellectual pursuits but are just about celebrating. Celebrating had its time and place and still has value on special occasions, but African American studies, women's studies, and the many other studies programs that now play a role in college, university, and national intellectual life, including—to speak to the immediate point—feminist literary criticism, are not about throwing a party. They may often be fun, and they may be proud, but as this chapter can show, they are now also as serious intellectual pursuits as any others.

By setting out to expose the abuses of patriarchy, early feminism and early feminist criticism sometimes seemed to see women mainly as objects and as victims. Partly in reaction to that exaggeration, more recent feminism increasingly draws attention to women's "subjectivity," their "agency," that is, their ability to imagine and shape their own lives. The term *subjectivity* has a variety of histories, but, for our purposes here, the relevant history is the structuralist notion of a subject versus an object in a sentence as a model for subjects versus objects in cultural practices. Subjects do, and objects are done to. Feminist criticism continues to pay attention to what is done to women, to women's role as objects, but it also pays serious

---

Some Antifeminist Myths about Feminism

1. It's all about victimization.
2. It's all about affirmation and celebration.
3. It's antilesbian.
4. It's antiheterosexual.
5. It's antipleasure; it's humorless.
6. It's for "radical kooks" and bra burners.

Myths 1 and 2, 3 and 4, and perhaps 2 and 5 are each opposites: That is how prejudice works. Many such myths come from people who feel their privilege or comfort threatened by feminism. Sometimes they find something in feminism—or in what they wrongly suppose is feminism—that they do not like, and then they try to use it to define all feminism. But any movement as wide-ranging and changing as feminism is too multidimensional to be defined by its least convincing advocates. Those who believe in myth 6 and similar expressions resort to derogatory name-calling as a substitute for argument about the issues. Burning bras might have been amusing, but there is no record of feminists burning bras anywhere except in the fantasies of antifeminists. As this chapter may show, feminism is not any one thing. Instead, it keeps changing as feminists debate among themselves.

heed to women as doers, as subjects and agents, seeing a complex dialogue between women as objects of patriarchy and women as agents of their own future. Popular critics of feminism sometimes complain about what they call "victim feminism," which shows how little they have kept up with contemporary feminist thinking. Contemporary feminism, while it continues to value the study of what patriarchy has done to women (and to men), has also gone far beyond that early focus to concentrate on what women do and, in the case of literature and literary criticism, on what women write.

SEX AND GENDER

Beginning in the 1980s and usually continuing through current feminism, feminists—along with many others influenced by feminism—use the terms *female* and *male* to refer to **sex**, and the terms *feminine* and *masculine* to refer to **gender**. In this way of thinking, sex comes from biology and anatomy, whereas contemporary feminist theory usually sees gender as the constructed product of culture rather than the natural, inevitable product of biology and anatomy. In the word *constructed* we can hear the influence of structuralism and deconstruction. Female and male refer to essences, whereas poststructuralist feminists think in terms of constructed gender rather than essences. Since the onset of third-wave feminism, then, the distinction between sex and gender has become a cornerstone of contemporary, nonessentialist feminist theory, because it suggests that gender proliferates into many different forms, like what Derrida calls the free play of signifiers or the free play of language. All this means that there are many different ways to enact gender, many different ways to be female or male, not one essentialist way. Feminists see this way of thinking as liberating. It means that it is ok for women to choose how to be women, whether that means going to college and working outside the home or working in the home to raise children, whether it means heterosexual desire or lesbian desire, driving a truck, baking cookies, wearing a pink dress or wearing jeans, studying physics or French, or any combination of these. And along the way, the hope is that feminism can also help men to feel at liberty to choose how to enact their gender.

With its interest in the multiplicity of gender, as opposed to an essentialist notion of what women are and can be, contemporary feminism draws from Derrida and deconstruction, although some feminists suggest that feminist thinking anticipates Derrida. In its opening to many different ways to be female and male, this strain of feminist theory has overlapped with, helped with, and been helped by the growth of lesbian, gay, and queer studies. As we saw in the previous chapter, it has also helped bring out the way that Freudian psychoanalysis tells a story about the construction of gender.

Meanwhile, to some feminists—in a strain of argument often associated with philosopher Judith Butler, though it did not begin with her—even the liberating distinction between sex and gender seems constraining. They argue that even sex is constructed, rather than inherent, because we cannot understand sexual anatomy apart from cultural ideas about gender, which structure how we construct anatomy. As it happens, anatomy books differ over the centuries in the ways that they present sexual anatomy (as Thomas Laqueur has shown), because how we see is shaped by how we think, and how we think varies across time and geography and even from person to person. In this way of thinking, sex is always already gender, that is to say, always already constructed. Each culture sees what it supposes is essentially female or male in different ways from other cultures, and even within a given culture we can find variations and differences.

FEMINISMS

For a time in the 1980s, many writings in feminist theory and criticism made a distinction between French feminism and Anglo-American feminism, a distinction that now seems exaggerated but still carries a legacy. Whatever its limits, the opposition between French feminism and Anglo-American feminism helped call Anglo-American readers' attention to provocative challenges coming from French feminists. Three influential writers, Hélène Cixous, Luce Irigaray, and Julia Kristeva, came to dominate Anglo-American readers' awareness of French feminism, although actually, as we might imagine, there are many other French feminist writers. Cixous, Irigaray, and Kristeva have differences among themselves, and their ideas have developed and varied across many writings, but they each see the predominant language as masculine, or *phallogocentric*, and they each try to imagine feminine alternatives to phallogocentric language.

Cixous [pronounced *seek-zóo*] argues that feminine writing, or *l'écriture feminine* (*écriture* is French for "writing"), has its source in the infant's prelinguistic relation to the mother, supposedly before the infant establishes boundaries and differentiations between the self and the rest of the world around it, that is, before the onset of what Lacan calls the symbolic. For her, the free play of language (we can hear Derrida's influence on Cixous) and linguistic celebration of the body evoke the prelinguistic relation to the mother. A woman's voice, for Cixous, "physically materializes what she's thinking; she signifies it with her body.... There is always within her at least a little of that good mother's milk. She writes in white ink" (Cixous, "The Laugh" 251). At other times, however, Cixous makes a point of saying that gender does not come directly from bodies, that men can be feminine and women can be masculine.

Irigaray advocates a specifically woman's language that she sees in the language of women's pleasures and in the bodily shape of women's sexuality. For Irigaray, who sometimes writes in poetic rhythms that enact the language she advocates, woman "touches herself in and of herself without any need for mediation, and before there is any way to distinguish activity from passivity. Woman 'touches herself' all the time, and moreover no one can forbid her to

Luce Irigaray (1930–).

do so, for her genitals are formed of two lips in continuous contact. Thus, within herself, she is already two—but not divisible into one(s)—that caress each other" (Irigaray, *This Sex* 24). As women, she writes, "We are luminous. Neither one nor two. I've never known how to count. Up to you. In their calculations, we make two. Really, two? Doesn't that make you laugh? An odd sort of two. And yet not one. Especially not one. Let's leave *one* to them: their oneness, with its prerogatives, its domination, its solipsism: like the sun's" (Irigaray, *This Sex* 207).

Kristeva describes what she calls the *chora* or *semiotic*, based on the fetus's prelinguistic relation to the mother in the womb. (Her use of the term *semiotic* differs from other people's use. Kristeva is actually Bulgarian, not French, but she lives in France and writes in French.)

In effect, Cixous, Irigaray, and Kristeva ask whether women and men think and write in contrasting ways, and, if they do, then why? They suggest that women as a rule, or perhaps as a tendency and not as a rule, do more than men to retain their prelinguistic, imaginary relation to the mother. Or perhaps differences between women's bodies and men's bodies, as Irigaray argues, lead to differing ways of thinking and writing. Some feminists react against the idea that women and men write differently and fear that to believe so is to resurrect the very stereotypes that feminists set out to oppose. In that vein, French feminism, as associated with Cixous, Irigaray, and Kristeva, is sometimes criticized as essentialist, as believing in an inherent, bodily femaleness rather than a culturally constructed feminine, that is to say, as seeing sex where other feminists say that we should see gender. Some readers see the French feminists, by contrast, as teasingly, exaggeratedly, even ironically essentialist for the sake of provocation.

Monique Wittig, another prominent if still not as well-known French feminist, far more explicitly challenges essentialist notions of gender, astonishing her audience, in a 1978 lecture, by announcing that "lesbians are not women." For Wittig, who wrote novels, theory, and hybrids of fiction and theory, the very idea of gender, including the very idea of women and men, depends on taking heterosexual norms for granted. Wittig rejects second-wave feminist claims for specifically women's culture, seeing such claims as depending on the sexist divisions between genders that they set out to oppose. She argues that lesbians have no place in the heterosexual way of thinking that naturalizes heterosexuality and centers on the experience of men; therefore, she believes, the very presence of lesbians exposes the fraud in those heterosexual assumptions. She thus asks us to abolish altogether the distinction between women and men. Though feminist and queer studies critics are gradually giving more attention to Wittig's ideas, her arguments have attracted less attention than the arguments of Cixous, Irigaray, and Kristeva, perhaps because Wittig's ideas are more radical and thus harder to fit into the everyday assumptions that, for better or for worse, continue to shape most critical practice.

While Wittig gets less notice, the linguistic, playful, theoretical, poststructuralist, and sometimes psychoanalytic interests of Cixous, Irigaray, and Kristeva are frequently seen as different from the more empirical and historical approaches taken by influential English-writing innovators from the same era of feminist literary criticism, such as Nina Baym, Sandra Gilbert, Susan Gubar, and Elaine Showalter, who are more concerned to recover a history of women's writing and its interests and dialogues than to pose a specially feminine language. For example, Gilbert and Gubar's *The Madwoman in the Attic: The Woman Writer and the Nineteenth Century Literary Imagination* (1979) sees Charlotte Brontë's novel *Jane Eyre* as a metaphor for the state of nineteenth-century women's writing. In Brontë's novel, Rochester proposes to Jane while he secretly remains married to Bertha Mason, the "madwoman" he keeps locked in the attic. Seeing Bertha, Rochester's secret wife, as a double for Jane, his proposed public wife, Gilbert and Gubar read Bertha's caged expressiveness, her madness, as a metaphor for how patriarchal culture viewed women's writing.

Feminist critics from outside the French/Anglo-American divide, such as the Norwegian Toril Moi and the Indian Gayatri Chakravorty Spivak (on Spivak, see Chapter 10), have launched major critiques of Anglo-American critical theory and literary critical practice, prodding Anglo-American critics to think more internationally and theoretically and to look critically at their own practices. Spivak, for example, notes that Bertha Mason is a Jamaican Creole, and Spivak therefore sees the British Rochester's caging of Bertha as figuring not only a cultural idea about women but also a colonialist idea about the colonized world and about the battered-down lives of colonized women. As critics who write in English and teach in English-speaking countries—currently the United States—such feminists as Moi and Spivak have reached English-speaking audiences more than many other international feminists. Alice

Walker, the African American novelist, along with bell hooks and Chandra Talpade Mohanty called needed attention to the way that many early Anglo-American feminists seemed to write about women as if all women were white. Concerned that such narrowness came to define feminism, Walker proposed **womanism** as an alternative. While some feminists—or womanists—still use the term *womanism*, it has a lower profile than the rethinking of feminist ethnocentrism that Walker, Spivak, hooks, Mohanty, and other critics of color have encouraged.

It is now almost as routine for women of every race and region where women have access to public intellectual life to call themselves feminists as it is for Anglo-American women to call themselves feminists. Indeed, French feminism, Anglo-American feminism, and the rest of the world's feminism have long since moved beyond the unfortunate binary that for some years seemed to oversimplify feminism into French feminism versus Anglo-American feminism, when actually, of course, feminists of all stripes learn from each other, and feminist thinkers come from every race and class and from all over the world.

HOW TO INTERPRET: FEMINIST EXAMPLES

We might imagine a variety of feminist approaches, for example, to Ernest Hemingway's novel *The Sun Also Rises* or Dorothy Parker's story "A Telephone Call" (not as widely taught as Hemingway's novel, but still a widely read, easily available classic). We could argue that Brett Ashley, in *The Sun Also Rises*, shows Hemingway's sexism, or his novel's sexism, because she is reduced to a mere sex object or because she makes a mess of her life. Or we could argue that the pitiful woman desperate for her lover to call in Parker's story shows Parker's sexism, or her story's sexism, because the desperate woman has made herself depend entirely on a man's affection (and implicitly not just on any man but on a cad) or because she too makes a mess of her life. Such arguments work in the typical manner of early feminist criticism, including images-of-women criticism, though at first such criticism paid less attention to writing by women. The point lies in interpreting characters (not so much form, ideologies, or language), and the goal is to ask whether they are good characters or bad characters. According to whether the characters are good or bad, fit or unfit role models for us as readers, such arguments issue a verdict for or against the novel or story.

While such readings were routine in early feminist criticism and remain on the table today, especially in classroom discussions, they now seem too simple. Even within images-of-women criticism, we can start to play with such readings in more challenging ways. We might see these works' portrayals of unfortunate women not as representing a belief that that is how women are, in their essence, but rather as critiquing that way of imagining women's possibilities and so suggesting that women can differ from Brett or from the anguished monologuist waiting for the telephone to ring. Suddenly, by that gambit, without changing our observation of details, we turn the interpretation upside down, and what at first looked like anti-feminist writings can now, from this other perspective, look like feminist writings. The possibility for such a reversal may work as a mere invitation to ingenuity, but it might also give us pause and encourage caution and modesty before we indulge in broad-brush rejections or endorsements along the lines of binary absolutes like antifeminist versus feminist.

Instead of leaping toward condemnation or praise, we might ask what happens to gender in these works, not only in the characters themselves but also in the form that renders them. "A Telephone Call" poses questions, for example, about the gendering of dialogue, of telephone calls, of asking questions ("What are you doing next Saturday night?"). There is nothing inherent in the form of dialogue to require that some people call while others are called or that we blame some people for calling while we blame others for not calling. Cultural convention draws those lines between categories of gender, but we could have drawn them in other ways or not drawn them at all. The rules are cultural constructions, not inevitable consequences of sexual difference. We might wonder at the *defamiliarization* (to use the Russian formalist term from Chapter 3) that allows readers to recognize and laugh at, and perhaps look critically at, patterns of gender that get so taken for granted that readers might not have thought much about them before—including patterns of rationalization or self-serving resort to religion, as when the woman in the story pleads with God to make her boyfriend call her on the telephone. Yet the character herself seems to see through her own self-deceptions. Even so, she cannot make her ability to see through them keep her from getting stuck in them. In these ways, gender comes freighted with cultural compulsion. We see how it confines us, yet we keep running headlong into those confinements, even when we know better. While the telephone—excitingly almost new at the time of this story (1928), at least for individual residences and single women—might seem to promise a bridge to more flexible structures of gender, its liberating potential ends up bowing down in subservience to the same old demeaning hierarchies. We might wonder how that compares to the new technologies of our own time. Here we have a woman who cannot converse, at least not to the person she wants to converse with, yet right before her is a technology that promises to open the gates of dialogue.

And at the same time, though the character cannot converse, Parker can, for her story reaches an audience. It comically shows a woman—Parker—writing this story in a way that defies the strictures that it laments women's inability to defy. Feminine agency and feminine reduction to mere object status thus sit together on a fence of alternating critiques and possibilities, like the narrator's flitting back and forth between the urge to call her lover and the conviction that it would be a disaster to call him. The continuously shifting options spoof the reduction of gender relations to a tortuous power imbalance that paints women as mere victims—and they set off a good laugh at it at the same time, leaving us to debate whether the laughter helps crack the barriers it spoofs, or not.

Brett Ashley in *The Sun Also Rises* may seem like an opposite figure, for she would certainly telephone her lover or any other man, straight or gay—or just walk over to him, but, even in their opposition to each other, both figures are provocative clichés of the feminine. Lady Brett parades through Hemingway's novel as a femme fatale and an iconic figure of Woman, whether endorsing such clichés, parodying them, or—deconstructively—both at once. But she is also portrayed as masculine, from her name to her short hair to her quenchless erotic initiative. Under this light, sex starts to reappear as gender, and gender no longer seems like so certain a category, for Brett blends and bends masculinity with femininity in ways that might make us question the conventional identifications between female and feminine and male and masculine.

At the same time, everything we learn about Brett comes mediated through the narration and focalizing of the narrator, Jake Barnes, and so in a sense characterizes his gender as well as hers and perhaps characterizes his more reliably than hers. Yet that obsessive mediation also makes his gender needily dependent on hers or on his perception of the relation between his and hers. His interest in her

masculine femininity and her feminine masculinity invites interpretations of him, but it also invites interpretations that, as the
reference to formal features such as his narration and focalization
may suggest, go beyond the old-fashioned criticism that only addresses character.

A variety of cultural issues arise in the preoccupation with
watching Brett, or with Jake's watching of Brett, or Jake's watching of
himself and others watching Brett, or Hemingway's watching Jake
watch. And they arise with our watching as well, or with the history
of many critics and readers watching so much watching and feeling,
compelled to use it to pit one character's model of gender against
another's, as if to weigh and judge them. Gender starts to appear as a
topic and means for a culture to debate its future, and before long, in
The Sun Also Rises, it connects to conflicting ways of thinking about
war, economics, sports, nationality, ethnicity, commodification, and
on and on. No interpretation can take on all the possibilities, but
any interpretation that gets beyond the basics will pursue its choices
far beyond the opening gestures I have pointed to here—and that
is where the interest lies. Feminist criticism is not about labeling
books as good or bad, sexist or nonsexist. It is about interpreting
them in light of the feminist rethinking of women and women's
position. By respecting women and by thinking through the implications of that respect, feminist criticism leads us to think through
anything in culture that has to do with women and gender, which
potentially is everything.

FEMINISM AND VISUAL PLEASURE

Laura Mulvey's "Visual Pleasure and Narrative Cinema" (1975), one
of the most influential articles in feminist criticism, can help us
consider feminist film criticism as well as feminist literary and cultural criticism. I will also use it as a point of departure to a variety of
issues that go well beyond what Mulvey's article addresses. Bringing
psychoanalysis and structuralist narratology together with feminism,
Mulvey describes classical Hollywood cinema as organized around a
binary opposition between a masculine spectator, the subject, and
what we might call a feminine spectated, the object. The spectator
enacts what, drawing on psychoanalysis, has come to be called the
gaze. The masculine subject gazes, and the feminine object is gazed
at. Mulvey describes this process as going beyond what we see on the

The Feminist Critique of Objectification

Mulvey's argument is a version of the standard, and to most readers probably familiar, feminist critique of objectification. Most people misunderstand that critique. They think that the feminist point is that objectification is bad, but objectification itself is not the problem. There is nothing necessarily wrong with objectifying something or someone. It is even inevitable. We all look at others and are looked at by others (even blind people look at others in the broader sense of perceiving others), and we often respond to looking or being looked at with indifference or with pleasure. Looking in itself, therefore, is not a problem. The problem comes with abusive objectification that reduces women (or anyone else) to little or nothing except their status as object. Mulvey associates classic Hollywood cinema and stereotypical masculine patterns of the gaze with abusive objectification.

screen to reach out and draw in the audience. Conventional film editing, the norm in classical Hollywood cinema and so pervasive a norm that most spectators are not even aware of it, aligns spectators in the audience with the masculine spectator in the film through subjective camera and shot/reverse shot editing. The expression *subjective camera* refers to camera work that looks as if through the eyes of a character, thus constructing a visual focalizer, like the focalizer in verbal narrative. As we saw in Chapter 3, *shot/reverse shot* refers to editing that invites us to look through the eyes of a character. Mulvey describes how the combination of subjective camera and shot/reverse shot editing leads audiences to look through the eyes of an actor and at an actress, identifying with the actor's gaze at the actress. The process that she describes is sometimes called the **masculinization of spectators**, because through gendering the camera and the editing, the conventions of film sway spectators—women and men both—into identifying with a masculine **subject position** (stance or point of view).

Mulvey also argues that classical Hollywood cinema tends to film men (those who look) in three-dimensional space, granting them movement to either side or backward and forward within the filmed space. By contrast, it tends to film women (the looked-at objects) in two-dimensional space. They often hold relatively still, suggesting stasis, especially while men look at them and while the audience is drawn into looking at them through the men's gaze. The women often appear in a framed space, perhaps standing in a door frame or before a window frame, underlining their position as two-dimensional static objects, like pictures in a picture frame. With the male gaze focused on women, this style of filmmaking, so standard and conventional that viewers do not usually even recognize it as a style, associates men with voyeurism, control, and authority, ex-pressed as a will to investigate and fetishize. Mulvey sees that will as sadistic for men and as confining for women.

For Mulvey, writing before widespread home video, DVDs, or movie downloading, the pattern she describes is specific to traditional film, shown to a large audience on a big screen in a dark theater:

> The mass of mainstream film, and the conventions within which it has consciously evolved, portray a hermetically sealed world which unwinds magically, indifferent to the presence of the audience, producing for them a sense of separation and playing on their voyeuristic fantasy. Moreover the extreme contrast between darkness in the auditorium (which also isolates the spectators from one another) and the brilliance of the shifting patterns of light and shade on the screen helps to promote the illusion of voyeuristic separation. Although the film is really being shown, is there to be seen, conditions of screening and narrative con-ventions give the spectator an illusion of looking in on a private world. (Mulvey 17)

Still, even though Mulvey points her argument specifically to film, related patterns are common in written literature, which often lin-gers over a narrator's or a focalizer's erotic gaze at a focalized char-acter and often at a focalized woman.

Mulvey declares boldly: "It is said that analysing pleasure, or beauty, destroys it. That is the intention of this article" (16). She sees traditional cinema as a corrupt pleasure, and she believes that film-makers can invent a new cinema beyond the sexism that defines the old cinema, if they reconceive film in a way that destroys its corrupt pleasure. She therefore calls for filmmakers "to free the look of the camera into its materiality in time and space and the look of the audience into dialectics and passionate detachment" while believing that "this destroys the satisfaction.... Women," she concludes, "cannot view the decline of the traditional film form with anything

Laura Mulvey (1941–).

much more than sentimental regret" (26). Mulvey thus calls for a radically new style of film that is not based on the "look," the "gaze," or subjective camera and focalizing narrative. The alternative style that she calls for would be fragmented rather than dreamily continuous and hypnotic. Characters—if there were characters at all—might step out of their roles to address the camera or the audience and break the audience's identification with the characters, splintering the subjective camera and editing typical of mainstream film.

Mulvey's argument—which she herself has gone on to rethink through later perspectives—has carried great force in feminist film criticism and beyond, in literary studies and in gender studies in general, but critics have also raised objections to her model. Even among critics who disagree with her, many of the ideas that Mulvey offered continue to propel critical discussion, even while the arguments take a shape opposite to what Mulvey suggested. In that sense, by reviewing the critiques of Mulvey's argument we can sample a good variety of additional feminist theory and criticism, using Mulvey's work as a bridge to more recent questions in feminist theory and in the many other strains of theory that contemporary feminism engages with.

Some critics see Mulvey as essentialist. They believe she paints gender as an absolute category rather than as a category that varies across different times and cultures. They read her as saying that this is what men do: they look, and they look in abusive ways; and this is what women do: they are looked at, and they remain passive. Mulvey can encourage that objection, but it also misses that she describes sexist patterns that she opposes. She does not see them as frozen in time and space, for she believes to describe them can help us change them.

Others object that Mulvey writes prescriptive criticism, because she prescribes that filmmakers produce certain kinds of films. She assumes that a given form—fragmented film without the gaze and without subjective camera and editing—will necessarily produce a given politics. More specifically, she assumes that traditional form necessarily produces a sexist politics and experimental form necessarily produces a feminist politics. That requires a belief in what communications theorists call **technological determinism**, the idea that a given technology produces a predictable result. For example, when people say that telephones will lead to equality by letting anyone call anyone else, that word processing will destroy writing, that fax machines, email, and cell phones will bring electoral democracy to China, or that the Internet will free people to challenge mainstream culture through an open exchange of ideas, they suppose that a given technology necessarily produces a predictable cultural change, and they usually say as well that the technology is valuable, or dangerous, depending on what they think of the change. Skeptics see technological determinism as a fallacy (along the lines of the intentional and affective fallacies proposed by new critics), because the same technology often produces dramatically different results. They see culture as determining the consequences of technology at least as much as technology determines the culture. From this skeptical perspective, Mulvey gets caught in the fallacy of technological determinism. As it turns out, the experimental film forms that Mulvey advocated soon became commonplace in, for example, music videos, but I doubt that any serious critic would propose that the fragmented, disruptive cinematic form typical of music videos has usually led to feminist filmmaking. The same form can work in a sexist or a feminist way, depending on how we use it, just as two poems can use the same meter and stanzaic form and yet produce dramatically different effects. The form in itself will not predict the outcome. But by buying into technological determinism, Mulvey essentializes form.

Mulvey has also taken criticism for supposing that the text (the film) shapes or determines the spectator (the audience, the reader). The film, she believes, constructs all spectators as masculine spectators, in effect converting women to a masculine subject position. More specifically, although she does not say so, in her model the film constructs all spectators as masculine heterosexual spectators. By taking the heterosexuality for granted and not making it explicit, Mulvey naturalizes heterosexuality. She ignores queerness. (More generously, we might say that she reads classical cinema as ignoring queerness.) She does not consider queer spectators of any kind— trans, bi, lesbian, or gay—or any spectators who take into account a variety of potential sexualities in themselves or in others. In Mulvey's model, spectators may or may not walk into the theater with any variety of desires in their minds or histories, but the film turns them all into masculine heterosexual spectators. Of course, that is part of the power and provocativeness of Mulvey's argument. But as many of her readers have insisted, it just isn't so. Some spectators, for example, will look at the feminine sex object on the screen and feel little or no attraction. Some spectators will feel attracted to the masculine spectator on the screen. In this sense, when Mulvey supposes that the text determines its spectator, she leaves out the possibility that the spectator also determines the text, as in reader-response criticism. Even masculine heterosexual spectators might see a film inviting them into an abusively objectifying model of masculine heterosexuality and respond by saying "No thank you," or respond with less enthusiasm than some other masculine heterosexual spectators. Queer spectators might simply not participate in the heterosexual invitation, or they might participate satirically. Indeed, Mulvey's approach, with its prescriptive sense of filmmakers as needing to provide good examples for their audience, leaves no room for irony or humor. On the screen, a heterosexual invitation can come across, in some spectators' eyes, as a parody of heterosexual presumptions, even as camp. Similarly, Mulvey does not anticipate the possibility of what has come to be called **critical spectators**, that is, active spectators who resist the system, as opposed to spectators who passively allow the system to seduce them into naturalizing its assumptions.

Different critics hold different beliefs about how easy or difficult it is to resist dominant cultural assumptions that film or any other media set out to draw us into. To some critics, resistance seems easy and routine. To others, the dominant assumptions are so entrenched that they make resistance almost impossible. In that case, much of what passes for resistance never adds up to much more than allowing us to think that we are resisting, so that we keep ourselves from realizing how little we really resist and how much more we remain compliant. As we will see in Chapter 8, Marxist theorists have developed models for how to think through this debate over how people do or do not resist prevailing cultural assumptions.

As part of Mulvey's underestimation of critical spectators, and in much the same way that she naturalizes heterosexuality, she idealizes the theatrical setting and naturalizes cultural patterns that actually vary greatly. Let us return, for example, to Mulvey's description of a traditional film shown to a large audience on a big screen in a dark theater, where the film seems to unwind magically and seduce the audience into a dreamy world of spectators isolated from each other, reduced to their individual relation to the film on the screen. Surely spectators are not always isolated. Many people go to the theater partly to enjoy their erotic relation to another spectator sitting next to them. Others spend an entire movie craning to peer around a taller person in front of them or lamenting a nearby loudmouth (all the more now that cell phones incite conversation during a film or at least ring or flash with light). We all recognize the difference between watching a movie with a large, talking, laughing audience and watching a movie in an empty theater or in the darkened theater that Mulvey describes as isolating the spectators from each other, reducing them to their gaze at the actresses and actors on the screen. When I was an undergraduate, before home video, in the heyday of new excitement about campus feminism and the heyday of film as a campus social outing, it was routine for spectators—not only women—to hiss at moments of a film that we found misogynist. That was part of the fun of going to movies, and it helped politicize spectatorship and make it a communal rather than an isolating pleasure. White, middle-class audiences typically speak back to a movie less than black audiences, especially in comedies that play with black social expectations. (Among many possible examples, I will mention Hollywood Shuffle.) All of us have seen films that speak from cultural assumptions that we do not share, whether in terms of race, class, sexuality, religion, or our personal histories, and, contrary to Mulvey's notion of the passive spectator, we sometimes—though Mulvey might say not often enough—explicitly reject a film's presumptions, even while the film unwinds before us as if magically. Sometimes, spectators yell out and make an entire theater angry or make it burst into laughter or both.

It may be that, as a rule, spectators remain too passive, too accepting of a film's cultural assumptions and, as Mulvey says, of the cultural assumptions embedded in the very technology of camera work and editing, including sexist assumptions. But spectators are not the passive victims that Mulvey supposes. Mulvey deserves credit for helping women get out from under the passivity they may have suffered from under sexist film practices, but her rejection of filmic pleasure comes out of an earlier, victim-focused stage of feminism. We can see why feminism went through that stage in its early years, even succumbing to what may now seem like antipleasure feminism, but women and men both have come a long way since then, even if not a long-enough way. Both on screen and in the audience, women, queer or straight, are not always passive victims of an abusive masculine heterosexual gaze. Women on the screen now more often move through three-dimensional space, even if sometimes in the explicit gender reversals of films like *Thelma and Louise* and *Million Dollar Baby*, which necessarily depend on the patriarchal expectations that they reverse or spoof. Even in classical Hollywood films, women are not only gazed at. They have their own gaze, whether looking back at those who look at them or just looking—on their own initiative. And women in movies or watching movies look at both women and men.

Mulvey herself looks. She describes how the erotic gaze at a woman, often a "performing woman,"

> takes the film into a no man's land outside its own time and space. Thus Marilyn Monroe's first appearance in *The River of No Return* and Lauren Bacall's songs in *To Have and Have Not*. Similarly, conventional close-ups of legs (Dietrich, for instance) or a face (Garbo) integrate into the narrative a different mode of eroticism. One part of a fragmented body destroys the . . . illusion of depth demanded by the narrative; it gives flatness, the quality of a cut-out or icon, rather than verisimilitude, to the screen. (19–20)

We can see the same process in verbal narrative when a focalizer's or narrator's eye slows the pace of narrative to gaze lingeringly at a focalized character. At such moments, the mobile focalizer halts, interrupting his mobility (I say *his*, since Mulvey writes about masculine gazers), and the static position of the immobile, flat feminine space gains ascendancy, with a mix of recovered power and constrained stasis. We can hear that sense of feminine power in Mulvey's excited description of such iconic figures as Monroe, Bacall, Dietrich, and Garbo, actresses whose characters often look at men as the men look at them. And sometimes they look at other women, as women spectators surely both gaze at the actresses and identify with their position of being gazed at and, sometimes, of gazing back.

As women look, they do not necessarily become any less women through their looking; they do not necessarily become "masculinized," as in the model that Mulvey proposes for classical Hollywood. Moreover, after Mulvey's article appeared, now that movies have reached the home and seemingly everywhere else, viewing habits have changed, as Mulvey herself has discussed in her more recent writing. The lights are on. The conversation often continues while the film shows. People walk in and out. We stop the film, replay it, slow it down, leave it on while we walk away, or leave it on as background for other activities, and often we watch it again (or at least play it again) over and over. Mulvey's technological-determinist formula might lead us to expect that such changes would loft us away from sexist film, but while popular film may not be as pervasively demeaning to women as it used to be, it is hardly a paragon of feminist equality. The broader culture, still saturated with sexism, continues to help shape how people produce and interpret film and other cultural processes, more than the technology itself determines them.

*   *   *   *   *

From the materials in this chapter, readers can probably see that it would be hard to think seriously about women and the feminine without also thinking seriously about men and the masculine, and so feminism has led to gender studies. And some feminists and women's studies scholars believe that feminism has reached a point where the women's studies programs that feminists built in colleges and universities, often against great odds, should now evolve into gender studies programs. Other feminists think that changing women's studies programs into gender studies programs will sacrifice or betray many of feminist scholars' hard-won advances. Especially in a world that continues to undervalue the role of women, they believe, we need to sustain women's studies programs as an enclave for intellectual work that otherwise might not get done. Yet other programs try to have it both ways, changing from women's studies programs to programs in women and gender studies or gender and women's studies. Among other things, the rubric of "gender" can seem to offer a safe place for queer studies, especially in public universities that may fear a taxpayers' backlash against queer studies. Intellectually, however, feminist studies and women's studies have generated so much momentum toward rethinking gender that it would be impossible to practice them thoughtfully without rethinking heterosexuality and queerness, as we have seen through the discussions provoked by thinking about feminism and film. Feminism and queer studies are not the same, but queer studies has found some of its intellectual momentum in feminism, and feminism in turn has drawn on the intellectual challenges of queer studies.

⇒ 7 ⇐

Queer Studies

Just as deconstructionists see everything as multiple and feminists see many ways to be a woman and many ways to enact gender, so queer studies suggests that there are many ways to enact gender and sexual desire. The growth of feminism helped prepare the ground for the growth of queer studies, which in turn led to rethinkings of feminism. We can see that multidirectional cross talk in the discussion of Laura Mulvey's ideas about feminist film theory in the previous chapter. Though Mulvey's "Visual Pleasure and Narrative Cinema" did not address queer studies, the feminist issues it posed gave critics new ways to pursue queer interpretations, which in turn helped rethink the feminist issues.

Again, as in feminism, the motive for queer studies comes not so much from a method per se, though it may lead to new methods, as from thinking about an identity category (or an unstable, shifting constellation of identity categories). It comes also from thinking about the way that, across history, cultures have understood or repressed queer acts, enacted queer identities, or abused or denied the existence of queer people. In this context, I will echo the introduction to feminism in the previous chapter and say that queer studies is a simple concept. It is about taking queer acts, life, and thought seriously and treating them respectfully.

Queer studies has grown out of and can include lesbian studies and gay studies, but queer studies does gay and lesbian studies with a difference. Lesbian and gay studies address sexual orientation and people who identify as lesbian or gay and compare them to people who identify as straight. In the process, lesbian or gay studies some-times takes on a sound of essentializing lesbians, gays, or straight people and pitting lesbians or gays or "homosexuals" against straights as binary opposites. Just as deconstruction tries to go beyond the binary oppositions that structuralists believe organize our thinking, so queer studies—drawing on and contributing to deconstruction—tries to go beyond the binary oppositions and essentialism that it sometimes sees as characterizing gay or lesbian studies. The concern is that some people use terms such as *lesbian* and *gay* or use lesbian or gay studies to suggest a belief in stable characteristics that can de-scribe all gays or all lesbians across geography and time and that definitively separate gays and lesbians from each other and from straight people. By contrast, the term *queer* suggests instability and continuous process. We might say that queer studies is a decon-structive version of gay and lesbian studies.

The desire for a deconstructive version of lesbian and gay studies speaks to the larger project of reconstructing ideas of identity and sexuality, moving away from **the naturalizing of heterosexuality** and away from **compulsory heterosexuality**. The naturalizing of hetero-sexuality is the assumption, typically made without thinking, that everyone is heterosexual unless labeled otherwise, that heterosexu-ality is the norm and anything else is a special case. Once, for ex-ample, a student in a theory class I was teaching cheerfully referred to the scene in the movie *Top Gun* where a group of hunky, bare-chested men play volleyball, calling it an episode that women get excited about watching. Without realizing it, she slid into naturalizing het-erosexuality by speaking as if all women were heterosexual. That could have been a good teaching opportunity, easily managed with a laugh. Besides noting that not all women might respond that way, I could have mentioned that the scene has also attracted interest from gay men and that the film is often read as rife with same-sex desire, but—fearful of embarrassing or offending the student by putting her on the spot—I didn't say anything. My caution naturalized hetero-sexuality yet again. Such moments have the effect of enforcing *compulsory heterosexuality*, a term popularized in a 1980 essay by the poet and essayist Adrienne Rich. Compulsory heterosexuality refers to the impression, explicit or implicit, that people should be het-erosexual or else something is wrong with them. Compulsory het-erosexuality can also take a direct form, especially for women; each year men and patriarchal economics pressure or force millions of women around the globe into marriage, rape, or concubinage. Even in its implicit form, compulsory heterosexuality costs many people—especially people with same-sex desires—great and needless suffering, and it has much to do with the tragically high suicide rate among queer youth. Insisting on compulsory heterosexuality is a way of protecting illusions that the increasing visibility of queerness puts in doubt. The naturalizing of heterosexuality casts a veil over a great deal of human desire, and in many ways queer studies begins simply by lifting that veil and acknowledging the range of human desire and the utter routine of the world beyond compulsory heterosexuality.

For queer studies, once the heterosexual/gay or heterosexual/lesbian binary breaks, then the line between heterosexual and queer no longer looks so firm as the conventional insistence on compulsory heterosexuality can imply. Within the binary model, same-sex desire is a quality that certain people have and others do not. Alternatively, same-sex desire and opposite-sex desire are potential in everyone. As you may recall from Chapter 5, Freud believed that infants are polymorphously perverse, meaning that they can find erotic pleasure in any body part. Perversity in this sense is not a moral judgment but a description of desire that persistently turns in unpredictably multiple directions, and polymorphous means it takes many forms. In this model, everyone has the potential for any sexual

Adrienne Rich (1929–).

orientation. But for most infants, the surrounding world structures and streamlines their polymorphous perversity into standardized patterns, such as gay, lesbian, bi, or straight. Whether Freud had that exactly right or not (and people disagree on that issue), the larger queer claim is that people's desire is more multiform than the rigid binary between straight and queer can account for.

Though compulsory heterosexuality and the naturalizing of heterosexuality would deny it, we see that multiform sexuality around us, and perhaps within us, routinely in our daily lives. Some men who identify as heterosexual find some "masculine" women attractive, perhaps an athletic woman or a take-charge woman. Some women who identify as heterosexual find attraction in a "feminine" man, perhaps seeing something refreshing in a freedom from machismo. Heterosexuals often find pleasure in staring at models of their own sex (for example, in fashion magazines and muscle or sports magazines). These simple examples might be multiplied many times over. The point is not to out anyone (see later in this chapter for more on outing) but instead to reconceptualize heterosexuality and queerness in less binarizing, less mutually exclusive ways. In tune with deconstructive feminism and gender studies, then, the point is also to challenge essentialized notions of what feminine and masculine might mean. Hence my earlier quotation marks around *feminine* and *masculine* mark stereotypes worth reconsidering. And the point is also to challenge the automatic assumption that feminine means a desire for masculine and that masculine means a desire for feminine, for, in the culture around us, each desire has a way of teasing itself to an interest, at least, in its opposite desire. The places that supposedly harbor the most intense gender conservatism—a beauty parlor, perhaps, and a football team and the military—are also entrenched bastions of erotically charged same-sex admiration. Meanwhile, other places that may seem the most skeptical of gender conservatism—a drag queen review, a butch–femme pairing—might also seem, ironically, to reinforce conservative notions of the gender binary by enacting stereotyped models of femininity and masculinity. Or perhaps they reinforce those models so ironically or so differently that they deconstructively undermine what they might seem to uphold. In this queering of daily life, every style of desire is only a turn of the corner away from becoming, at the same time, or instead, the opposite of what it might seem.

Just as such a way of thinking can threaten conservative models of gender and sexuality, so it can also threaten essentialist models of lesbian and gay or straight identity, models that claim a stable sense of what lesbian is, what gay is, what heterosexual is, and how each supposedly remains firmly separated from the others. From within such models, the term *queer*, with its insistent, deconstructive instability, can seem to obscure differences between gay and lesbian or between same-sex desire and heterosexual desire or between the differing cultures and histories associated with each group.

For that reason, some people interested in what I am here calling *queer studies* resist the term *queer* in favor of saying *gay* or *lesbian*. In practice, however, lesbian, gay, or lgbt (lesbian, gay, bisexual, and transgender) studies often mean more or less the same thing as queer studies. While *queer theory* implies a more deconstructive, theoretical approach and *queer studies* implies a more practical approach, people sometimes put aside these differences, as I mostly do here, and use the terms interchangeably. Individual critics may or may not keep up these distinctions, depending on the context and their preference. The differences can matter, but when other issues come to the fore, some critics blur the boundaries.

In the early euphoria of new dialogue between deconstruction and queer studies in the 1980s, it sometimes came to seem that queer theorists turned their deconstructive energies on the categories of gay and lesbian, making it seem as if deconstruction were a special quality of gay and lesbian identities and not of straight identities. In response, the novelist Dorothy Allison and queer studies scholar Esther Newton comically but trenchantly produced a call to "Deconstruct Heterosexuality First" (Duggan 7). By now, queer studies has gone much further to meet that call, and all identities are up for discussion. Thus the question still common in the general populace, *What makes people gay or lesbian?*, is partly a way of avoiding the question *What makes people straight?* Many straights want to avoid that question, because to recognize their heterosexuality as a construction is a way of recognizing that they did not and perhaps do not have to be heterosexual. It could have turned out differently. In a similar way, in the early euphoria of dialogue between deconstruction and race studies, it came to seem as if critics eagerly produced deconstructive readings of black identity while leaving white identity as if it were a stable quality, unchanged across time and place. Just as we can hardly understand queer identities without thinking of straight identities, and vice versa, so in an American context, certainly, the same mutual dependence holds for black and white identities, and black and white identities are only part of the American or the global scene. Before long, however, there arose a provocative and by-now-massive scholarly enterprise of whiteness studies (see Chapter 10), often led by African American writers and taking its cue from history at least as much as from deconstructive philosophy. In these ways, the growth of queer studies and its dialogue with deconstruction is part of a panoply of other dialogues across many different, sometimes overlapping identities, each thinking through many of the same issues.

Following an argument especially identified with philosopher Judith Butler, especially her book *Gender Trouble: Feminism and the Subversion of Identity* (1990), many cultural critics express the constructedness of sexual and other identities by describing identity as performed rather than as a static essence. Because no two performances come out the same way, performance suggests variation and continuous process rather than an interior core of essential selfhood. At its most celebratory, the idea of identity as performance can suggest that anything goes, that people can choose whatever performance they want. But even performances work from a script. We do not make up from scratch the range of possible performances. Instead, we inherit models of gender, sexuality, and identity, and the surrounding culture often forces or pressures those models on its members, even as its members sometimes try to mix ways of repeating the inherited models with ways of inventing new variations.

We build models of gender through repetition, Butler argues. Performing gender, and watching it performed, in more or less the same way over and over, produces a taken-for-granted idea that certain ways are natural ways and right. Yet, repetitions are never perfect. We never do the same thing exactly the same way twice. And some repetitions vary from the model more than others. Thus, even as repetition irons in the model of an essentialized notion of gender, it also undermines that model, proliferating what it repeats into a series of variations. While we can see patterns in the ways that people perform gender, then, we can also see repetitions that change the patterns and even, with a sense of humor, repetitions that spoof the patterns. Butler proposed drag as one way to spoof seemingly rigid patterns of gender. A drag queen, for example, can seem to spoof masculinity by offering a campy, comical, fabulous variation on masculine gender, and at the same time a drag queen can spoof femininity by exposing the repeated patterns of femininity as a performance that bears no necessary relation to the sexuality of the performer that they supposedly represent.

Butler's claim about drag, though only a small part of her overall discussion, set off arguments about whether drag inevitably chal-

Judith Butler (1956–).

lenges conservative models of gender. Instead, drag might reinforce the models that it seems to spoof. For as people watch a drag queen, they might respond by thinking that, after all, she, or he, is not really a woman, and so they might intensify their belief that, after all, he is really a man and that there is an essential difference between men and women, corresponding to an essential difference between masculinity and femininity, exactly the opposite of what Butler argues. When a drag queen performs, he mimics a structuralist poetics of femininity. That is, he mimics repeated patterns of dress, gesture, and speech that a traditional model of gender associates with femininity. While the mimicry can mock those patterns, as Butler supposes, it can also intensify people's belief that those patterns, in a woman, *are* femininity. In that sense, drag can work in opposite directions at once, perhaps more in one direction for some and more in another direction for others.

Moreover, the performer cannot control the outcome. To Butler's chagrin, some readers took her as arguing that people can choose their own performances of gender, an argument sometimes described as *voluntarism*. But if, as Butler argues, there is no core identity of gender, then there is no one home to do the volunteering, for, in Butler's deconstructive argument, people do not have a preexisting self that then performs identity. Instead, the performance of identity constructs the self. Or, in more poststructuralist lingo, the performance of identity constructs the subject. The subject or self is not the cause of what people do. It is the effect of what people do and, still more, of what people keep doing. Gender, like subjectivity, is not an essential core but a constant production. People produce gender and subjectivity not *by* the ways they express them, as if the signifiers and signifieds were separate causes and effects, so much as *in* the ways they express them.

People can partly, but not freely, perform gender in ways that spoof and undermine the preexisting menu or structuralist poetics of possibilities for gender, for observers do not necessarily read gender in the way that its performers desire. A dyke comfortable with her own performance can be read by some people as a man or as a failed woman. A comfortably gay man can be read by some people as an inept performer of his true gender, as another failure. In a world that naturalizes heterosexuality, a lipstick lesbian and a gay man in a business suit can be naturalized as straight and rendered invisible as queer or can be misread as not accepting their own queerness. As much as we influence how we perform gender and how others read our performance of gender, we do not control how people read our performances. We do not even control how we ourselves read them, for, like any audience, within our individual selves we can multiply the models of interpretation, mixing the radical and the conservative and even making competing interpretations give urgency and meaning to each other.

HOW TO INTERPRET: A QUEER STUDIES EXAMPLE

For example, in the movie *The Crying Game* (1992), Dil repeatedly explains herself to Fergus by saying such things as "A girl has to have a bit of glamour" and "A girl has to draw the line somewhere." In effect, she proposes a structuralist poetics of femininity. Each time she calls on that poetics by explaining her actions and preferences as matching what a girl has to do, she performs a feminine role. But by calling attention to her performance as a role, she also suggests an ironic possibility that not all girls have to have a bit of glamour or have to draw the line in the same way and that she or some other girl might consider drawing the line some other way. Once Dil is revealed as a he or for all those who suspect all along that she is a he or who know from watching the movie before or hearing about it before that she is a he, then Dil's remarks about what a girl has to do multiply in their already multiple meanings. A girl may have to do certain things, by one model, but a guy may not have to do those things. Or a guy who is also a girl or is performing girlness might feel even more pressure to do them or might find pleasure or relief in doing them. Or he might find pleasure in vexing Fergus's more conservative notions of what gender requires from Fergus or from men or from couples. When Fergus desires Dil, supposing she is a woman, or a woman performing a woman, and then discovers that she is a man, or a man performing a woman, then Fergus can find himself rethinking his understanding and performance of his own desire. Audience members might go through the same rethinking, if they have specularized Dil in the way that (as we saw in Chapter 6) Laura Mulvey proposes that audiences specularize movie showgirls as feminine heterosexual objects and icons. Fergus discovers that he has been performing heterosexuality, and his newfound sense of his heterosexuality as performance can compromise its stability as heterosexuality. Suddenly, things he did not understand before cascade into a series of newfound recognitions, such as his memory of Jody's (Dil's previous boyfriend) words about Dil, his own bonding with Jody, and his conflicted feelings about his attraction to Dil and his unlikely commitment to pursue her.

As Jody, Dil, and Fergus perform their gendered identity and sexuality, they also perform and show the mobility of their colonialist identities. As a black Briton, Jody can fit among the colonized, but the new, would-be postcolonial Britain invites him to join the colonizers by enlisting in the army. By joining the colonizers, Jody sacrifices his chance to join his potential peers and allies among the colonized Irish. The power of the metropole offers an attraction too strong to resist. Meanwhile, the potential allies among the colonized are not so welcoming. Except for Fergus, when the Irish Republican Army fighters look at Jody they see only his collaboration with the colonizers. From their perspective, he is just like the other colonizers or, in a sense, worse, for by joining the colonizers' army he has consented to their rule. He has, in effect, colonized himself. Or so it might seem. For when Jody points Fergus to Dil, another black Briton, he upsets the equation. Just as he breaks a racialized taboo in following the Irish white woman, allowing a heterosexual interlude to deflect Fergus from recognizing that Jody might also desire a man, he breaks several taboos in directing Fergus to Dil: taboos of nationality, of race, and of gender. Each intensifies the others.

In these ways, *The Crying Game* trades on Fergus's heterosexual desire and queers it, or reveals it as always already queered. It asks whether a queer desire drives Fergus's heterosexual pursuit of Jody's girlfriend, who too conveniently performs the ostensibly heterosexual stereotype of the showgirl chanteuse. Queer studies often proceeds by taking ostensibly heterosexual practices and unveiling a queerness within them, making *queer* into a verb. When Fergus pursues the girlfriend of another man, in a sense he also pursues the other man. He tries out the position of erotic relations, mediated or once-removed, with the other man, and all the more so when Dil turns out to be more like Jody than Fergus anticipated. As Fergus found himself unexpectedly facing and touching Jody's penis, so he again unexpectedly faces and touches Dil's. Similarly, even among heterosexuals the familiar pattern of competition between people or literary characters for the same man or woman can end up expressing desire, not only for the person they compete for, but also, potentially, for their rival, as they bond with their comrade in the chase. More generally, once we think of gender as performance, then queer and straight practices do not run along independent of each other. Instead, like the opposite but not really so opposite poles of any binary, they define and depend on each other, and in a sense they actually inhabit each other. Just as Marilyn Monroe or John Wayne, Mae West or Ernest Hemingway, perform heterosexuality so extravagantly that they overperform it, so—like the stereotypical gunslingers and tough-guy detectives of film and fiction—they end up performing a role so conspicuously scripted and iconic that it carries the possibility of flipping into its opposite and spoofing the heterosexual confidence that it supposedly exemplifies. Queerness ends up queering straightness.

QUEER STUDIES AND HISTORY

In the spirit of deconstructive queer studies that sees practices and beliefs as changing across time, scholars study queer history. From one approach, the notorious trials of Oscar Wilde in London in 1895 look like a landmark in the public recognition of queerness, particularly for gay men. Wilde, the brilliant playwright, poet, wit, and aesthete (champion of art for art's sake), was convicted of "gross indecency," a euphemism for gay sex. Through the Wilde trials, a gay male subculture came into the wider public eye and consciousness, which many historians see as transforming an awareness of gay acts to an awareness of gay identity and culture.

In that vein, in *The History of Sexuality, Volume One: The Will to Knowledge* (1976), Michel Foucault proposed that the very idea of homosexuality as an identity is a relatively recent invention. While people have always engaged in practices that we now associate with queerness, Foucault argued that those practices did not generate or represent an identity until a medicalizing discourse obsessed with repressing sexuality arose in the nineteenth century. Ironically, the zeal to repress sexuality produced a massive discourse of sexuality, including psychoanalysis, that centered identity on sex. In Foucault's thinking, then, acts do not represent or emerge from preexisting identities. Instead, a pattern of thinking emerged that imposed identity on acts. Eventually, the identity came to be taken for granted, as if it came from the acts themselves rather than from ways of thinking about the acts. Before the invention of homosexuality, according to Foucault's controversial thesis, people would engage in same-sex acts, but they would not be homosexual. Beginning with the invention of homosexuality in the nineteenth century, what you did became what you are, whether straight or queer. (For more on Foucault, see Chapter 9.)

Not all historians agree with Foucault. They continue to debate how we should interpret the relation between the long history of queer practices and the history of queer identities. It remains clear, nevertheless, that the interpretation of queer practices has changed across time and space. In ancient Greece, erotic love between men and boys was honored among the aristocracy, including the military and the leaders of culture and government. While scholars continue to sift the evidence and debate the details of ancient Greek pederasty, the Greek example shows how ideas about sexuality vary. For example, acts considered gay or lesbian in the twenty-first century West do not necessarily look that way in other cultures and times. In many countries, for example, public hand-holding among same-sex heterosexuals is routine. Passionate expression of love between heterosexuals of the same sex was routine in the nineteenth-century

United States. In some countries, a man may penetrate another man anally without being thought of as gay. Most people do not realize that the sexual categories and assumptions of their own time and place have a history. They are not essences. They have changed over time, and they continue to change.

The very term *homosexual* did not appear until 1869. In the late nineteenth century, it came into prominence as a diagnosis for what many doctors then considered a sickness. Because of its history as a medical term connoting illness, many people now reject the term, and I do not ordinarily use it in this book. (In an influential series of statements beginning in 1973, the American Psychological Association declared its judgment that "homosexuality" is not a disorder or illness.) The relative newness of the term, historically, corroborates the idea that queerness as a distinct identity, or an identity in something like its current or recent form, did not emerge until well into the nineteenth century. At least it corroborates the idea that during that time gay and lesbian identities went through dramatic changes, whether in themselves or in the public awareness of them or both. The word *heterosexuality* did not appear until 1880, suggesting that our concept of heterosexuality is not an essence, but, instead, as structuralists might say, part of a binary that makes the concept of heterosexuality depend on the concept of "homosexuality," and perhaps vice versa. From a poststructuralist perspective, however, or simply, in the eyes of many historians and cultural critics, from a historicist perspective, that binary—though often

---

Stonewall

One evening in 1969 in New York's Greenwich Village, the police raided a gay bar, as they had countless times before. But this time, the customers and a gathering crowd at the bar, called the Stonewall Inn, fought back. And they fought back successfully, first by hundreds and then by thousands. "Stonewall," as the event has come to be known, or sometimes the Stonewall riots or the Stonewall rebellion, inspired queer political groups such as the Gay Liberation Front, and it marks a turning point in the development of "gay pride" and the organized, public assertion of queer rights.

The Stonewall Inn.

supposed stable—varies so widely between times and places and between and within groups of people and individuals, that it looks dramatically unstable.

In 1980, Adrienne Rich famously proposed a way to describe that instability for women. She suggested that there is a *lesbian continuum*, "a range—through each woman's life and throughout history—of woman-identified experience" that fits somewhere on the lesbian continuum, regardless of whether "a woman has had or consciously desired genital sexual experience with another woman" (648). Rich's proposal attracted considerable interest, partly because, by naturalizing lesbianism and seeing it as routine, ordinary, and pervasive, it turns the tables on the naturalizing of heterosexuality and partly because some feminist and lesbian critics find it oversimplifying. They fear that it desexualizes lesbianism or mutes its specificity and that the concept of a continuum can reestablish its opposite poles, leaving only a subtler form of the old binary between straight women and lesbian women. It might also invite others to propose a heterosexual continuum, the same continuum as it appears from the other side of the binary. Regardless, in the 1970s and 1980s especially, Rich's notion and the ideas of other lesbian feminists helped turn feminism and gender studies away from naturalizing heterosexuality, so that lesbian studies influenced feminism even as feminism and gender studies influenced lesbian and queer studies.

Meanwhile, within queer studies—or some would say outside it— there has always been tension between lesbian and gay studies. Many scholars see it as the productive tension of an alliance, while others resent the potential for gay studies or lesbian studies to overshadow the other or to overshadow or be overshadowed by queer studies. In a still patriarchal culture, some critics see gay studies as especially at risk of overshadowing lesbian studies. At their best, each of these possibilities helps keep scholars—and gay, lesbian, and queer people more generally—more alert to the consequences and nuances of their practices and assumptions. Meanwhile, these potentially productive tensions have increasingly found themselves mirrored in similar suspicions and provocation between, on the one hand, lesbian, gay, or queer studies and, on the other hand, transgender studies, an emerging area of interest and scholarship that overlaps with each of these other categories while still laying claim to its distinctiveness.

OUTING: WRITERS, CHARACTERS, AND THE LITERARY CLOSET

In the classroom, the hardest idea for me to get across about queer studies is that queer studies, and especially queer literary criticism, is—as I like to put it—not about **outing**. Outing is the controversial process of publicly exposing people for living in the **closet**, that is, for keeping their queer desires private rather than public. To many people's thinking, outing is a terrible violation of privacy. Though the practice remains controversial, a modicum of consensus has developed that suggests that outing is abusive—except when it comes to outing people who abuse their position in the closet to advocate homophobic public policy. For example, queer activists threatened to out closeted members of the United States Congress who voted against the interests of queer people. The controversy is vexed because the very concept of the closet and of outing presuppose a homophobic cultural setting. If the cultural environment were not homophobic, then no one would want to hide in the closet, and it would make no difference whether someone were outed or not. But in a homophobic setting, those who look on outing with suspicion fear that it may hurt people, or that people at least believe that they could be hurt by being outed, by coming out of the closet, and they believe (as I do) that it is no one else's right to make that decision for someone else. Nevertheless, staying in the closet can help perpetuate a homophobic cultural environment by helping to sustain the public perception that there is something wrong with being queer. By coming out of the closet, people can help make queerness visible as an ordinary part of what is routinely all around us.

When journalists say—as they often do—that someone in the public eye is "openly" or, even worse, "admittedly" lesbian, transgender, gay, or queer, they slam the closet door in the guise of sliding it open. They spotlight queerness as something to be ashamed of. Similarly, the U.S. military tries to paint queerness as shameful through the policy of "Don't ask, don't tell." Such practices help make the environment that leads, for example, to the epidemic of queer teen suicides. It is a form of queer-bashing, however unwitting. In the process, such language also fetishizes the status of in versus out of the closet, making the process of fingering someone's sexual "preference" (as if it were a consumer choice) the binary be-all and end-all of much of the broader public's dialogue about queerness. In that binary obsession, people can get reduced to "they are" or "they are not" queer, as if it were always that simple and as if the on–off switch on that overly simple binary defined everything that matters about someone. You never see a journalist describing someone as openly—let alone admittedly—heterosexual. For example, when an American president—George W. Bush—called for cluttering the U.S. Constitution with an amendment banning same-sex marriage, news reports did not describe him as openly heterosexual, implying that he bore some undue bias because of his own history. But when Massachusetts Representative Barney Frank speaks out on the same

issue (and on many other issues), news reports routinely introduce
him with the "openly" or "admittedly" tag.

Besides making for shoddy journalism, such a practice encourages a crudely oversimplified notion of queer literary and cultural
criticism. It leads students—and many critics—to suppose that
queer criticism is about pointing out that particular writers are or
were lesbian or gay or that certain characters are lesbian or gay. I call
that a form of outing. But the goal of queer criticism is not to out
writers or characters. A focus on outing—even without using the
term *outing*—can actually go against the ideas and goals of queer
studies. For one thing, to "out" writers or characters or to allow
outing to seem like the organizing motive of queer criticism re-
inforces, rather than undermining, the binary between queer and
straight, because it suggests that we can divide everyone up into two
categories: They are queer or they are not queer. Usually (depending
on how we do it), to out writers or characters by announcing that
certain writers or characters are lesbian or gay can invite the assumption that all the rest are straight, as if everyone were straight
unless otherwise noted. It also risks reducing queer writers or characters to their sexuality, in a way that we do not typically do for
straight writers or characters. And it suggests a transhistorical essence for such categories as *lesbian* and *gay*, as if such terms applied
in the same way to all times and all people and as if everyone fit
perfectly within those terms and understood exactly how they fit
in them. To call Shakespeare gay—or to say that he was not gay—
supposes that, 300 years before the Wilde trials or almost 400 years
before Stonewall, Shakespeare's way of understanding his identity
and sexuality would fit snugly into the assumptions and practices of a
later age.

To be sure, in many ways they might have fit the assumptions of
a later age, and historians debate what has remained continuous
in queer and straight life and what has changed. Increasingly, for
example, critics argue over whether we can determine Shakespeare's
sexual orientation or at least the sexual orientation of the speaker in
his sonnets, who passionately addresses most of his love sonnets to a
man, while sometimes writing of his love for a woman and sometimes
of his love for both the man and the woman. For some critics, it seems
presumptuous to apply our own categories of "sexual orientation"
to so different an age. To others, the gay or bisexual stance of
the sonnets seems explicit. We can also recognize many characteristics associated with later gay stereotypes in some of Shakespeare's

characters, such as Richard II, and in characters of other playwrights from his time, such as Christopher Marlowe's Edward II, a partial model for Shakespeare's Richard II. In that sense, to argue against outing writers and characters risks encouraging a practice that could slide into denying the queerness of writers or characters, which would also undermine the goals and practices of queer criticism. But there is a difference between focusing on outing, which can reduce queerness to something that critics point at and finger like an essence logoed on the forehead, and recognizing queerness as an integral, sometimes shaping part of a picture but not necessarily in itself the goal and end-all of literary interpretation. Now and then, these opposed concerns may clash, but that can make for a productive dialogue that helps keep queer criticism queer by keeping it unstable and self-questioning.

HOMOSOCIALITY AND HETEROSEXUAL PANIC

The category of the **homosocial** speaks to these questions about changing notions of sexual practices and identities over time and how those changes influence our understanding of literature, including character and literary plot. The term *homosocial* refers to intense relations between people of the same sex that might not be sexual but that through their intensity can suggest an erotic charge. In a famous and influential 1975 article, "The Female World of Love and Ritual: Relations between Women in Nineteenth-Century America," feminist historian Caroll Smith-Rosenberg describes the intense friendships typical of many ostensibly heterosexual nineteenth-century American women, often expressed in intensely passionate letters and diaries that seem, to later ears, erotic but that bear no evidence of sexual relations. Such friendships were routine for many ostensibly heterosexual men as well as women. Some of them must have included sexual contact, but apart from homosocial kissing and hugging, most of them probably did not.

Historians are left to ask what changed to make such once-commonplace friendships unusual or even taboo and what changed to make the passionate language of such friendships, once routine among ostensible heterosexuals, now sound erotic—sound "homosexual" rather than homosocial—whether lesbian or gay. By themselves, the Wilde trials cannot explain the change, but they can signify a shift in people's sense of possibility, a shift that the Wilde trials grew out of, catalyzed, and made visible. Visibility and public awareness make a difference. In some ways, of course, they make things better by showing both the queer and straight public the ordinariness of queer life. But in the face of continuing homophobia and even queer-bashing, visibility and public awareness also pose a threat to lesbians and gays and to anyone else whom a homophobic culture might suppose is lesbian or gay. That threat, in turn, appears to have changed the profile of homosociality, because the same acts and expressions of passionate affection that once could happily co-incide with a heterosexual self-identity soon came to look lesbian or gay in a culture that often saw lesbian and gay life as an abomination.

As a result, homosocial friendships changed, at least in the Anglo-American and western European world. They lost much of their passionate language and openness of touch, but they did not disappear. Indeed, **homophobia** and the continuation of homosociality have much to do with each other. Homophobia refers to a prejudice against and fear of so-called homosexuals. The term takes the heterosexist idea that "homosexuality" is a psychological problem and turns it upside down, lifting the burden of psychological disorder ("phobia") from queer people and putting it instead on heterosexuals who fear and object to queer people. Where homosociality remains powerful, in such places as football teams, monasteries, convents, and the military, homophobia is especially strong (which is not to say that it succeeds in stamping out queer acts or emotions—far from it). As the literary critic and queer theory scholar Eve Kosofsky Sedgwick has argued in *Between Men: English Literature and Male Homosocial Desire* (1985), homosociality also plays a key role in heterosexual relations and marriage.

Sedgwick argues that in crucial ways marriage has, historically, been a homosocial institution, much as that might at first seem counterintuitive. Marriage and heterosexual relations, say Sedgwick, have traditionally been a homosocial exchange **between men**. She draws on the structuralist argument by Claude Lévi-Strauss that cultures structure themselves through the **traffic in women**, also called the **exchange of women**. Working from assumptions that now leap out at us as sexist, Lévi-Strauss proposed that men structure their relations with each other—which he saw as the relations that define culture—by using women. The women cement or figure alliances among men, and they figure masculine status. The feminist anthropologist Gayle Rubin, in a landmark article called "The Traffic in Women: Notes on the 'Political Economy' of Sex" (1975), offered a feminist rereading of the exchange of women that considered its consequences for women, the objects of masculine exchange. When I first describe the exchange of women to students, they usually look at the idea with skepticism. Americans are used to thinking of that as something that other cultures do, not their own culture, which they see as envisioning marriage through romantic heterosexuality, not through dowries or arranged marriages. But students start to get more of a feel for the exchange of women if we mention the familiar notion of the "trophy wife," including Thorstein Veblen's idea about men using women for conspicuous consumption, men's way of showing off their success to other men. Still more, students see the point if we refer to the tradition of the father of the bride "giving" the bride to the groom, as if a wedding were a deal between men, as it often is and as, in many parts of the world and points in history, it is explicitly.

Traditionally, classic British comedies and novels end in marriage, as if marriage were the goal and end of all that matters, especially for women. Sedgwick proposes that male characters negotiate and use those marriages and the brides to shape their homosocial relation with other male characters, not simply to shape a heterosexual relation between husband and wife. In many a Shakespearean comedy, for example, and not only when the characters finally marry each other at the end, men use marriage to resolve their conflicts with each other. For Sedgwick, the homosocial includes the homosexual, because the bias against homosexuality reroutes it into homosociality. Men use women to shape men's relations with other men in a variety of ways across a variety of cultural activities and literature, from explicit instances, as in Robert Browning's "My Last Duchess" and Shakespeare's *The Taming of the Shrew, Much Ado about Nothing,* and *The Tempest,* to surreptitious instances, as in Henry James's *The Portrait of a Lady,* to many variations in between. In Nathaniel Hawthorne's *The Scarlet Letter,* for example, Roger Chillingworth and Arthur Dimmesdale use Hester Prynne to negotiate their relation to each other, without their fully understanding or saying so, so that generations of readers unattuned to the exchange of women or unattuned to erotic emotions between men have often missed that reading. Yet contemporary readers, increasingly attuned to queer possibilities, see it far more often and provocatively. Drawing on the discussion of feminist interest in women's agency in Chapter 6, we might read Shakespeare's *The Merchant of Venice* as showing women's reaction against men's using women to shape relations between men. We could see Portia as controlled by her father's directions for her marriage, or we could see her as using the song to turn her father's directions to her own purposes and then taking charge through the

Eve Kosofsky Sedgwick (1950–).

trial and the rings. Similarly, Desdemona in Shakespeare's *Othello* resists her father's plans for her and thus shows feminist agency, or we could see her resistance as a disaster that ends up reinforcing the value of patriarchal wisdom. Often the interest lies in the ways that the traffic in women is not a done deal but instead gets negotiated, successfully or not, by women as well as by men.

In *Between Men* and later works, Sedgwick also discusses the concept of **homosexual panic**, which develops from her discussions of homosociality. Homosexual panic refers to the fear by straight people or by people of uncertain sexuality that others might think they are lesbian or gay in a homophobic culture. Homosexual panic is a powerful cultural force. It leads, for example, to queer-bashing, whether through harassing acts and language or through physical violence, as heterosexuals fear that they are or might be or could be thought queer. In response, they sometimes project their fear of their own queerness or potential queerness onto others and then try to reassure themselves by abusing that queerness as if it were not part of themselves. They want to see it as utterly separate from themselves in a binary so falsely firm that it must forever be propped up to keep it from toppling over. We might see antiqueer legislation as a form of homosexual panic, including laws against equal rights in housing, employment, benefits, hospital visitation, and so on. Opposing such rights is a form of reassuring the opposers about their own threatened heterosexual status. From this perspective, the idea that heterosexual marriage must be protected by legislation exposes a fear that it is vulnerable, that heterosexuality cannot stand up by itself but instead needs to hold itself up by putting down nonheterosexuality. That can remind us that heterosexuality needs and depends on nonheterosexuality. Without queerness to compare it to, heterosexuality cannot be recognized as heterosexuality.

Homosexual panic is an especially helpful concept to introduce to college students, who will make up many of the readers of this book, because it does a great deal to shape the lives of many adolescents and young adults. In a world where many people conflate femininity and masculinity with the strict binaries of stereotypically heterosexual femininity and masculinity, adolescents and young adults and people of other ages as well frequently feel pressed to prove their masculinity, femininity, and heterosexuality, perhaps by acting or dressing a certain way on Friday or Saturday night, by drinking or by drinking as much as or more than the next person, by putting on the right swagger in the locker room, or maybe by a queer-bashing wisecrack that tries to say: *They* are like that, but *I* am not. Or maybe by staying silent when someone else makes a wisecrack. We see it academically when straight students fear that if they talk about or ask a question about queer studies in the classroom or in a paper, or if they check queer studies books out from the library, or if someone sees them looking at queer books in a bookstore or looking at queer websites or even reading this chapter, then someone might think they are queer. In fact, the term *homosexual panic* is misleading. We might better call it heterosexual panic, since it refers to a panic by (more or less) heterosexuals. Already-out gays and lesbians are immune to homosexual panic, because other people already know that they are queer. The new visibility figured in the Wilde trials made homosocial acts look like queer acts in a queer-bashing world, thus intensifying homosexual panic and reshaping the pleasures and anxieties of same-sex friendship. If we think critically about homosexual panic and recognize the ubiquitous ordinariness of queer

life, then we can help the panicky heterosexual reply, in response to worries about what "someone might think": *So what?* And if it doesn't really matter for most of ordinary life, then maybe those other people won't presuppose that I am or that I'm not, and maybe I won't presuppose about them either, and *it's ok.*

Daily life, movies, popular culture, and literature are fraught with homosexual panic, with people and characters desperate to prove a stereotypically heterosexual masculinity or femininity or, more subtly, so self-conscious about the desperation to prove it that their desperation also provokes curiosity about what they fear. The desire to prove people's heterosexuality seems especially intense and controlling an ordeal after the shift represented by the Wilde trials. It is intensely visible, for example, in Ernest Hemingway's fiction, where characters (both female and male) often live in fear of and fascination with queerness and their own femininity and masculinity.

"That's so *gay!*"

In recent years, the expression "That's so *gay!*," meaning "That's so *stupid!*," has grown common, especially among younger straight people. If asked, they sometimes hurry to say that the expression has nothing to do with gays or queers, that it's just an expression. But what does it express?

Many people also say, "That's so *Jewish!*" or "That's so *retarded!*," intending the same meaning: "That's so stupid." People who never imagine that they themselves might join in queer-bashing routinely use these expressions or stay silent when they hear other people use them. The widespread use of an expression like "That's so *gay!*" can direct us, whatever our sexual orientation and behavior, to think about what role such a phrase or the sentiments it expresses might play in encouraging queer depression and even the tragically high rate of suicide among young queer people. It also encourages homosexual panic. It says that *you* or someone else might be gay, but *I* am not, so you don't have to worry about me, and I don't have to worry about me. In that way, ironically, the expression "That's so *gay!*" worries very much.

HOW TO INTERPRET: ANOTHER QUEER
STUDIES EXAMPLE

In Shakespeare's *A Midsummer Night's Dream*, the opening scene shows men trying to control the fate of women, and that control may seem to draw on men's right to exchange women, but we do not see any actual exchange negotiated, and the patriarchal system remains far from perfect or complete. Egeus wants his daughter, Hermia, to marry Demetrius, but we never learn what Egeus might get in return, so that Egeus's wish never emerges certainly as an attempted exchange. Hermia and Lysander, her choice for a husband, protest Egeus's arrangement. That puts Theseus, Egeus, and Demetrius on one side, with Lysander on the other side, so that men do not fit into a general conspiracy of men exchanging women. Nor do they exclude Hermia from the discussion; she gets her say, just as they do. Thus men's exchange of women lies implicitly on the table, but it is also up for debate. Then Lysander goads Demetrius and the reigning assumptions about sexuality, saying: "You have her father's love, Demetrius, / Let me have Hermia's; do you marry him" (Shakespeare, *Midsummer Night's Dream* 1.1.93–94).

Lysander's verbal jab protests men's efforts to control women's desire. It also suggests that something might be going on, erotic or otherwise, between Egeus and Demetrius and that they want to use Hermia as the proverbial feminine pawn as they negotiate their relations between themselves, of whatever kind. It has two additional, contradictory effects. On the one hand, it throws before us an aggressive, homophobic syllogism with something like the following bitter logic: (1) Marriage, love, and sex between men (three separate things here implicitly blended together) are obviously ludicrous. (2) You—Demetrius and Egeus—are calling for Hermia to marry Demetrius out of your love for each other, rather than from any love for Hermia. (3) Therefore, your plan for Hermia to marry Demetrius is obviously ludicrous. The upshot of such logic, apart from its immediate meaning for the fates of these particular characters, is to skip past the initiating assumption and allow it to linger unchallenged in the background, namely: Same-sex desire is ludicrous. Caught in the flow of plot and drama, an audience can get swayed by the logic for the characters, the conclusion in number 3, and allow the broader cultural logic and assumptions to hover in place as unnoticed yet active cultural dictates. (That is what Marxists call ideology, as we will see in the next chapter.) Cultural assumptions

like that can rumble through an audience's emotions, setting off homosexual panic and punishing people for potential same-sex desires.
After the play concludes, an audience's concern for the characters'
fate may end or diminish, but the cultural logic underlying the dialogue and plot continues to help regulate the unthinking logic and
momentum of daily life, and in this case that logic is homophobic.

On the other hand, when Lysander suggests what we could take as
the obviously ludicrous possibility that Demetrius marry Egeus, it
might not in every respect and to every member of the audience seem
as ludicrous as the homophobic logic demands. In that sense, the
point is not so much what Lysander's bitter wit may suggest for the
other characters as it is the deconstructively unstable multiplicity of
Lysander's comment, more for the audience than for the characters.
The point is not to out the characters. Demetrius and Egeus, or, if not
them, then maybe two other men, could love each other or could feel
for each other sexually, and maybe they sometimes negotiate their
feelings for each other through the exchange of women. Or they could
put aside the exchange of women and negotiate their feelings for each
other more directly. If we open our eyes, then we might see that some
men already express their feelings for each other more directly; and as
that is the case for men, so it is also the case for women. That is to say,
even homophobic assertions that queerness is ludicrous can turn
themselves upside down and expose their own ludicrousness when
juxtaposed against the nonludicrous routine of queer life. Indeed,
such questions might lead to more questions, particularly for *A
Midsummer Night's Dream*, which soon goes on to experiment with a
host of sexual shenanigans, rapidly shifting erotic allegiances, an ostensibly heterosexual couple (Oberon and Titania) fighting over their
passion for a lovely changeling boy, and Titania falling head over
heels for someone who, by class and species, lies outside her culturally
assigned range of appropriate lovers. A work of art, literature, or
popular culture, such as *A Midsummer Night's Dream*, can expose,
reflect, and help provoke an instability of cultural logics and assumptions about all sorts of things, by all means including queerness.
None of this has much to do with saying that Shakespeare or Egeus or
Demetrius is—or is not—gay. Queer criticism is about the cultural
logics of queerness and heterocentrism, not about outing or pin-
pointing the supposed sexual orientation of writers or characters.

*   *   *   *   *

If you wish to think about possibilities for queer criticism, then
you can ask yourself what underlying cultural assumptions about

queerness seem to be at work in a literary text or in another cultural text, such as a political speech, a law, a court ruling, a movie, a song, a website, a TV show, a concert, or a painting. You can find those assumptions in references to queerness. You can also find them in references to heterosexuality. Who desires whom, and what suggestions seem to be at work about who should or should not desire whom, and what are the consequences of those desires? Do characters or plots seem to take anything for granted about the possibilities for who is attracted to whom? How do they enact their taking-for-granted, and does their taking some things for granted have the effect of silencing, calling attention to, or resisting other possibilities? Is heterosexuality naturalized? If so, is it comfortably naturalized, or do you see faultlines in the effort to naturalize it?

How do characters with queer desires respond to the cultural resistance to queer desire? Can they ignore it? Do they oppose it? Do they internalize and accept it, or find themselves caught between ignoring, opposing, and adopting such attitudes? Do you see any homosexual panic or any encouragement of homosexual panic? Do men conduct their relations with each other by manipulating women? Do women go along?

How do assumptions about lesbian, gay, and heterosexual desires compare to each other? Do illicit heterosexual desires receive a different treatment from illicit same-sex desires? Can illicit heterosexual desires in any way serve as a stand-in for illicit same-sex desires? Do characters or the texts themselves take pleasure in or find fear in identity as a performance that may in some ways float free from a sense of identity as an essence? How does the text understand masculinity and femininity, and does it assume connections between certain patterns of masculinity or femininity and other patterns of sexual desire? Do those patterns work, or does something resist them? Do some characters or actions not fit into conventional patterns of masculinity or femininity or patterns of masculine or feminine desire?

When the text ponders questions like this, does it worry over them soberly, or does it tease them or laugh over them? How does the focus on seriousness or laughter or the mix of seriousness with laughter speak to cultural debates and assumptions about queer possibilities and the resistance to them? What variations do you see within these debates and within the work's assumptions or the characters' assumptions about sexual identities and about same-sex and opposite-sex desires?

❊ 8 ❊

Marxism

You might wonder why we would care about Marxism today. Didn't it die when the Berlin Wall fell in 1989? That is what many Americans believe. Actually, well over one out of five people still live in Communist countries, most of them in the People's Republic of China but many of them in Vietnam, North Korea, Laos, and Cuba, and Communist parties or their descendants are active in many other countries. But while contemporary Communism varies widely, contemporary Marxist criticism has little to do with Communism. Many Marxist critics see the Soviet, Maoist, and other Communist ruling parties since the Russian Revolution of 1917 as having hijacked the socialist ideals of Marxism and merged them with totalitarianism, often forming what is called *state capitalism* (which concentrates power in the hands of party and national leaders, as it was once concentrated in the hands of capitalists). Marxist critics often see contemporary Communists, not least the Chinese Communists, as blending state capitalism with corruption and, in recent years, with local versions of plain-old capitalism. For these reasons, though we might do well to take Communism seriously, this chapter on Marxism has little to do with Communism.

In the mid-nineteenth century, Karl Marx and his colleague Friedrich Engels developed the ideas that came to be called Marxism. Without attempting to give a full account of Marxism, this chapter introduces the elements of Marxism, and especially contemporary Marxism, that matter most to current literary and cultural criticism.

Karl Marx (1818–1883), London, 1861.

For Marx, human history begins with the desire for food and shelter. Marx took a **materialist** perspective, as opposed to the idealist perspective of traditional European philosophy from Plato to Hegel. That is to say, he understood the world as made up of natural, physical things, including food and shelter, rather than idealistic or spiritual abstractions like beauty, truth, and the supernatural. He believed that life shapes consciousness, as opposed to consciousness shaping life. Thus he saw the material, economic world as a **base** and the rest of the world as a **superstructure** produced by that base. Marx's notion that economics is the cause of everything else is called **economic determinism** or **economism**.

As people joined together to produce food, shelter, and clothing, they assigned different work to different people, which began what Marx called the *division of labor*, which in turn led to different classes with competing interests. When agriculture grew enough to make surplus crops, that led to trade, until gradually capitalism replaced feudalism. The new class of capitalist merchants, the **bourgeoisie**, exploited the class of workers, the **proletariat**. For Marx, this process culminated in his own time, at the height of the industrial revolution and the growth of factories, with a small number of owners and a large number of workers. He saw the world as divided between a class of people who labor to produce goods and who sell their labor and another class, people who have capital, use their capital to purchase the labor through wages, and exploit the labor to accumulate wealth for themselves.

For Marx, **capital** is not simply money that can be exchanged for goods or labor. It is money that is used to purchase goods or labor for the purpose of making a profit. Typically, the profit comes from purchasing goods and then selling them again. One hundred dollars, therefore, is not capital unless it is used to buy something with the goal of selling it again for more than $100. Hence *capital* refers to money that is used to make more money, which is used again to make more money and on again in continuous circulation.

Capitalists understand their practices as only natural, because capitalists privilege capital over labor, whereas Marx privileged labor over capital. Rather than seeing history as a series of wars and changing ideas, he saw it as an ongoing class struggle between those who labor and those who own. Marxists often use the term **dialectic**

The Bourgeoisie and the Proletariat

The terms *bourgeoisie* and *proletariat* often confuse readers not familiar with them. I have seen such variations as *bugoisie* (which sounds like an insect) and *proliterate* (which of course would mean something else), so you may want to note the spelling. *Bourgeoisie* is a noun, with *bourgeois* as the adjective, and *proletariat* is a noun, with *proletarian* as the adjective, so we might say that the bourgeoisie usually think in bourgeois ways, and the proletariat usually thinks in proletarian ways. The first syllable of *bourgeois* or *bourgeoisie* rhymes with *store*, though some people pronounce it *boo*. Regardless, the term *proletariat* applies only after the massive growth of wage labor that began with the industrial revolution. While the term *bourgeoisie* might sometimes fit the merchant class before the industrial revolution, neither of these terms typically applies to preindustrial conditions, such as Elizabethan England or the world before the renaissance.

to evoke that ongoing struggle. The concept of dialectic has a long history in philosophy, but for Marxists it usually refers to the way that contradictory arguments and economic forces engage with each other (as in dialogue) to produce something else. In particular, Marx supposed, the back and forth of contradictory ideas and class conflict, which Marxists call *dialectical materialism* or *historical materialism*, would eventually resolve into a socialist future. The proletariat would spontaneously rise up in revolution, overthrow capitalism, and establish a socialist state without class or private property.

Marx did not anticipate the ways that capitalism would adapt to the clamor for socialist change that he and those he influenced began. Through a variety of reforms—increased voting rights (by class, gender, and race), unions, child-labor laws, a limited work week, income tax, unemployment compensation, welfare, social security, and so on—capitalism adapted. In the eyes of people more or less like today's liberal Democrats in the United States or social democrats in Europe, such reforms make almost as much progress as we can reasonably hope for, though they require continuous effort to sustain them, tinker with them, and adapt them to changing conditions. To conservatives, such reforms often go overboard and threaten to convert capitalism into socialism, while to democratic socialists (who have a higher profile in Europe than in the United States), the reforms seem like mere reforms and do not go far enough. Regardless, no one any longer expects the proletariat to lead a spontaneous revolution and create a classless, propertyless state. Instead, contemporary socialism favors democratic change. And contemporary Marxist criticism is often less about provoking social change than about using Marxist ideas to interpret culture. Some critics lament that contemporary Marxist criticism is not enough about social change. Indeed, most of the ideas we will review from Marxist criticism could also work for a right-wing or a liberal critic as well as for a Marxist critic. The difference between a true Marxist critic and another critic who draws on Marxist ideas is simply that the Marxist critic uses Marxist ideas while keeping in mind the ultimate purpose of revolution or at least of dramatic, socialist-directed change.

Under the division of labor in industrial capitalism, Marx argued, much as Henry David Thoreau argued in *Walden,* workers are subjected to the **alienation of labor.** In earlier times, people made their own clothes. Even people producing goods for the market, such as farmers, blacksmiths, and shoemakers, saw the process through from beginning to end and could see and take pride in the completed product without feeling alienated from their own labor. Factory workers, by contrast, work on only one small part of a product and may never see the finished product, let alone use it themselves. Today, we do not make our own Nikes or Levis, build our houses or apartments, plant and harvest our pizzas or cheeseburgers or sodas, or design and assemble our iPods and cell phones. Instead, hundreds of thousands of people from around the globe play a role in making each of those products, and, like us, they are alienated from their labor.

In precapitalist times, workers used the objects they produced, and so those objects had what Marx called **use value**. In alienated labor, workers produce objects for sale on the market, and so those objects, which Marx called **commodities**, have what he called **exchange value**. Exchange value in the widely dispersed and often-distant market seems more abstract than use value, and so laboring for exchange value redoubles the alienation of labor. Meanwhile, Marx argued, exchange value takes on a power of its own, for commodities have the capacity to enhance desire, leading to what Marx called a **commodity fetish**. If Marx looked around him in the middle of the nineteenth century and saw a world mesmerized by commodity fetishism, surely that concern has magnified many times by the twenty-first century, and many critics, from the conservative new critics to contemporary Marxists, have wondered about the role of art and literature as commodities as well as about the role of art and literature in competition with commodities. Some commodities achieve exchange value not so much because of their use for those who purchase them as because of the status they represent. Your cool shoes, for example, may have no more immediately practical value than my uncool shoes and may even have less; but if they are the latest thing, then they signify status and bring you what Marx called **sign exchange value**. For most practical purposes, your Rolex may not work any better than my Timex (especially after someone steals the Rolex); but because you have the sign exchange value of a Rolex and I do not, people will think you are special and I am . . . an English professor. The growth of a commodity economy and a commodity culture takes us steadily further from practical, unalienated labor and use value, leading people to value each other mainly as producers and purchasers of commodities, and so, in effect, in a process that Marx called **commodification**, people themselves are commodified, valued not as people but instead as numbers, statistics, and cogs in an abstract economic machine.

For many years, Marxist criticism made little difference for most literary critics. It tended to work at a rather general level, identifying a writer with the writer's class and seeing the work as reflecting the writer's class interests. To most critics, especially those not so sympathetic to Marxism in the first place, that felt clunky and oversimplified. In the 1930s, with the growth of Communism, the Great Depression, and the rise of the left internationally, Soviet leaders and many of their followers in other countries called for *socialist realism*, literature that explicitly endorsed a romantic vision of the common people and a Communist vision of their future. That kind of prescriptive criticism, criticism that tells writers (prescribes for them) how to write, seemed unreflective and inartistic to many artists, writers, and critics. Meanwhile, many left-wing writers in the English-speaking world called for a proletarian literature and debated what that might mean. At its crudest, it echoed socialist realism, and proletarian literature often continues to be remembered in socialist realist terms. In its subtler modes, it could call instead for art that encouraged people to think critically about capitalist assumptions or socialist possibilities without necessarily speaking to readers didactically or idealizing the proletariat, who, of course, far from offering a socialist vanguard, are often as committed to capitalism as the bourgeoisie. After World War II, as western Europe and the United States turned against the left to pursue the Cold War and with the rise of new criticism and its attention to formalist detail, it often seemed to Americans and western Europeans that Marxist criticism cared little for the nuances and particulars of a literary text and was unresponsive to its literary art and aesthetics.

Meanwhile, mostly apart from Anglo-American eyes, two major Marxist theoreticians, Georg Lukács and Antonio Gramsci, pursued work that would later figure largely in the thinking of Marxist literary criticism. Lukács, a Hungarian philosopher, literary critic, and politician entangled in sometimes-brutal Communist party politics, served as People's Commissar for Education and Culture in the Hungarian Soviet Republic of 1919, the world's second Communist government, which lasted only four months, and as Minister of Culture in the anti-Soviet government of 1956, which lasted less than two weeks before the Soviet tanks rolled in. Unlike the new critics, who during the same years celebrated innovative literary form without taking much interest in social meaning, Lukács, as a Marxist, gave special attention to the social meaning of literary form. Lukács expanded on Marx's notion of **reification** (from *res*, Latin for "thing"). Sometimes called *thingification*, reification refers to the way that commodification reduces social relations, ideas, and even people to things, thus intensifying alienation. Things take on their own momentum, independent of human life, evoking the bewildering fragmentation of alienated, capitalist modernity. Amidst commodity fetishism, things take over human life as people lose touch with the actual labor of the proletariat that global corporations "outsource" to a distant, unseen elsewhere.

Controversially, Lukács decried modernist fiction, such as the novels of James Joyce, Franz Kafka, Robert Musil, William Faulkner, and Samuel Beckett, because he believed that the fragmentation of modernist form decadently and uncritically reproduced the alienated reification of modern life. He saw the modernists as writing for form and technique rather than for social representation, and he saw their form, as in modernist stream of consciousness, as swept up in merely individualist virtuosity. By contrast, he championed what he saw as realist novels, such as the fiction of Sir Walter Scott, Stendahl, Honoré de Balzac, Leo Tolstoy, and Thomas Mann, because he believed that realism, though produced by bourgeois writers, represented not modernist fragmentation but, rather, the totality of society, including history and dialectical class conflict, which can lead readers beyond reification to revolutionary class consciousness. The dialectics of realist fiction, readers might infer, contrasts with the triumphant proletarianism of socialist realism, which replaced boy-meets-girl with boy-and-girl-meet-tractor to make the working class live happily ever after. But especially in the 1930s, when Lukács was beholden to the Communist advocates of socialist realism, he could not put the case so bluntly.

Antonio Gramsci was a leader of the Italian Communist Party. Imprisoned by the Italian Fascist dictator Benito Mussolini, Gramsci wrote most of his influential works in prison, sometimes in secret, and under censorship that forced him to couch many of his ideas in an indirect, fragmented way that his readers must struggle to decipher. Gramsci's prison notebooks, smuggled off to Moscow and published long after his death, have held great interest for contemporary Marxists, especially because he criticized the classical Marxist notion of economic determinism. He distinguished between what he called the *state* (government and politics) and *civil society* (culture), and he concentrated his writings on civil society, which appeals to cultural critics who want to explain things in cultural terms rather than explaining everything by economics. Writing in Fascist Italy in a Fascist prison, Gramsci wanted to understand how the right had risen to such dominance. He wanted to understand why the proletariat had not revolted, as Marx predicted they would. Yet more, he wanted to understand why the masses, for the most part, not only held back from revolution but actually supported the far right, against what Gramsci saw as their own interests. This question has remained central for Marxist thought, because Marxists need to understand why the masses do not overthrow capitalism to set up the socialist system that, according to Marxists, would make the world a far better place for the masses.

Gramsci reasoned that the right maintained its **hegemony**, its dominating influence and power, not so much by violence or **coercion**, as we might expect, as by leadership that won the seemingly spontaneous **consent** of the masses. The government can step in with coercion if necessary, through the police and the army. But according to Gramsci, the more effective way to sustain hegemony comes through cultural leadership. The bourgeois capitalists' cultural prestige makes their way of thinking seem like common sense to the masses, so the masses come to identify with bourgeois ways of thinking, leading them to consent to bourgeois dominance. For example, we might think of the seemingly irresistible drive to consumerism. We could argue that instead of choosing their purchases, people have the drive to consume imposed on them, culturally. The menu of "consumer choices" is chosen for us; but the feeling of a menu deceives people into thinking that they consent, that they have choice and are only doing what they individually want, even when they purchase a mass-produced product that they have been made to want via marketing and peer pressure, which create a demand that was not there before, and even when the products pollute the environment and come from factories that help prop up antidemocratic, misogynist, repressive, corrupt governments. When I buy a pair of shoes (let alone the many pairs that so many of us buy, because the menu of consumer choices makes us feel a need to buy again and again), I do not usually think I am choosing to support a system that starves women and keeps them from voting while corrupt oligarchs live in luxury. I think I am choosing some cool shoes. But perhaps I have been swayed into letting the delusion of consumer choice keep me from realizing that I am acting against the interests of working-class people around the world, people who under a different system could be my allies.

Antonio Gramsci (1891–1937).

We might change bourgeois cultural dominance, Gramsci argued, not by a spontaneous proletarian revolution, which no longer seemed likely, but, instead, by changing people's cultural assumptions, a gradual process of making alliances with other groups to form a "historic bloc" that can eventually achieve its own hegemony. At the helm of that process of cultural change Gramsci saw what he called **organic intellectuals,** not the traditional intellectuals who think they are different from and better than other people, but, instead, leaders who arise from within the people and can use civil society—education and the media—to express the people's ideas that the people might not be ready to express for themselves. With his focus on process and cultural change, therefore, Gramsci moved away from the classical Marxist sense of inevitable revolution and to a sense of *praxis* (practice), a sense that the future will come through the doing of it, through alliances and contingencies, rather than through absolute and abstract theoretical laws. In this way, his thinking has held appeal for Marxists influenced by structuralism, who see everything through its relation to something else, and for Marxists influenced by deconstruction, who see culture as a continuous shifting of multiple forces.

In the middle decades of the twentieth century, a group of Marxist philosophers pursued what they called *critical theory* (in a narrower sense of that term, versus the broader sense that is the overall topic of this book). Associated with the School for Social Research at the University of Frankfurt am Main, in Germany, they came to be known as the Frankfurt School. Led by Max Horkheimer, Theodor W. Adorno, Herbert Marcuse, and, in the next generation, Jürgen Habermas, they sought to reinterpret the relation among reason, art, modernism, and public debate. With the proletariat not leading a revolution, as Marx had predicted, the Frankfurt School sought to understand how capitalist ideology deters revolutionary consciousness, concentrating their attention, like Gramsci, on the superstructure, on culture rather than on economic determinism. Fleeing to the United States to escape the Nazis, they later reestablished themselves in Germany after World War II. While in the United States, they saw technology and the commodifying, commercial "culture industry" (the entertainment industry—movies, music, the media, sports, and so on) reproducing capitalist ideology from one generation to the next, drawing the consuming masses to take capitalist assumptions for granted. In the world of corporate entertainment, they lamented, art becomes another commodity, encouraging political complacency instead of revolutionary or critical thinking. Adorno saw the discontinuities of modernist art as a reprieve from the false promises of Enlightenment rationalism. In the shock of Nazism and World War II, he reacted against traditional art and beauty as ways of painting over the horror of modernity. Adorno called instead for a modern, avant-garde art that would disrupt traditional complacency, an argument not accepted by those who see art and beauty as relatively independent of the corrupt cultures that sometimes produce them. Habermas, more appreciative of Enlightenment rationality, sees Enlightenment models of public debate, which he famously dubbed the **public sphere**, as offering a space between the state and civil society and offering the best alternative to the threatening fragmentation of modernist art and life. He values the role of "communicative reason," as opposed to poststructuralist and postmodernist skepticism. While Habermas sees the corporate mass marketing of politics as displacing the public sphere's rational debate, others have argued that he idealizes the historical public sphere, neglecting the many groups that it excluded, such as women.

Walter Benjamin, who was more loosely associated with the Frankfurt School and who seems to have committed suicide while fleeing the Nazis, took a more sympathetic approach to the relation between technology and culture. Granting that technology displaced the traditional "aura" of the work of art, he also saw new technologies as potentially encouraging critical thinking, depending on how they are used. While the Frankfurt School philosophers, especially after arriving in the United States, saw corporate, mass, consumer culture as producing conforming consumers, Benjamin thought that it could also produce critical consumers. The Frankfurt School thinkers were themselves critical consumers, though we could still argue that critical consumers are the exception rather than the rule.

CONTEMPORARY MARXISM, IDEOLOGY, AND AGENCY

Gradually, many forces converged to form what we might almost call, ironically, a revolution in Marxist criticism, including the disappointment with Communist governments; the growing theoretical challenges from structuralism and deconstruction; a radicalizing professoriate in the wake of the Civil Rights movement, the war in Vietnam, and the growth of feminism; and the persistence of the British left, which—compared with the American left—has a longer and stronger tradition of leftist critique. Amidst continuing debate and controversy, there gradually arose what came to be called *new Marxism, post-Marxism* (the prefix *post* suggests a later Marxism and a dialogue with poststructuralism), or *contemporary Marxism*, which sets itself against the earlier Marxism that it sometimes calls *classical* or, more dismissively, *old* or *vulgar Marxism*.

More contemporary Marxism in this mode looks critically at the base/superstructure model of classical Marxism, sometimes observing that, though Marx proposed that model, in some of their writings Marx and Engels also sought more flexible ways of understanding the relation between economics and culture. As we have indicated, in classical Marxism (at least as new Marxists describe it and certainly in the classrooms and officially sanctioned thinking of Communist countries), the base is economics, and everything else—including art, literature, music, politics, and popular culture—is the superstructure. The base is the cause and the superstructure is the effect, the direct reflection of the base. That model can seem clunky, because many people think that attributing so much to one cause, economics, oversimplifies the variety and unpredictability of human behavior, especially for the arts. We typically think of music, literature, and the visual arts as enclaves of imaginative unpredictability too quirky to be explained in any one way. For that reason, as Marxists—often in the tradition of Gramsci—looked more skeptically at economic determinism, their rethinking of Marxism appealed to many literary and cultural critics.

In that context, literary and cultural critics turned with special interest to the writings of the French Marxist Louis Althusser, especially his contributions to an ongoing discussion about what Marxists call *ideology*. In "Ideology and Ideological State Apparatuses" (1970), Althusser famously defined ideology as "the imaginary relationship of individuals to their real conditions of existence" (162). Althusser used the term *imaginary* in Jacques Lacan's sense of the term, as we introduced it in Chapter 5 on psychoanalysis. But Althusser's phrasing can also make sense to readers unfamiliar with Lacan's special use of the term *imaginary,* if they understand that Althusser saw ideology as an unconscious process.

Confusion arises because, like other Marxists, Althusser did not use the term *ideology* in the usual way we do in English, outside the lingo of Marxist and critical theory. In ordinary English usage, ideology refers to a conscious political program. For example, in an infamous moment at the 1988 Democratic National Convention in the United States, Michael Dukakis, accepting the Democratic nomination for president, bluntly declared: "This election is not about ideology—it's about competence," uninspired words that sent heart attacks racing through the Democratic electorate, until there were not enough Democrats left by election day for Dukakis to beat George Bush (Bush the elder), the least ideological president in recent times. I retell this anecdote to underline the ordinary meaning of the term *ideology* as a conscious political program. But for Althusser, **ideology** refers to an *unconscious* set of beliefs and assumptions, our imaginary relation to real conditions that may not match what we imagine. According to Althusser's notion of ideology, therefore, we mostly misunderstand the world around us and the reasons that lead us to act in the ways that we act.

For example, many college students, especially the humanities-oriented, culturally and intellectually ambitious college students who will often read this book, if asked why they went to college,

Louis Althusser (1918–1990).

might say that they go to college to learn, to grow culturally, intellectually, and imaginatively, perhaps even—as the well-worn phrase
puts it only half ironically—to discover themselves. From an Althusserian perspective, however, those students are deluding themselves, because the real reason they went to college is, as I will put it
deliberately in less inspiring terms, to reproduce the managerial
economy.

No one will get excited to hear that. But the truth is, most of the
students reading this book will become middle managers. They will
be the easily replaceable cogs in the vast machine of the managerial economy that reproduces itself from generation to generation.

They will not change things much, at least not on a big scale. They will make small adjustments to help reproduce the system better rather than to change it. But the kind of people who take the classes where they might read this book are not likely to feel a thrill surging through their veins at the thought that their future is to reproduce the managerial economy. If universities advertised, "Come to our great university and major in English so that you can reproduce the managerial system," potential students—if they survived the dumb-founded perplexity that such an advertisement might produce—would immediately turn about face and go somewhere else. It sounds dull and uninspired. But from the notion of ideology that I am describing here, the dull and uninspired life of small adjustments and middle management is exactly those students' fate. That is also why the culture at large, let alone the individual universities, dares not admit that fate to itself or to would-be students. By encouraging students to believe that their fate is to grow and learn and to discover themselves culturally and intellectually, the system baits them into a much duller fate that they would refuse to go along with if they knew its real conditions. Thus students' imaginary relation, that is to say, their unconscious relation, to real conditions tells them that their motives are discovery. But the real conditions that actually drive what they decide to do are the far more impersonal managerial economy's built-in structures of self-replication, which allow it to reproduce itself from generation to generation. That system needs to remain unconscious and imaginary, because if it were conscious, no one would go along. It recruits its next generation of managers by encouraging them to believe that they act out of individual selfhood, whereas the real conditions are that individual selfhood is a delusion that makes it possible for them to act out of socially (not individ-ually) determined motives that they remain unconscious of, obliv-ious to. They must remain unconscious of or oblivious to those motives, or they would not go along. English majors would become revolutionaries instead of managers, and then the whole system would fall apart. (Or else the former English majors would languish in prison.)

The engine that keeps the system reproducing itself is what Al-thusser famously called **interpellation**, not the most elegant choice of terms. Literally, *interpellation* means "calling," and Althusser sug-gested that the system calls to us, or **hails** us (in the sense of saying "hello!") and we answer. When we answer, we become **subjects** of interpellation, like subjects to a queen or king or subjects to the law.

And so we get drawn into ideology more by what Althusser called *ideological state apparatuses* (ISAs), echoing Gramsci's term *civil society*, which include the schools, media, churches, families, unions, and entertainment culture, than by the repressive state apparatuses (RSAs), echoing Gramsci's term the *state*, which includes the police, courts, prisons, and military. The ISAs can recruit us into ideology more subtly than the RSAs, making us imagine that we have chosen the actions that real conditions have chosen for us. Thus, when an advertisement or the broader consumer culture that advertisements participate in asks us which new car (or new shoes or deodorant or flavor of ice cream or cell phone plan) we want, we think it through and then choose this one or that one. We may even think—and the system encourages us to think—that we have a genuine choice and that our choice expresses our individuality. In the process, we have been interpellated or hailed into unconsciously accepting the assumptions underneath the question, accepting our imaginary relation to real conditions. We do not respond by saying "Wait, I don't need a car (or new shoes, deodorant, ice cream, or cell phone plan)." And we do not say that the system that baits us into thinking we need them leads to an economic structure that distributes income and political power unequally and abusively. Instead of expressing our individuality, we let a screen of bogus individuality (a prepackaged set of options) block us from realizing that we are acting more or less like everyone else.

In this sense, *interpellation is the process of being passively, unconsciously drawn into dominant social assumptions.* (Note the spelling of *interpellation* so that you do not make the common mistake of confusing it with *interpolation*, a completely different term.) At those rare times when we can step outside interpellation enough to see it, we might say that at the point where the interpellation takes place, such as the point when the flashing neon sign makes most of us think we need that ice cream or new car, the ideology *congeals* (one of Althusser's less important but more evocative terms). That is to say, it becomes palpable, like oil (or, as I think of it, like peanut butter or even like slime). A question or thought such as "Is she married?" for example, when we are asked about someone whose sexuality we do not know, can interpellate us into supposing that she and everyone else is heterosexual or wants marriage and should want marriage. In that way, the naturalization of heterosexuality is a form of interpellation, like the naturalization of whiteness, the assumption that people are of course white unless indicated otherwise. Interpellation is the engine that reproduces taken-for-granted (unconscious) cultural assumptions from generation to generation, preventing radical change.

Such is the Marxist and Althusserian theory of ideology, at its grimmest and most inflexible. But it is not always so completely grim.

Subjects and Subjectivity

The terms *subject* and *subjectivity* sometimes cause confusion, because, depending on the context, they have different meanings. For clarity's sake, let us begin with what we do *not* mean in critical theory by these terms. When we say *subject*, we do not mean it in the sense of topic (as when people ask what topics or subjects interest you). And when we say *subjectivity*, we do not mean it in the sense of bias (as when people say that someone's view is biased or subjective). Those are perfectly acceptable meanings, and sometimes people use them in critical theory. But using the terms that way can cause confusion with the usual and more technical meanings of the terms in critical theory.

In the usual and more technical sense, the term *subject* has two different but related meanings. One meaning we have already seen in our discussion of structuralism. Based on the grammatical model of a sentence, the subject is the agent, the one who does, as opposed to the object, which someone does something to. In that sense of the term, the subject holds a position of relative or potential power, similar to a self or an individual but not the same as a self or an individual. Those who equate subjectivity with selfhood miss the point. The terms *self* and *individual* suggest a romantic individualism, whereas the term *subject* refers to a position, specifically to a position that can be held by a group as well as an individual, such as when we speak of feminist or Asian American subjectivity. In this sense, we might think of subjectivity as a structuralist, impersonal answer to what, from the perspective of structuralism, can seem like an overly personal and romantic notion of individuality and selfhood.

Althusser, by contrast, uses the term *subject* to refer to having less power, as in being subject to the law or subject to a queen or king, or, for Althusser, subject to a dominant ideology. Althusser's use of the term focuses on how the subject is interpellated and made into a subject by being interpellated. The subject's delusion of selfhood and individuality keeps it from recognizing that it is a subject, not a self or individual. Thus in the structuralist sense of the subject of a sentence or agent, the term *subject* suggests a degree of control and power, and in the Althusserian sense it suggests being controlled and having less power, but in both senses it offers an alternative to the romantic and consumerist notion of selfhood and individuality.

After all, the students reading this book no doubt vary a great deal. Some of them come to college because, in the world where they grew up, college is just expected. Others come from a world where hardly anyone expects them to go to college, and they have overcome enormous obstacles to graduate high school, let alone move on to college. Some of them think they can avoid middle management by becoming teachers, but of course that just makes them part of the machine that manufactures the raw material of other students into middle management or into more middle management makers (that is, into more teachers). Others, however, will do almost anything they can to avoid working in middle management. Perhaps most of those avoiders will eventually change their minds, as practicalities mount later in their lives, but some of them will hold out. Yet others, meanwhile, consciously go to school specifically in the hope that school will lead to a job in middle management. The picture is thus intricately diverse. The grim view explains a lot, but it might not explain everything. Few English majors will become revolutionaries, but many of them—including some of the middle managers—will work in politics or social services, whether within their jobs or beyond their jobs, and many of them will vote. None of that seems likely to lead to revolution, but it might sometimes contribute to incremental changes for the better, and, over the years, changes might build on changes. Maybe the system will revise itself only as much as it needs to keep reproducing itself, or maybe some of the changes will add up to more than a mere reproducing of the system. You may think that people sustain enough individuality, perhaps a little here and a little there, to change the system but Marxists would probably not put it that way. Instead of looking to individuality as the potential route to **intervention** (the technical word for changing the system or at least for trying to change it) or **agency** (the ability to make things happen), Marxists would probably look to what they call **relative autonomy**, a related but decidedly different term that refers to the superstructure's partial independence from the base. *Relative autonomy* suggests at least a little independence from the clutches of the system, from interpellation, but such independence does not have to come in the form of individualism. Given the Marxist interest in thinking socially, not just individually, relative autonomy, agency, and intervention can come from groups, not just from individuals. For example, if you somehow find a way to think critically and resist interpellation, at least now and then, your ability to resist may remain modest, may be only relative, which makes the term *relative autonomy* far less romantic and less deceiving than the term *individuality*. And you may get that relative autonomy not just because you are, romantically, a unique person (patting yourself on the back), but because you are part of a group of people whose history and partially collective thinking help you learn to think critically or even interpellate you into what we might think of as a subideology, a way of thinking different from and potentially counter to the dominant ideology. Maybe it is an economic group, such as the working class, or a racial group, such as African Americans, or a religious or regional identity, a campus organization, an immigrant, ethnic, or national identity, or a political organization. Whatever the group, and possibly with whatever dash of individuality some people may add to the mix, your relative autonomy, though only relative and not complete, and your exposure to a sub- or counterideology help you to think critically about the dominant ideology, leading to agency and intervention. Those who do not understand relative autonomy rush to convert it into bourgeois individualism. They end up using the Marxist term *relative autonomy* in romanticizing ways that turn it back into the capitalist individuality that the very notion of relative autonomy seeks to undermine, much as those who do not understand the term *subject* use it as if it meant the same thing as *individual* or *self*, which misses the point of the term.

It is easy to say where ideology comes from. It comes from a culture's dominant assumptions, its hegemony. It is harder to say where relative autonomy comes from, but it seems to come from imperfections in the overall system of any ideology. Especially in light of deconstruction, any system seems incomplete, imperfect. Gaps in the dominant system, wrinkles or loose threads in the hegemony, make its imperfections visible, which leaves openings for relative autonomy. It works both ways, however, because relative autonomy also produces gaps, wrinkles, and loose threads in the system. When we pull on a loose thread, we sometimes hit a knot, so that not much more comes loose, but sometimes we find ourselves pulling out more and more thread until the system begins to unravel.

We might see the Marxist term **false consciousness** as the opposite of relative autonomy. *False consciousness* refers to a way of thinking that is so interpellated into oppressive ideologies that it leads people to act against their own interest. For example, when you ride a motorcycle, you put yourself at so high a risk of injury or death, especially when you ride without a helmet, that, though you think you are acting cool, you might reach that thought out of a false consciousness that keeps you from seeing that riding a motorcycle, and, even more, riding without a helmet, is against your own interest. More provocatively, we might say that when American voters support amending the United States Constitution to ban flag burning, their false consciousness makes them think they are acting in a wonderfully patriotic way, but the real conditions are that they undermine their own national polity by trivializing the Constitution and jeopardizing free speech. Or we might say that by advocating lower taxes, my false consciousness leads me to believe that I help myself by reducing my tax burden, whereas the real conditions are that I damage the larger cultural and social world, including my own life in that world, by sabotaging schools, libraries, public transportation, police and fire departments, and a host of other public services.

Among Marxists, however, the notion of false consciousness has a bad reputation, because it can seem presumptuous to suppose that we can put ourselves in a superior position that allows us to understand other people's interests better than they understand their interests themselves. In that light, each of the examples listed earlier is loaded and arguable (though I myself stand by them). Other people might respond that by riding a motorcycle, they use less gasoline and therefore help the broader good by acting more environmentally. Or they could say that banning flag burning keeps us from trivializing the Constitution's protection of free speech and so helps uphold genuine debate. Or, from a common right-wing perspective, reducing taxes makes governments healthier by encouraging them to cut waste and privatize public services, and it boosts the economy by rerouting private money from taxes into investment. For these reasons, Marxists often criticize the notion of false consciousness, though at least some degree of false consciousness has to be assumed, or else there is no way to explain why people have not made the radical changes that Marxists call for, even though those radical changes, according to Marxists, would be in people's own interest.

This leaves us with relative autonomy, agency, and intervention on one side of a continuum and ideology, interpellation, and false consciousness on the other side. We can see critics or cultural commentators who focus more on the relative autonomy, agency, and intervention side of the continuum as more optimistic Marxists and see those who focus more on the ideology, interpellation, and false consciousness side as more pessimistic Marxists. (In the case of Althusser, different readers have put him at different positions on the spectrum, sometimes varying according to which of his essays or which parts of which essays they weight the most.)

Let us suppose, for example, an imaginary thirteen-year-old girl—let's call her Danielle—who listens to hip-hop and especially likes to listen to misogynist hip-hop. From the more pessimistic way of thinking, Danielle is a victim of false consciousness, interpellated into the commercial ideology of consumerism that leads her to buy and listen to her misogynist CDs or her MP3 player and maybe even share her music with her girlfriends, helping to interpellate both herself and her friends into ideologically, unconsciously accepted and abusive assumptions about women and commercial culture. From the more optimistic way of thinking, all that might still make sense, but it is not the whole story. Danielle might buy misogynist CDs or download misogynist hip-hop onto her latest-model iPod, and she might listen to that music with her girlfriends, but she might not pay much attention to the lyrics. She might even interpret the lyrics as ironic, as making fun of misogynist ideas (actually, a notorious defense of misogynist hip-hop that I rarely find convincing). Regardless, whether or not she pays much attention to the lyrics, the role that those lyrics play in her imagination might be modest

compared to other uses she finds for her music. She might listen to the music partly as a signifier of resistance to authority, perhaps in the form of parents, teachers, or her general sense of what people in authority think is right for a thirteen-year-old girl to do. While such resistance can seem juvenile or adolescent, we might be harsh to dismiss it as self-destructive. Instead, we can see it as beginning to include, and as carving a path to, genuine cultural criticism—including agency, intervention, and relative autonomy—as Danielle matures. By sharing her music with friends—listening together, talking about the music, reading rap websites, and swapping fanzines—Danielle may also bond with other girls in ways that allow her to set up a community of girls that helps give her the means to resist or criticize some of the misogyny of daily life, despite the misogyny of the lyrics. Maybe the music even inspires her to experiment with making her own music or writing lyrics, perhaps nonmisogynist lyrics or lyrics where the play with misogyny achieves an ironic or satiric sound more convincing than many of us think it has in commercial hip-hop.

In these ways, the interest for a critic lies not so much in plastering on a label of ideology, interpellation, and false consciousness or a label of relative autonomy, agency, and intervention and then calling that the end of the story. Instead, the interest comes in the intricate negotiations across the interlocking possibilities in any particular cultural activity, including poems, movies, novels, plays, clothing styles, music, political campaigns, sports, websites, magazines, and so on. As critics, any of us may tend to lean more toward the optimistic side or more toward the pessimistic side. (I lean more toward the pessimistic side.) Or we may prefer both equally or vary widely from case to case, but the interest usually comes in how we interpret the particulars rather than in imposing a predetermined tendency.

In light of this overview of Marxist and Althusserian notions of ideology and the resistance to ideology, we can return, for another example, to the discussion of Laura Mulvey's "Visual Pleasure and Narrative Cinema" from Chapter 6. When Mulvey interprets classical Hollywood cinema as masculinizing its audience, as unconsciously coaxing its viewers, whether women or men, queer or straight, into an abusive masculine heterosexuality, we can now see her as arguing that classical Hollywood film interpellates or hails its audience into a particular sexist ideology. Mulvey then tries to make an intervention, tries to crack the shell of that ideology so that, by exposing it to our conscious scrutiny, we can generate enough relative autonomy to resist its enticements and begin to imagine alternatives. Powerful though dominant ideologies are, once we notice their workings and bring them to consciousness, we have begun to look, at least partly, from outside the ideologies, and that makes it possible to resist them. If Mulvey herself underestimates the ability that many audience members already have to say no to the film's persuasions, then that can remind us that her critical autonomy is relative, not complete.

Similarly, the German Marxist playwright Bertolt Brecht called for a new style of acting, which he dubbed the **alienation effect**, which would encourage readers *not* to identify with the actresses and actors on the stage or the roles they played. Contrary to the usual Stanislavskian, or "method," acting that asks performers to absorb themselves into their roles and invites audiences to lose themselves in a trance of realism, Brecht asked for staging and acting that calls attention to itself as performance. Let the lights go on, he said (versus the classical Hollywood assumptions of a darkened theater, as described by Mulvey), and let the lights be visible, and let the performers act in ways that expose their role as actresses and actors, so that audiences can have a critical distance that allows them to question ideological assumptions instead of letting interpellation smother their skepticism. We might transfer Brecht's argument about staging into parallel arguments about poetry or fiction that calls attention to itself as performed, constructed writing instead of encouraging audiences to see the literary text as a passive window to or transcript of unquestionable truth and realism.

Evolving patterns of historical change and contemporary Marxism's rethinking of classical Marxism often reinforce each other. In classical Marxism, because the base of economics determines everything else, class, an economic category, was thought to determine race, a cultural category, just as the base determines the superstructure. In the eventual classless state that Marxists predicted, race would disappear. But as antiracist, anticolonial, and postcolonial thinking increasingly set off massive cultural change, it grew harder to see race as produced entirely by class. While in many countries whites tend to have more economic privilege than people who are not white, so that race and class often seem parallel, nevertheless people of all races belong to every class. Race is therefore a relatively autonomous determinant of cultural variation, of who we are and what we do. Racism may feed off economic exploitation, but economic exploitation also feeds off racism.

Similarly, so long as Marxists tried to explain everything by economics, they had a difficult time accounting for gender, since people in the same family, and hence in more or less the same economic position, do not all share the same gender. For that reason, classical Marxists often ignored feminism and specifically ignored women's concerns. But as feminism revolutionized cultural criticism, feminists convinced Marxists (and sometimes the Marxists and the feminists were the same people) to see gender, like race, as a relatively autonomous determinant of culture. Much as in the relation between racism and economic determinism, misogyny feeds off economic exploitation, but economic exploitation also feeds off misogyny. In the new Marxism, cultural categories such as gender and race shape our lives in a dialectical relation with economics.

In tune with the rethinking of economic determinism, the French sociologist Pierre Bourdieu, who was critical of Marxism, expanded the traditional Marxist notion of capital to include **cultural capital**. Most people think of their aesthetic taste as something they choose for themselves. But in Bourdieu's model, developed especially in *Distinction: A Social Critique of the Judgment of Taste* (1979), we do not freely choose our aesthetic style, our taste in music, clothing, movies, or home décor, or even our style of speaking. Instead, class position, defined not so much by economic capital as by the related qualities of family and formal education, goes a long way to determine aesthetic taste. Drawing on extensive sociological study in France, Bourdieu argues that working-class taste tends to favor realism and escapism in literature and favor realistic or functional painting and photography. Elite taste, by contrast, favors—and has the luxury to favor—an appreciation for form and style in themselves in literature, music, abstract painting, and artistic photography. Those with less formal education tend to favor matter, while those with more formal education tend to favor manner. It often requires more education and aesthetic experience to appreciate an art that imitates or plays off other art than to appreciate an art that imitates nature. Just as cultural capital produces an elite taste in art and elite patterns of speech and behavior, so those tastes and patterns of speech and behavior produce cultural capital, so the social stratification reproduces itself from generation to generation. Thus cultural capital, and not simply economic capital, makes working-class people stay in the working class and makes upper-class people—defined now by their aesthetic taste and not merely by their economic wealth—stay in the upper class. For Bourdieu, then, art serves a social function: It reproduces and legitimates social hierarchies.

The most widely read contemporary Marxist literary theorist and critic is Terry Eagleton, whose broad learning, steady eye on the political consequences of aesthetic and critical practices, and spirited style, together with a massive output of criticism and theory, nearly defy summary. For more than a generation of critics, Eagleton's books have sorted through the ideas of his predecessors in critical and literary theory, especially Marxist theory. He played a leading role, for example, in bringing Althusser to an Anglo-American audience. Meanwhile, his literary criticism has ranged across a host of mostly well-known British writers, from Shakespeare to the present, with particular attention to the historical and political embeddedness of literary writing. As a theorist, he is probably more influential in the model he sets for attending to theory and its political consequences, as seen from the left, than for any one theoretical argument, and deliberately so, for he prefers to direct theoretical debate to the purposes of Marxist political change, as opposed to letting theory shape politics.

The most influential American Marxist literary theorist is Fredric Jameson. After early books that introduced central European Marxist theory and offered a Marxist critical introduction to structuralism and Russian formalism, Jameson continued on to a massively dialectical weaving of Marxist theory, structuralism, and formalism with poststructuralism, psychoanalysis, and the study of popular culture and capitalist globalization. His governing Marxist slogan is "Always historicize!" (Jameson 9). Jameson sees literature and other cultural productions and movements as shaped by unacknowledged social meanings that he calls the *political unconscious*, evoking a social dimension to psychoanalysis and to bourgeois culture's investment in repressing its recognition of its own desperate motives. In *The Political Unconscious: Narrative as a Socially Symbolic Act* (1981), Jameson criticizes the bourgeois belief that art is pure and separate from history and politics. He sees that way of thinking as impoverishing bourgeois life, in the same way that the bourgeois interest in individuality desperately tries to separate bourgeois subjects from the social world. Jameson thus follows how literary form evokes the growth of bourgeois culture and aesthetics from realism to its disintegration into modernist and postmodernist fragmentation. In postmodernism, as he argues in his influential essay "Postmodernism, or, the Cultural Logic of Late Capitalism" (1984, 1991), modernist fragmentation multiplies itself until parody, with its bite of cultural criticism, gives way to postmodernist pastiche, imitation without the political bite of parody. The fragmentation of modernist style implied a critique of capitalist commodification, Jameson argues, but the cultural logic of late capitalism and postmodernism is the ascendancy of commodification as an end in itself. Modernist styles degrade into postmodernist codes, into conglomeration without direction, randomly cannibalizing the history of style in a purposeless hodgepodge of kitsch, schlock, and clutter, an effort to escape history that is itself a sign of history.

To bring Marxist insights into a film or a literary text that has characters and a plot, we might ask whose labor makes it possible for the characters to do the things they do and makes it possible for them not to do the things they do not do and how much the text makes that labor visible. In many stories, for example, as often in the novels of Henry James and Edith Wharton as well as many other writers and filmmakers, the characters lead privileged lives but never dirty their hands with the work that makes their privilege possible. If labor is invisible or rarely visible, that can interpellate readers into assumptions regarding who matters, what activities we should value, and how we might think about labor and class. Or perhaps the novels or movies themselves critique their own characters' obliviousness to the work that upholds their privilege. When a character in a nineteenth-century novel or a historical movie rides in a carriage and the carriage appears magically, as if by itself, or attracts little or no additional mention, then at that point the ideology congeals. It hails readers into the assumption that the privileged life of carriage-takers is somehow better and more valuable than the laboring life of those who care for and harness the horses, maintain and fetch the carriage, drive it, keep their mouths shut, and clean up afterward. Some novels and stories, by contrast, such as Elizabeth Gaskell's *Mary Barton*, Harriet Beecher Stowe's *Uncle Tom's Cabin*, Rebecca Harding Davis's "Life in the Iron Mills," and Richard Llewellyn's *How Green Was My Valley*, call attention to those workers, writing from the workers' point of view or showing them mistreated. This is not to say that *Uncle Tom's Cabin* is better than Henry James's *The Portrait of a Lady*. Rather, it is about understanding some of the cultural and ideological assumptions that works of art and other cultural acts reflect and contribute to.

HOW TO INTERPRET: MARXIST EXAMPLES

Let us conclude with two examples, beginning with a reading of Edwin Arlington Robinson's "Richard Cory" (1896).

> Whenever Richard Cory went down town,
> We people on the pavement looked at him:
> He was a gentleman from sole to crown,
> Clean favored, and imperially slim.
>
> And he was always quietly arrayed,
> And he was always human when he talked;
> But still he fluttered pulses when he said,
> "Good-morning," and he glittered when he walked.
>
> And he was rich—yes, richer than a king—
> And admirably schooled in every grace:
> In fine, we thought that he was everything
> To make us wish that we were in his place.
>
> So on we worked, and waited for the light,
> And went without the meat, and cursed the bread;
> And Richard Cory, one calm summer night,
> Went home and put a bullet through his head.
>
> (Robinson 9–10)

Richard Cory attracts the gaze of the working-class poor, the "people on the pavement" who "looked at him." They seem to know little about his internal life, but they project onto him the antithesis to themselves, for he is a "gentleman," meaning a man wealthy enough that he does not work. Short of money, they must crimp on meals, cursing the monotony of their diet of bread without meat. Yet though he can eat better than they can, he is still "imperially slim," as if to suggest that the wealthy have some kind of mysteriously inherent superiority, much like the mystique of royalty. His class position shows all the way up to his "crown," and he is "richer than a king," richer than those who achieve their wealth naturally, by divine right. In other words, the imperially crowned kings and Corys of the world do not labor to earn their wealth; they simply are wealthy. Nothing in the poem acknowledges that Cory's wealth comes from the labor of others. In that way, the poem mystifies the privilege of capital, taking it as natural, rather than explaining or thinking critically about the economic system that produces inequality.

Still, the poem criticizes the owners of capital, even satirizes them for their inability to appreciate their privilege. From the focalized stance of the poem, "we" work hard, and "we" suffer. Our suffering is real, but Cory's woes are the effete suffering of the privileged, whose internal angst comes across as one of wealth's privileges. The "we" of the poem want to be in Richard Cory's "place." Perhaps, having lived their hard lives, they would know how to appreciate his privilege better than he can. Or if wealth corrupts them, then at least their history of hard times would help them better appreciate the opportunity to make their suffering as refined as his.

Yet, even as the poem criticizes the Corys of the world who own the capital and who profit from the labor of others, the "we" of the poem cannot criticize the structure that produces the unequal distribution of wealth that Cory represents. They can criticize the person but not the system. Ideologically, they have been interpellated into taking unequal distribution as the natural order of things. That allows them to think they are resisting the way of the world when they make fun of Cory, but making fun of Cory keeps them from realizing that they still accept the system he represents. After all, when Cory bids them "Good-morning," their pulses flutter. Instead of looking doubtfully on his condescension, they let his greeting hail them, interpellate them, into his mystique and the social hierarchy that it masks. In that way they consent to their own degraded position, so alienated from their own labor that they refer to it merely as work without caring to mention what kind of work, and certainly they give no hint of any pleasure in their work. Instead of doing something to change the system, they passively wait for the light, hoping that Cory's mystique will someday be theirs. They have been interpellated into a craving to get theirs, and that craving shuts off the impulse to think critically about the overall system that keeps them and others like them from getting it. With so little to challenge it, the system can reproduce itself from generation to generation, occasionally changing who fills the position of the rich Richard Corys but not changing the overall structure.

If it is all that bleak, then the "we" of the poem are utterly victims of false consciousness, deluded into believing that if they work hard enough and crimp on their meals enough, then someday, maybe, they too can grow wealthy like Cory, when of course they never will. With the hard finality of its devastating last rhyme, this is not a

poem that offers much hope. If we insist on finding relative autonomy regardless, then perhaps we might see the merest hint of possibility for breaking outside the suffocating grip of ideology and false
consciousness in the poem's crafted meter and pointed rhyme, offering at least a glimpse of aesthetic values not entirely run down by
the hard lives of the poem's half-starved workers.

Critics sometimes ask how to bring Marxism together with questions about gender, and so we can look at one more example that
brings those two ways of thinking together. Kate Chopin's "The
Story of an Hour" (1894) begins with the following sentence:
"Knowing that Mrs. Mallard was afflicted with a heart trouble, great
care was taken to break to her as gently as possible the news of her
husband's death" (Chopin 352). These opening words seem likely to
interpellate readers into a variety of ideologies, sets of cultural assumptions that readers participate in unconsciously, that is to say,
without stopping to think about it or to recognize the ideologies. The
character is defined by her marriage (the first word to describe her is
"Mrs."), labeled by her husband's name and not by any name that she
brings to the marriage. She comes across as delicate and vulnerable,
at least in the eyes of those who see her as Mrs. Mallard. We get a
sense of women as vulnerable and as dependent on men and marriage. But the story drops us so firmly into the middle of an ongoing
narrative that, at least on a first reading, we probably get swept up
into the suspense and allow such ideologies of gender to absorb us
without our recognizing it. That is how ideology works (how it interpellates and hails us), and in retrospect we might say that when we
return to the story and recognize how it begins in those assumptions
about femininity, we can perhaps see that right at the beginning of
the story the ideology has already congealed.

But Mrs. Mallard, it soon seems, might not be so utterly vulnerable
and dependent as the opening sentence can suggest. She has her own
room, and she can go away to it and even close and lock the door. In
her own space, she exudes a bodily solidity and self-sufficiency: She
sinks down into a "comfortable, roomy armchair," throws her head
back on a cushion, and gives way to "physical exhaustion," with "her
bosom" rising and falling "tumultuously" (352–53). The woman in
this story languishes indoors, finding refuge in domestic privacy and
physical repose, while the men move about outdoors, following another silent but suggestive ideology of gender binaries. Working first
through Mrs. Mallard's languishing corporeality and then through
the emotional shift that gradually overwhelms her, the story even-

tually cracks the shell of its interpellations into the dominant ideologies of gender by leading Mrs. Mallard to a new and suddenly critical view of her dependence, along with a newfound delight in her imagined future of independence, marked abruptly by the shift from the interpellating "Mrs. Mallard" to the more personal "Louise" (354).

And then, in the shock at the end, her feeble heart catches up to her. Thus the story follows the interpellation, then exposes it, and then kills the character off for exposing it—and it runs readers through the same emotional slalom. When the story submits, then rebels, and then punishes its rebellion, where does that leave its relation to the patterns of ideology that it exposes? In some ways it ends up suppressing resistance, critical thinking, and feminine independence. Louise's independence might even degrade into mere petulant selfishness as she thinks (in free indirect discourse) that "she would live for herself" (353). Or perhaps the story rethinks such options as feminine independence, critical thinking, and resistance to patriarchal ideology, not so much by suppressing them as by bringing them to light in ways that refrain from romanticizing them as easy, complete, or free from internal contradictions. After all, dependence has its pleasures as well as its burdens. When Louise enjoys her independent life in her own room, she yearns for freedom and implicitly yearns for a mobility that this story associates with men, not with women. The men's movement in the world outside—Richards in the newspaper office and from the newspaper office to the Mallard house, Brently Mallard out on what could be a business trip, the "peddler...crying his wares" (352) in the street below—all suggest the labor that pays for Mrs. Mallard's room in a house big enough to have an upstairs and a downstairs. By hinting at the labor behind her luxury, the story enjoys her luxury but does not idealize it. We do not know whether she envies the men's labor, but she profits from it, and she envies their mobility.

When the story exerts so much effort at unearthing Louise's desires, then, it is hard not to see the story as making a feminist intervention. But after the devastating conclusion, it is also hard to tell whether the story finally lands more on the side of endorsing an ideology of feminine dependence or more on the side of yearning for relative feminine autonomy. Perhaps it is too simple to characterize the story as all on one side or all on the other. Even so, the dialogue between opposed possibilities can end up legitimizing the skepticism about dominant gender roles that the story also punishes. Meanwhile, to think of the story as punishing Louise's relative autonomy might underestimate the story's humor, a sense of comic irony that lightens the closing tragedy and keeps alive, for readers, the hopes that finally die for Louise.

Given that "The Story of an Hour" was first published in *Vogue* magazine in 1894, a fashion magazine aimed at upper-middle-class women in New York City, the emotions in this story are commodified. Chopin sold the story to the magazine, which sold it to readers, who read it for their own pleasure in its emotions and because the editors used the story as bait to sell the magazine. The editors sold the magazine to readers and to advertisers who used the magazine to sell fashion to women like Louise Mallard, who typically depended on their husbands or fathers to fund the fashions that the story helped market to them. Thus the story, as a commodity within a commodity that marketed yet more commodities, helped reproduce the same dependent position of women that it also struggles to think about, partly resisting and partly embracing.

For those who see popular culture as leading us away from questioning dominant ideologies, the commodification of "The Story of an Hour" would seem to deflect readers from thinking critically about their own immersion in commodity-obsessed consumer culture. But for those who see popular culture as encouraging relative autonomy, "The Story of an Hour" might work against some of the consumerist principles that must have led *Vogue*'s editors to put it in their magazine. Women's fashion, after all, need not be entirely about commodification. It can also be about women's aesthetic expression. In that sense, the story as a commodity can also help set up a forum for women's artistic expression, commodified or not. And the story's questioning of women's dependence on marriage might make female readers question their economic reliance on men, including their reliance on men for access to the fashionable world of feminine expression and communal feminine pleasure.

In these ways, it is hard to sort out the story's cultural consequences for its readers, who after all may vary a good deal, both from reader to reader and even within individual readers. Those individual readers—as anyone versed in deconstruction can tell us—are rife with their own internal contradictions. And so, even if we could poll a cross section of readers, what those readers say that they think, in a world of ideology, might not accurately reflect the emotional resonance that the story carries for them. But "The Story of an Hour" can help us see how relative autonomy and hidebound ideology can tangle into each other. How we interpret that tangle will vary with our purposes and predilections, anywhere from seeing rebellious thinking as terribly defeated to seeing the door to its temptations opened just enough so that, however abruptly the end of the story tries to slam shut the door, it cannot keep skeptical thoughts from slipping in and inviting us to recognize and rethink ideological assumptions.

*   *   *   *   *

As we will see in the next chapter, historicism and cultural studies continue to work with the questions and debates they inherit from Marxism.

✺ 9 ✺

Historicism and Cultural Studies

While deconstruction grabbed headlines in the popular press, igniting controversy and shaping the debates of literary criticism, a restlessness was stirring through literary studies. The new critics, structuralists (in their early mode), and deconstructionists (in their early mode), different though they were, shared a formalist approach to interpreting literature. They gave little attention to history and culture, preferring to concentrate on literary form. Sometimes they even suggested a sneering condescension to historical and cultural interpretations of literature, looking down on such ways of reading as if they were naively old-fashioned. Many critics felt that formalism betrayed the social and historical interests that help make many readers and critics care about literature in the first place. Other critics shared the formalist interest of the new critics, structuralists, and deconstructionists, seeing literary form as integral to the very idea of literary study, and yet they felt that a concern with history and culture should go along with an interest in form, complementing it rather than opposing it.

Critics hungered for a way to draw on what they had learned from deconstruction and to bring it together with cultural and historical inquiry, and out of that hunger emerged what came to be called *new historicism*.

NEW HISTORICISM

New historicists see literary studies, from the new criticism through deconstruction, as tending to evade history or as using history only for what new historicists call *old historicism*. To new historicists, old historicism relegates history to mere *background* and *context*, with the literature merely *reflecting* the history. We have all been students in classrooms—and some of us have been teachers in classrooms—where the teacher begins by providing historical background and then leaves the history as mere background without going on to pay much attention to it as we talk about the literature. To new historicists, old historicists also see history as certain and stable, as a set of secure facts, which allows us to make such claims as "the Elizabethans believed" such and such, claims that, after deconstruction, seem too general and confident to new historicists.

By contrast with old historicists, new historicists try to read history and literature together, with each influencing the other, and without a stable sense of facts. For new historicists, history is just as uncertain and complex as literature. Apart from the basic facts (though maybe for basic facts too, as we will soon see), it simply will not work to make claims about history by saying that this or that happened or the Elizabethans believed such and such and leave it at that. Just as it would be too simple to make broad-brush, absolutist claims about a literary text ("*Romeo and Juliet* is about the beauty of true love"), so it would be too simple to make broad-brush, absolutist claims about history ("the Elizabethans believed in deference to authority, represented by the great chain of being"). When we study literature, after deconstruction, we take into account that there are always multiple perspectives and that different perspectives lead to different interpretations. It is not a matter of throwing up our hands and saying that anything goes. But it is a matter of saying that multiple things go, and that we will distinguish among those multiple things on the basis of what interests us (perhaps feminism or figurative language or questions about class or focalization and so on) and on the basis of whether we can put together an interesting argument to back up our interpretation. For new historicists, those same principles that we bring to literary interpretation should also direct how we read history. It is not just about saying that here is the historical background and then applying that historical background, as if it were a mere lump of inflexible facts, to the supposedly more nuanced challenge of interpreting literature. For new historicists, the history already has as much multiplicity and nuance as any work of literature (and maybe more, to say the least). Moreover, literary texts influence the sociohistorical world that influences the literary texts, so that the textuality of history and the historicity of texts shape and reshape each other in a continuous cycle of mutual influence.

New historicists thus see themselves as recovering history for literary studies, after the move away from history in new criticism, structuralism, and deconstruction. By studying history with the close attention to its multiplicity that we associate with deconstruction, new historicists see themselves as merging historical study with deconstruction, rescuing literary study from its tendency to ignore history and rescuing historical study from its tendency to oversimplify, to see things as absolute and definite (a mistake that the best historians would not make, but still a problem in much historical study and especially in old historicist literary study).

From a new historicist perspective, the facts that old historicists rely on may not be so reliable as raw facts. New historicists argue that what makes a fact depends on the perspective we look from; it is a construction, not an essence. To illustrate the point, let us consider some routine "facts." The sun rises in the morning and sets in the evening. Summer comes in June, July, and August. Columbus discovered America in 1492. Gold is heavier than paper. George W. Bush was elected president in 2000. As many readers will know, there is considerable dispute about whether George W. Bush was elected president, though in a controversial decision the United States Supreme Court ruled in his favor. From another perspective, the sun does not rise or set, but the earth rotates on its axis, making the sun appear to rise or set—at least on a sunny day. Summer comes in June, July, and August north of the equator, but south of the equator it comes in December, January, and February. In 1492, the name *America* did not even exist, and what Columbus did is no discovery if discovery means being the first person to find something. Untold millions of people knew about "America" before Columbus, and they did not think of it as the "New World" either. By tagging

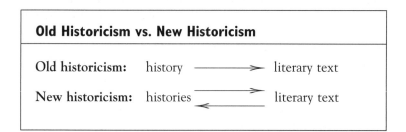

Old Historicism vs. New Historicism

Old historicism:	history ⟶	literary text
New historicism:	histories ⇄	literary text

Columbus as the discoverer of America and the New World, we keep ourselves from looking through the perspective that would characterize him as an invader and conqueror, and as a brutally genocidal invader and conqueror. But surely, you may respond, there is no question about some facts. Surely it remains a fact that an ingot of gold is heavier than a sheet of paper. But a sheet of paper in one gravitational field (such as the earth's) may be heavier than an ingot of gold in another gravitational field, or in weightless space, or some paper—maybe your birth certificate when you apply for a passport— is heavier, metaphorically, than gold. Or, more ideologically, we might question why we resort to scientific facticity as the last bastion of facts and truth. From another perspective, we might choose God instead of science as our ideal realm of truth and fact. And from another perspective, we might choose love or beauty or the need for food and shelter. What we choose to represent facts and what perspective we look from determine what we choose to call facts, which allows new historicists, drawing on poststructuralism, to see history itself as contingent (meaning that it depends on variables) and constructed rather than as a stable absolute or essence.

With the new historicists, then, the last seventy years of literary studies come full circle. The new critics called for close attention to the text rather than to history or the social world. With structuralism and deconstruction, critics developed increasingly sophisticated methods to study texts closely. But many critics missed the social dimension that the new critics tried to get away from. New historicists, therefore, drawing on the increasingly prominent Marxist ideas discussed in Chapter 8, try to restore literature to its social history while retaining the tools of deconstruction and poststructuralism that can help us see social history in its multifarious intricacy.

In the late 1980s, feminist critics pointed out that the early works of new historicism usually ignored developments in feminist criticism and gender studies. While that was a sorry oversight in much of the early new historicist scholarship, there is nothing in new historicist method that calls for slighting feminist thinking and gender studies, and before long, feminist criticism, gender criticism, and new historicism often worked together, as indeed they can, for every topic and every approach has a history, and every history has to do with people who live their lives partly through gender.

The critics most identified as founding figures of new historicism are Louis Montrose and especially Stephen Greenblatt. Greenblatt coined the term *new historicism*, but he used it casually and never liked it as the name of a critical method. He prefers to call the method *cultural poetics*, drawing on the structuralist sense of *poetics* as the study of a larger system (not necessarily a poetic system). Greenblatt's work first attracted widespread interest with a book called *Renaissance Self-Fashioning: From More to Shakespeare* (1980). (*More* refers to Thomas More, the British Renaissance politician and writer.) In that book, Greenblatt provides subtly literary and historicist readings of a series of British Renaissance writers, focusing on how their culture shaped their sense of selfhood or subjectivity. People who know little or nothing about new historicism have supposed that Greenblatt's title refers to how the self fashions itself, which turns Greenblatt's historicist and partly Marxist, Foucauldian method upside down (on Foucault, see later in this chapter) and converts it into a routine bourgeois celebration of capitalist individuality, thus missing the point. Greenblatt explains that he started to write about how the self fashions itself, but ended up writing much more about how the self is fashioned by, is almost passive before, broader cultural forces.

Sometimes, Greenblatt and other new historicists who followed in his wake dramatized the way that their approach differed from earlier, less historicist criticism by writing about historical matters at length before they began to discuss a literary text. They often began an article or book chapter with a provocative anecdote based on an obscure but startling historical source. In Greenblatt's most influential works, *Renaissance Self-Fashioning* and *Shakespearean Negotiations* (1988), that strategy showcased the turn to history and playfully jabbed at the routines of the usual ahistoricist criticism. To skeptics' eyes, the history overwhelmed the literary interpretation, and the dramatic anecdotes tested readers' patience by showing off the critics' historicist erudition without getting to the literary texts. But for readers who have the patience to read through to the end or who appreciate Greenblatt's historicist curiosities and his skill at making unexpected and revealing cultural connections, Greenblatt eventually gets to the relation between the history and the literature. He tries to sort out what he calls "the circulation of social energy," the way that literature comes not only from individual authors but also from the cultural controversies of an age, with the controversies provoking the literature and the literature interpreting the controversies, in a continuous cycle of exchange and influence.

Stephen Greenblatt (1943–).

Some critics have complained that in Greenblatt's interpretations, the literature itself ends up confirming the dominant ideologies rather than contesting them, and sometimes those critics complain that new historicism as a whole, following Greenblatt's model, underestimates the capacity for literature to change the world. In Marxist terms (as reviewed in Chapter 8), they find that Greenblatt and his new historicist colleagues put too much weight on ideology, interpellation, and even false consciousness and not enough weight on relative autonomy, agency, and intervention. If so, however, that balance (or imbalance) owes to Greenblatt's own predilections, not to anything necessarily inherent in new historicist principles.

Over time, as new historicism has grown more routine, lost its newness, and evolved simply into historicism, Greenblatt's idiosyncrasies, however interesting, matter less than the general principle that literature and history shape each other, as opposed to the old-fashioned habit of seeing literature as a passive reflector of history. After all, if we care about literature, then it might seem odd to see it, even implicitly, as merely passive, merely reflecting other things in what new historicists sometimes call the *reflection model* of literary criticism. If literature only reflected the rest of the world, then we would have no reason to read literature. On the other hand, if it did not reflect the rest of the world at all, then it would have no capacity to comment on the world. We value literature and other aesthetic productions in part for their nuanced (Marxists might say their dialectical) combination of reflecting and rethinking the rest of the world. New historicism has tried to craft a model for criticism that takes that combination of reflection and rethinking into account, both in literary art and in the art of criticism.

Shakespeare's comedies, for example, and other comic dramas of Shakespeare's time and for many years afterwards typically end with many of the characters falling in love and marrying. The term *comedy* referred not to humor, as it does today, but to a happy ending. And happy endings, drawing on the naturalization of heterosexuality, tended to be defined by marriage. Sometimes, most famously in *Romeo and Juliet*, the characters fall in love and marry at a young age. But historian Lawrence Stone's landmark *The Family, Sex, and Marriage in England, 1500–1800* (1977) argues that marriages in Renaissance England typically came comparatively late, that parents, kin, or friends typically arranged the marriages, and that they arranged marriages not for love but for economic reasons. Infants from the upper and middling classes were often sent out to wet nurses, and children usually left their parents to work as servants or apprentices or go to school. Parents and children died young (compared to our own time), and living arrangements for all classes were crowded and without privacy. For all these reasons, Stone argues, sexual and emotional attachments minimized warmth and intimacy.

For a historicist literary critic, then, Stone's argument raises problems, because the history and the plays do not match. That mismatch throws up a roadblock for old (or traditional) historicist criticism especially, because traditional historicism relies on the reflection model, and in this case the literature does not reflect the history. (At least the literature does not reflect the history if Stone has got his history right. Some historians dispute Stone's findings.) But because new historicism challenges the reflection model's implication that literature passively reproduces its surrounding culture, Stone's findings might offer an opportunity for new historicist literary criticism. New historicists could argue, for example, that the difference between the plays and the cultural pattern suggests that the plays talk back to the cultural pattern (exercising relative autonomy and agency, making an intervention). Perhaps the plays seek an escape from the expected pattern, or perhaps they parody it or experiment by exploring alternatives. Or, by a model that sees less disruption of and more compliance with the dominant expectations, comic drama portrays a fantasy world that has little to do with what actually goes on in daily life and therefore cannot much disrupt or pressure daily life. Or more than one of those models applies at the same time, potentially in conflict with each other and underlining the internal contradictions within comic drama's relation to its culture and to the dominant ideologies of its culture. We might see those competing forces as balancing each other out, almost in a social version of new critical balance. Or we might see them in poststructuralist disequilibrium, with the resistance to the dominant ideologies overwhelming the simultaneous urge to comply with those dominant ideologies, or with the urge to comply overwhelming the resistance. Our choices among such a wide palette of options would probably depend on how we observe and interpret a host of individual details about cultural history, the language and performance traditions of the actual plays, and the dialogue between the plays and the history.

Perhaps these new historicist alternatives to the reflection model end up relying on the reflection model all over again, because they still show the literature responding to the history. But they replace direct reflection with indirect reflection, with mediated reflection. From that perspective, new historicism does not replace the reflection model so much as it sophisticates the model. Regardless, it gives critics a new set of questions, a set of questions that continues the dialogue between more pessimistic and more optimistic models of Marxist interpretation, as we reviewed them in Chapter 8.

As historicism has grown more familiar in literary studies, some critics, especially in Renaissance studies, have called for *presentism*. Traditionally, to call a critic a presentist was a put-down. It accused the critic of imposing thinking from the present onto literature from the past in ways that distort the past. For example, in the pejorative sense of the term, a presentist might miss the point to call Chaucer a feminist or to see an environmentalist sensibility in *Moby-Dick*'s portrayal of whale hunting or a gay sensibility in its comical same-sex bed scene. On the other hand, scholars who now advocate presentism might well want to know about the relation between Chaucer and feminism or between *Moby-Dick* and gay studies or environmentalism. They argue that we can never know the past in itself. We can only view the past through the lens of the present. Therefore, they believe, to disavow our interests in the present would distort our view of the past more than to own up to our interests frankly. In that way, presentism can offer a strategy for doing historicism better, with an alertness to how our view of history depends on our position in the present. Or it can make a deliberate strategy out of keeping a measured distance from the past and asking, not what happened then, but how what happened then looks through the lens of our interests now or how what happened then speaks to what is happening now. Instead of trying to reconstruct an Elizabethan performance of *Hamlet,* a presentist stage production might ask how to perform or interpret *Hamlet* for our own time. Whichever of these strategies a presentist or historicist chooses, they all trouble the binary between the present and the past, in different ways encouraging us to study each in relation to the other.

But studying history is not as easy as it may sound. Some of the early new historicists, English professors and graduate students still learning how to work with history, were accused of relying on Stone's work too heavily or relying on this or that other small array of secondary historical scholarship. Over the years, in the wake of new historicism, historicist critics have grown into better historians, but the intense historical study that goes with historicist criticism is a challenge in itself. To expect critics to learn and research every-thing we expect from a literary critic *plus* everything we expect from a historian is asking a lot. New historicism, to put it plainly, is hard work. We might also wonder how it can translate into the classroom. Many students do not know much history. Some students even turn to literature in part to get away from studying history. Would his-toricist teaching require literature students to read less literature so that they could read more history? Or would the history help bring the literature to life, intensifying the students' ability to appreciate and engage with the literature? There is no one-size-fits-all answer to these questions, but they hint at the obstacles and the excitements in historicist criticism and teaching.

MICHEL FOUCAULT

New historicists drew heavily on the writings of the poststructuralist philosopher Michel Foucault, a major figure often grouped with Roland Barthes, Jacques Derrida, and Jacques Lacan to represent the first and leading wave of poststructuralist (and more or less Parisian) innovators. Foucault's writings bring a wide and changing range of methods to a wide range of topics, far more than we can address here, but we can pick out a few concepts that have carried notable influence in literary and cultural studies.

Foucault wrote about the relation between knowledge and power. He argued that we internalize patterns of expectation from the surrounding culture, absorbing the culture's expectations so much that we take them for granted and suppose that they come from our own thinking. Typically, we think of knowledge as responsive to something outside itself. In that model, if a person has knowledge, that knowledge is knowledge of an essence exterior to the person. Foucault argued almost the opposite, that knowledge constructs what it purports to know. It is mediated by history, rather than being pure knowledge of unmediated raw truth. Foucault called this kind of knowledge **discourse**.

In Foucault's sense of the term, a discourse is a practice that produces what it purports to describe. A discourse is a common pattern of culturally internalized expectation rather than the supposedly pure or essential truth that people traditionally mean by the term *knowledge*. When Foucault used the term *discourse*, he did not exactly mean languages or systems of representation, the related sense of the term *discourse* that (as we have seen in earlier chapters) is its other meaning in structuralism and poststructuralism. He meant something closer to the Marxist notion of ideology that we reviewed in Chapter 8. But Foucault was suspicious of Marxism, because he did not believe in the Marxist truth that Althusser called "real conditions." He understood Marxism as clinging to a suspect model of economic determinism, whereas discourses do not necessarily come from economics. For example (as we have seen in Chapter 7), we can recognize discourses of gender, internalized patterns of cultural expectation about femininity and masculinity that, as the philosopher Judith Butler has argued, construct through repetition what they purport to know. People may suppose that women move, talk, and dress in a certain variety of ways and men move, talk, and dress in a different variety of ways, but the discourse of gender (including the ways that people move, talk, and dress) constructs that knowledge through repeated actions and expectations. If people did not repeat that discourse in their actions and expectations, then they would not continue to believe in it and see it as knowledge. And indeed, we do not repeat that discourse perfectly and at all times, and to the extent that we do not repeat that discourse we open a path for alternative, less dominant ways of understanding gender. In that way, discourses are not absolute, but nevertheless they wield great power. The discourse of gender does not describe gender, as we might think before Foucault, as if gender were there before the discourse. Instead it produces the gender that it purports to describe. Perhaps you can see similarities between Foucault's sense of discourse as producing, rather than describing, and Derrida's sense that language and systems of representation generate so much momentum that the signifiers spin free from any particular signifieds.

Foucault worked out these ideas by studying institutions, such as insane asylums, medical clinics, and prisons, that regulate behavior socially and psychologically through discourses of madness, illness, and punishment. In *Discipline and Punish: The Birth of the Prison* (1975), Foucault proposes that the Panopticon, a prison designed (and never built) by the English philosopher Jeremy Bentham (1748–1832), offers a model of modern culture. Bentham designed the Panopticon with prison cells circling around a guard tower so

Michel Foucault (1926–1984).

that a guard in the tower can watch each prisoner, but the prisoners cannot tell when a guard watches them. Therefore, Bentham reasoned, prisoners, knowing that a guard might be watching at any time, would protect themselves by policing their own behavior, whether or not a guard is actually watching. Indeed, the prison would not need a guard to watch all the time, because prisoners would internalize the rules that the guard enforces, and so the prisoners would police themselves.

To Foucault, modern society works like the Panopticon. To stay with the earlier example of gender and to use the terms that Foucault has provided critical theory and cultural studies, our discourses of

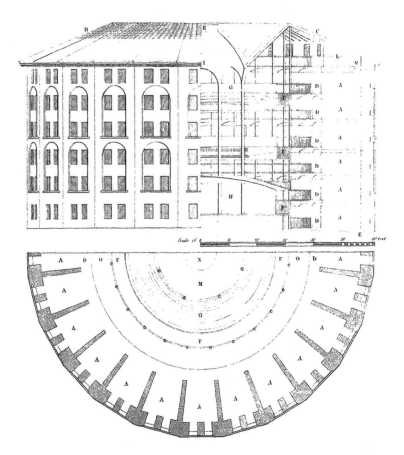

Jeremy Bentham's design for the Panopticon, 1791.

gender *regulate, discipline, police, and surveil* (as in keeping under surveillance) behavior and beliefs, producing and reproducing stereotypical ideas of gender. People internalize those ideas so deeply that no one else has to make people believe or live by those ideas, because people surveil themselves (police, discipline, regulate themselves), making sure that they abide by the dominant discourses of gender. You can probably think of ways of dressing, walking, talking, or gesturing that signify femininity and masculinity and that many people absorb so thoroughly that they police themselves, restricting potential impulses to act in what the dominant discourse paints as the wrong way. To Foucault, such self-disciplining works more powerfully than coercion. (If you recall Chapter 8, then you might hear Foucault's ideas echoing or at least paralleling Gramsci's notion of the state versus civil society or Althusser's notion of RSAs versus ISAs.) Knowledge itself, then, to Foucault (such as knowledge of gender expectations), is a means of surveillance, regulation, and discipline, a discourse that produces what it purports to describe. In this model, the subject is not a person or individual, a knowing, self-understanding agent of free will. Instead, the subject is a place where discourses come together.

Similarly, in *The History of Sexuality, Volume One: The Will to Knowledge* (1976), Foucault (as we began to see in Chapter 7) discusses the discourse of sexuality as a means of power and social regulation. As people internalize the discourse of sexuality, it regulates and administers people's lives. He criticizes what he calls "the repressive hypothesis," the Freudian notion that we suffer from repressing our sexuality. He argues that sexuality, in the era of supposed repression, is anything but repressed. With the massive medical and educational discourse about sexuality, it is a central obsession, and the discourse of sexuality, the will to knowledge of sexuality, emerges as a power to regulate sexuality, not to repress it. It regulates sexuality in part by identifying certain sexual behaviors as "other," especially homosexuality. Thus to Foucault power produces discourse rather than repressing it. Instead of asking the traditional questions about who has power or what people want to do with power, Foucault asks how power constructs subjects, making subjects effects of power. Foucault proposes that before modernity, a variety of sexual acts were recognized. Still, those acts did not determine identities as homosexual or heterosexual. But the modern discourse of sexuality, Foucault argues, constructs subjects as queer or straight according to their behavior, thus converting behavior into identity.

Foucault's readers have varied in how much potential they see Foucault allowing for resistance to the power of dominant discourses. They vary in part according to which works of Foucault they concentrate on and perhaps according to what they want to see Foucault as saying. Sometimes it seems that Foucault sees power as so pervasive that we have little chance to resist it. At times, nevertheless, he sees power as generating its own resistance, because any discourse of power—such as the discourse of gender—will necessarily be imperfect and incomplete. People do not always dress, walk, talk, and gesture the way that the discourse of gender tells them to. Sometimes, Foucault sees power as generating resistance merely to squelch it, but at other times he sees the resistance as opening a potential for change, though he does not develop that sense of resistance in much detail. We can line up these two opposite views of power and resistance (or of Foucault's ideas about power and resistance) with the more pessimistic and more optimistic Marxist models reviewed in Chapter 8, the models that offer, pessimistically, ideology, interpellation, and false consciousness or, optimistically, relative autonomy, agency, and intervention.

Indeed, despite Foucault's suspicion of Marxism, his influence on literary and cultural criticism sometimes merges with or parallels the influence of Marxism on literary and cultural criticism. Foucault's ideas, for example, influenced Greenblatt when Foucault visited the University of California at Berkeley as Greenblatt and others were working out the ideas that led to new historicism. Those who look skeptically on what they see as Greenblatt's habit of underestimating resistance to dominant ideologies sometimes match that reading of Greenblattt with a similar reading of Foucault. By contrast, the sense that dominant ideologies can indeed be resisted tended to come out of the more optimistic version of Marxist thinking that often came to be identified less with new historicism and more with cultural studies.

CULTURAL STUDIES

The term **cultural studies** can confuse people, because it sounds so general, and many critics who know little about the term's history use it in a general way to refer to any study of culture or to any study of aesthetic production (film, art, literature, music, and so on) that goes beyond the study of form to include study of the surrounding culture.

But the term *cultural studies* has a specific meaning and history, for it refers to the cultural studies movement associated with the Centre for Contemporary Cultural Studies at the University of Birmingham in Great Britain. It can also include the heritage of weaving together literary studies with the study of popular culture, cultural history, Marxism, and the working class that emerged through the writing of Raymond Williams, a practice that Williams called **cultural materialism**. Cultural studies and cultural materialism developed along similar lines, though at first cultural materialism, like the new historicism, gave more attention to literary history, often including Shakespeare. Indeed, cultural materialists succeeded in bringing their ideas to a wide audience in part because, led especially by Jonathan Dollimore and Alan Sinfield, they wrote provocatively about Shakespeare, the most widely studied topic in English studies. I will use the term *cultural studies* broadly, allowing it to include cultural materialism, its close cousin.

Founded by Richard Hoggart and later directed by Stuart Hall, the Centre for Contemporary Cultural Studies developed cultural studies into what we might describe as an effort to bring Marxism together with poststructuralism, psychoanalysis, and—eventually—feminism for the study of contemporary popular culture. As we might expect, not all Marxists appreciated the idea of bringing Marxism together with poststructuralism, because, from a Marxist materialist perspective, poststructuralism can seem to sidestep material culture in favor of "discourse." But thanks partly to the influence of cultural studies, the growth and evolution of contemporary Marxism changed poststructuralism, leading it away from the socially disconnected language play of early deconstruction to make it engage deeply with politics and material culture, even when it understands material culture as a form of discourse. Students from many countries traveled to study at Birmingham and then often returned to their home countries, spreading the ideas and methods of cultural studies and the influence of Hall's intellectual leadership. (On Hall, see also Chapter 4.) A Jamaican who moved to Britain at the age of nineteen, Hall has played an active role in the politics of the British left, advocating nuclear disarmament and later critiquing the right-wing policies of Prime Minister Margaret Thatcher.

In line with the interest that cultural studies takes in popular culture, Hall saw a particular need for the socialist left to understand why the right appealed to the popular electorate. From a left position, as we have seen, when the general populace elects a right-wing government, they vote against their own interests. The left, there-fore, needs to interpret the working class's readiness to elect right-wing politicians against the left's expectation that the working class would lead resistance to the dominant, right-wing hegemony. (Here, as through much of this chapter, I am drawing on the Marxist concepts and terms outlined in Chapter 8.) For that reason, cultural studies scholars investigate how dominant ideologies tend to reproduce themselves through interpellation, so that working-class youth, for example, aspire to working-class jobs like the jobs of their family and friends, instead of seeking revolutionary change.

As they studied popular culture, such as music, TV, movies, and magazines, cultural studies scholars often came to see a degree of relative autonomy in popular culture. Instead of looking down on popular culture and seeing it as separate from and inferior to the elite culture of canonical literature typically studied in English departments, cultural studies scholars came to respect its intellectual, aesthetic, and even political seriousness. They often study what they call *subcultures*, such as youth culture, immigrant culture, Black British culture, working-class culture, or smaller groups that fit within or combine such categories or that gather around a specific kind of music (for example, Black British dance hall reggae), a set of magazines (for example, preteen girls' magazines), a specific TV show (for example, *Star Trek* and "Trekkies"), or any other genre of popular culture, from advertising to shopping malls to film. By taking the people and pleasures of popular culture seriously rather than scornfully, cultural studies scholars shifted the study of popular culture from the study of how its fans are dupes of the broader cultural hegemony to studying how they use popular culture to speak back to and perhaps even resist or begin to resist the expectations of dominant ideologies, such as consumerism, sexism, racism, capitalism, class elitism, and so on. In that way, cultural studies scholars came to identify with the more optimistic pole of the continuum between pessimistic Marxism, which believes that dominant ideologies are too powerful to allow much resistance to them, and optimistic Marxism, which sees more opportunity to crack the shell of interpellation and resist dominant ideologies. Over the years, so many cultural studies projects focused on the resistant side of popular culture that eventually the readiness of cultural studies scholars to find relative autonomy and resistance in popular culture came to seem rote and predictable rather than carefully thought through. In turn, then, scholars responded by moving away from rote optimism and developing an increasingly nuanced sense of the relation between popular culture's compliance with dominant ideologies and its resistance to dominant ideologies.

For example, if we return to Danielle, the hypothetical thirteen-year-old girl from Chapter 8 who listens to misogynist hip-hop, we can see how cultural studies draws on Marxism to interpret popular culture and subcultures, such as youth and music cultures, with a nuanced respect for the routines of ordinary people and ordinary life, taking seriously both the ability to resist dominant ideologies and the ability to make trouble for dominant ideologies or at least to begin to question them. The reading of Danielle in Chapter 8, though included under Marxism, comes from cultural studies. It draws on the ability of earlier cultural studies scholars to take popular culture and its participants seriously and to recognize the thinking in popular culture, including the potential resistance in cultural activities that, before cultural studies, many scholars saw as ignorant, duped compliance with consumerism and triviality.

At first, cultural studies, apart from its cultural materialist component, did not usually address literature, still less elite (or "literary") literature, as opposed to the literature of popular culture. Literature scholars now draw on cultural studies, however, and integrate it with literary studies in a variety of ways. Whether drawing on Foucault, on cultural studies, or simply on related trends in literary criticism, they often read literary writing in relation to other cultural activities, including both popular and elite culture, and usually without the sense, once routine but now usually seen as dated, that "literary" writing is inherently superior to popular culture. "Literary" writing may often make for better "literary" literature, in the cultural context of what we expect from "literary" art, but it is not inherently, essentially better for all purposes. The methods of interpreting literature that this book describes can usually work equally well for interpreting popular culture, and the methods that cultural studies scholars bring to popular culture can usually work equally well for interpreting literature. The same interchangeability also applies, of course, when we read literature and popular culture together. In the wake of cultural studies, new historicism, and Foucault, even literary critics who interpret older writing will often look to the popular culture of an earlier age; or, if they study a time more or less before popular culture, they will still look at literature as part of a wide range of cultural history and cultural expression. If they draw on the new historicist critique of the reflection model or the cultural studies

alertness to agency in cultural expression, then literary critics will not read literature simply as reflecting cultural history. Instead they will read literature as part of the culture, in some ways passively reflecting it and in some ways speaking back to it, from within it, and helping to change it or contributing to a broader array of cultural conversations that, collectively, can begin to change it.

Cultural change, however, is hard to measure, and it is even harder to pick out the exact agents that lie behind cultural change. If a feisty sonnet criticizes a dominant ideology or discourse, how can we tell that it has cultural agency? Shakespeare's Sonnet 130, for example, concludes by insisting on the speaker's love for his mistress, after beginning with these famous lines:

> My mistress' eyes are nothing like the sun;
> Coral is far more red than her lips' red;
> If snow be white, why then her breasts are dun;
> If hairs be wires, black wires grow on her head.
>   (Shakespeare 1867)

We could say that the speaker's insistence on his love for a woman who does not fit the stereotypical patterns (or discourses) of western European beauty resists an ethnocentric model (a discourse) of beauty and feminine value or of abusive masculine objectification of feminine beauty and that therefore this poem makes an intervention, shows a degree of relative autonomy, or exercises resistant agency.

That is a plausible argument, and I find it convincing. But by drawing on the strategies of cultural studies and historicism, we can push the argument much further, so that I can only give a taste of the possibilities in the short space available here. For another scholar might argue that the sonnet's resistance to standardized forms of feminine beauty is so conventionalized (we even have a name for the convention, calling this an *anti-Petrarchan* sonnet), that it does more to repeat a familiar literary form than to protest a discourse or a social ideology. That would suggest the kind of formalist argument that tends to read form as if its art insulated it from the social con-nectedness that historicist and cultural studies scholars insist on, so we might respond by saying that such insulation is not possible or that the mere existence of a conventionalized, oft-repeated form shows not a lack of resistance in anti-Petrarchan sonnets but rather a breadth of resistance calling out for such forms as anti-Petrarchan sonnets to give it expression. Still, a skeptic might respond by saying that it seems fanciful to find cultural protest in this sonnet if there is no evidence that readers in Shakespeare's time interpreted the sonnet that way, especially if we think of ourselves as historicist and cultural studies critics. Indeed, historicist and cultural studies critics often must rely on how they think that readers might or could have responded, especially when there is no direct evidence from outside the text about how actual readers responded.

That reliance on speculation raises a variety of questions. It could make us shrug our shoulders and give up on historicism. Or it could send us to archival research. Maybe, for example, we can find responses that readers wrote in the margins of a literary text, or comments in letters or diaries, or, for more recent times, book reviews that give an individual reviewer's opinion about a literary work. Or, though we might not find responses to a particular text, such as Shakespeare's Sonnet 130, we might still find discussions of ideas like those in Shakespeare's sonnet—perhaps even in other sonnets or in responses to other sonnets. Or, drawing on cultural studies' interest in contemporary culture, we could, like a presentist, study how the sonnet works in our own time, with or without supposing an analogy between how it works in our own time and how it worked in the poet's time. We could set up focus groups or surveys, or we could read students' papers, observe class discussions, or survey published criticism. For example, we might find (as I have found) that in the contemporary classroom many students of color come upon this sonnet with a sense of delight that intensifies their interest in Shakespeare—and not only students of color but also, in the contemporary classroom, many other students who live their daily lives—as their parents or grandparents often did not—alongside students of color whom they see as peers. At the least, we need not give up on the fragile possibility of supposing ways that readers might have responded, based on the possibilities implied in the text itself in relation to our historicist understanding of the surrounding culture, because the skills of close reading that the new critics taught us can also prove suggestive for cultural interpretation. Moreover, even when we have a record of responses from actual readers, whether historical readers or contemporary readers, we might say, drawing on psychoanalysis and deconstruction, that what those readers say about their responses is itself only their own interpretation of their responses. Readers are not fully conscious of their own responses, and any textualization of their response—a remark scribbled in a margin, a comment in a letter or diary, a book review, class discussion, student paper, or work of professional literary criticism—is itself a text as subject to multiple readings as the literary text itself and thus in many ways no less uncertain than what we derive from educated speculation about how readers *might* respond. (For more on readers' responses, see Chapter 11.)

HOW TO INTERPRET: CULTURAL STUDIES, HISTORICISM, AND LITERATURE

By bringing Marxism together with structuralism, deconstruction, psychoanalysis, and other movements in contemporary critical theory, cultural studies developed along a parallel track with new historicism, despite differences between the two groups. Cultural studies, a predominantly British movement, tended to address contemporary popular culture, and new historicism, a predominantly American movement, tended to address literature from the past. Drawing on an optimistic strain of Marxism, as we have seen, cultural studies tended to take notice of the possibility for agency, relative autonomy, and resistance to dominant ideologies, whereas new historicism, drawing on a more pessimistic strain of Marxism and on Foucault, often noticed ways that dominant ideologies or discourses overwhelmed the possibility for resistance or allowed resistance but used the resistance to prop up the dominant ideologies by showing how they can crush the resistance. In short, by returning to the continuum reviewed in Chapter 8 between, at one pole, more optimistic, Marxist notions of resistance that put weight on relative autonomy, agency, and intervention and, at the other pole, more pessimistic notions of resistance that put weight on ideology, interpellation, and false consciousness, we can say that new historicism tended to land on the pessimistic pole and cultural studies on the optimistic pole (Table 9.1).

In the 1980s, as new historicism and cultural studies rose to prominence, some commentators tried to inflate these differences among allies and paint new historicism and cultural studies as great antagonists. But as each group rose to prominence, its advocates also read the work of the other group, and each learned from the other and evolved to the point that the supposedly vast difference between the two groups faded. (I would go so far as to say that Table 9.1, though once accurate, is now obsolete.) Cultural studies scholars did not often take up literary studies, and there was never much demand

Table 9.1. Cultural Studies vs. New Historicism

CULTURAL STUDIES	NEW HISTORICISM
contemporary	historical
popular culture	elite literary culture (Shakespeare, etc.)
more optimistic about resistance	more pessimistic about resistance
British	American

for them to do so, for there is no shortage of literary scholars or literary scholarship. But literary scholars on both sides of the Atlantic and in many countries increasingly study popular culture, including popular literature, often relating popular culture to elite literature in the same ways that they relate history to elite literature. Meanwhile, cultural studies scholars, as we have seen, grew suspicious that their tendency to see possibilities for resistance had calcified into a habit rather than a thought-through practice, while literary scholars drawing on new historicism grew suspicious of new historicism's tendency to underestimate cultural agency and relative autonomy. The two movements learned from each other and, before long, blended together more than they retained their differences.

To suggest, briefly, how things stand in light of this dialogue and partial blending of historicism (no longer new) and cultural studies, let us return to Dorothy Parker's "A Telephone Call," discussed in Chapter 6 on feminism, and Kate Chopin's "The Story of an Hour," discussed in Chapter 8 on Marxism. We might see "A Telephone Call" as compliant with the ideologies (or discourses) of gender that it portrays or as resisting those ideologies by mocking its character's compliance with them. We might see "The Story of an Hour" as mocking and punishing Louise's independence by killing her off or as sympathetically identifying with her and showing how sadly the unequal system of marriage constrains her. Regardless, it would not make for a satisfying or even a convincing literary critical argument to say that these stories could be one thing or could be the opposite thing and then to shrug our shoulders and leave it at that without daring a more decisive interpretation. Deconstructively, we already know that the stories could be, and are, more than one thing. But we can also see, deconstructively, that those opposite pessimistic and optimistic readings do not balance each other out in stable equilibrium, like a new critical paradox. They do not even have the same cultural consequences across the varying spectrum of cultural settings. For example, in Dorothy Parker's "New York to Detroit," a story similar to "A Telephone Call," the lonely woman finally calls her absent lover and hints that she is pregnant. The pessimistic and optimistic possibilities of these stories, then, carry a different weight in a setting that makes abortion or, for "The Story of an Hour," divorce legal or socially acceptable and a setting that makes abortion or divorce illegal or socially unacceptable. In that way, cultural settings and cultural history play an integral role in literary interpretation. Our interpretations, therefore, will do well to refuse a timid formalist balance that merely says that it could be this or it could be that. We will do better as interpreters when we stand for something that we care about and believe in as we interpret how the combination of competing possibilities plays out in the material circumstances of actual historical and cultural conditions that we care about as readers and critics.

That is not easy, for, as we have seen from the Marxist critique of ideology, we do not choose what we care about all by ourselves. A vast range of conscious and unconscious cultural forces shapes or helps shape our choices. And so as we ask ourselves what we care about most, we have to think critically about what drives our choices, but we can never fully answer that question. And sooner or later, however much our choices might be pushed along by forces beyond ourselves, we still have to choose. Historicist and cultural studies criticism, typically in combination with the other methods of criticism discussed in this book, offer us the chance to put our chosen commitments to work by thinking through the relation between literature and the historical and cultural conflicts and changes that we care about deeply.

☀ 10 ☀

Postcolonial and Race Studies

In the middle of the twentieth century, not that long ago, the world turned a somersault. A small number of nations had colonized a huge proportion of the world's land and population. Roughly one out of every five people in the world lived in British India alone. Just as most of Latin America had wrested independence from Spain and Portugal in the early nineteenth century, so in the middle of the twentieth century most of Africa, the Caribbean, and South Asia broke free from the rule of colonial powers in a wave of change that promised to rock the world but ended up not rocking it so much after all. Colonialism turned out to be far more entrenched than anti-colonialists anticipated or hoped, and the world ended up not all that different, or not different enough for anticolonialists, from what it was before.

At its peak, the British Empire ruled roughly one-quarter of the earth's land and population. Economically and culturally, British power fed off British conquests. But until the last few decades, the study of British history and especially British literature typically paid little attention to colonialism. We can understand why, because, in many ways, colonialism was so brutal that if the conquering peoples owned up to it, that might have led them to reject colonialism and give up the privileges of power. In that way, Westerners had a stake, however unconscious, in not owning up to colonialism, and certainly in not thinking about it critically.

Postcolonialism thus has a long history, but postcolonial studies, especially Anglo-American postcolonial literary studies, gathered force in the late 1970s, especially with Edward Said's *Orientalism* (1978) and then a series of influential articles by Gayatri Chakravorty Spivak and Homi K. Bhabha. These critics' work, and the work their ideas responded to and helped provoke, spoke to a powerful sense of need as readers faced up to changes in world politics and the growing recognition of English as a language of international literature and international daily life. Postcolonial studies emerged as a driving force in literary studies and helped reshape scholarship and teaching across the humanities and social sciences. It offers the possibility—not yet fulfilled—of making literary study as international as literature itself, and so it holds a powerful appeal for readers who care about the state of the world and its writing. Because of its attention to racial and national politics, postcolonial studies has also held special appeal for students, readers, and critics interested in the study of race and in the study of racial, ethnic, and national minorities, including, in the United States, African American studies, Latina/Latino studies, Asian American studies, and American Indian studies. Scholars in all these areas often see analogies and overlapping questions between their own concerns and the concerns of postcolonial studies.

POSTCOLONIALISM

The term *postcolonial* has grown routine, yet it has also led to confusion and debate. Scholars of postcolonialism often write about the colonial as well as or instead of the postcolonial, and in many ways we still live in colonial times, not postcolonial times. The term's suggestion of kinship with poststructuralism, corroborated by the poststructuralist approaches of the most prominent postcolonial theorists, such as Said, Spivak, and Bhabha, attracts suspicion from scholars who want more certainty than they see poststructuralism likely to encourage. Nevertheless, despite its distortions and deceptiveness, the term has emerged as a convenient label for the study of colonialism, postcolonialism, and, more broadly, cultural and political relations between more powerful and less powerful nations and peoples.

Postcolonial literary studies considers writing from colonizing peoples, colonized peoples, and—increasingly—formerly colonized peoples. The colonizing nations are sometimes described as "metropolitan," and the colonies themselves are sometimes divided into two different kinds (each with its own array of variations): **settler colonies** and **occupation colonies**. (Occupation colonies are sometimes called *exploitation colonies* or *colonies of conquest*.) In occupation colonies, such as colonial India and Nigeria, the colonists remain a small proportion of the population. Typically, they leave their metropolitan homes to do their work exploiting the colony, and then they return home and other colonizers replace them. In settler colonies, such as Australia, New Zealand, Canada, and the United States, the colonizers move in permanently, and they or their descendants often grow far more numerous than the people they colonize, whose numbers the colonizers often reduce by disease and by abuses that sometimes reach the level of genocide. Sometimes the settlers forcibly or culturally limit outnumbered indigenous peoples to specific areas, where they are surrounded by settlers in **internal colonies**, such as Indian reservations or reserves, South African bantustans, and, by loose analogy, urban ghettos. Scholars have debated whether to include settler colonies in postcolonial studies at all. The settlers often act like occupiers and identify with their metropolitan homelands, yet they also develop a sense of difference from or even resentment of their homelands. Sometimes, as in the United States, they even lose their awareness of being settlers and act as if the indigenous peoples have disappeared. Regardless, the division into two groups, settler colonies and occupation colonies, can fog differences between different examples in the same group, and some examples, such as Ireland, Algeria, Kenya, Hawaii, and South Africa, do not fit clearly into either group. In the Caribbean, the two patterns combine, as native peoples were decimated and absorbed or replaced by forcibly imported slave labor in plantation economies, with the colonists otherwise acting much as they act in exploitation colonies. These distinctions thus remain up for debate, and they probably serve us best if we question them and keep them provisional.

Following the independence of India and Pakistan (including what is now Bangladesh) in 1947, the wave of newly independent nations inspired excitement and hope across South Asia, Southeast Asia, Africa, and the Middle East. Some countries had to fight the colonial powers before achieving independence, but most won independence peacefully. Some countries went on to set up successful democracies, while others met a more checkered fate, shifting back and forth between elected and imposed governments. In many countries, local oligarchs and dictators betrayed the promise of independence by exploiting the divisions and disarray left by colonialism. Such leaders reproduce many of the abuses of colonialism, including the concentration of capital and resources in a few privileged hands, undemocratic government, ethnic and racial demagoguery, the exploitation of labor and the environment, the displacement of local populations, and restrictions on speech and civil liberties. Under their leadership, postcolonialism transforms into **neocolonialism**. Neocolonialism updates the ravages of colonialism, merely splitting the profits between the local oligarchs and the colonial powers, now represented not only by colonialist governments but also by colonialist, international corporations, often turning the rage for "globalization" into colonialism under another name.

All these shifts in politics and economics, including the cosmetic adjustments that change little beyond the color of some of those who reap the profits, underline that colonialism is a matter of how people think as well as a matter of military power. The shifts of recent history leave the world not so much divided between colonizers and colonized as (in postcolonialist lingo) **hybrid**. Cultural hybridity comes from the way that colonized people and colonizers have taken on many of each other's ways of living and thinking. For just as many colonizing peoples moved to the lands they colonized, so millions of people from colonized and formerly colonized countries, under the pressure of war, forced displacement, or economic disaster or in search of economic and educational opportunities or change, have migrated to the metropole and to other formerly colonized countries. With enormous (in postcolonialist lingo) *migrant, diasporic,* or *exiled* populations, with the mixing of peoples and cultures, and with global trade and communication, the metropolitan countries and the colonized countries have both changed. The metropolitan countries, however, tend much more to deny the ways that international dialogue, migrant populations, the descendants of migrants, and the commerce between cultures have changed the metropole. They also often see the changes in colonized nations and populations as peculiar, amusing, or threatening mixtures that compromise the authenticity of supposedly exotic locales, as if historical change were a feature of the metropole but not of the rest of the world.

*   *   *   *   *

In the 1930s, a group of French-speaking black poets and intellectuals in Paris, inspired partly by the American Harlem Renaissance, put together a literary and political movement that they called

244   How to Interpret Literature

Négritude. Led by the Senegalese Léopold Senghor and the Martinican Aimé Césaire, the Négritude writers called for pride in blackness. They believed that black people, whether from Africa or the
African diaspora, share a "collective personality" that differs radically from the European colonizers. Senghor went on to become the
first president of Senegal, and Césaire served many years as mayor of
Fort de France, the capital of Martinique, and, when Martinique became a French province, as the island's representative in the French
National Assembly. The European colonizers saw the people they
colonized as barbaric, but the writers of Négritude reversed that view
and saw the European colonizers as the true barbarians.

The Nigerian playwright and Nobel Prize laureate Wole Soyinka
criticized what he saw as a defensiveness in the Négritude movement's assertion of black pride. Controversially, he responded to
Négritude by declaring, "A tiger does not proclaim his tigritude, he
pounces" (quoted in Jahn 265; see also Soyinka 126–39). Among
critics of Négritude, the Martinican psychiatrist Frantz Fanon stands
out. Fanon was one of the most provocative and influential theorists
and practitioners of anticolonial resistance. After fighting with the
Free French Forces against the Nazis in World War II and then
studying medicine and psychiatry in France, Fanon sought work in
Africa and was appointed to direct an Algerian psychiatric hospital.
In 1954, he joined the National Liberation Front to fight for Algerian independence from France. A student and friend of Césaire,
Fanon sympathized with the Négritude movement, understanding
how racist colonialism could provoke a prideful counterreaction,
especially after colonialism had gone so far to strip colonized peoples, including blacks, of their sense of racial self-respect and a proud
history. While he valued the pride rekindled by Négritude, he objected to what he saw as its romantic oversimplifications. Pan-
Africanism and similar transnational movements, he feared, depended on a romantic delusion of sameness that threatened to mask
the variety of African and black peoples. Fanon believed that in the
guise of rejecting colonialist prejudice, the poets and philosophers of
Négritude reinvigorated the same stereotypes that the colonizers
believed in, except that the Négritude movement celebrated a supposed sensuality and communalism that colonizers saw as depraved
and uncivilized.

Though the colonizers taught native peoples to believe in and
internalize the colonizers' racist sense of native peoples' inferiority,

Frantz Fanon (1925–1961).

Fanon argued that anticolonial violence cleansed native peoples of their fear and self-doubt. Because colonialism was violent, he believed that it would take violence to overthrow colonialism. He did not believe that the colonial powers could grant independence. Independence must be won. When the colonial powers tried to sit down with the colonized elite and negotiate independence, he believed that the elite represented their own interests, betraying the masses and positioning themselves to rule the common people as the colonizers had before them. Fanon warned that betrayals from the native elite, together with the false pride of Négritude and similar movements, would allow recently colonized peoples, led by Europeanized native intellectuals, corrupt capitalists, and dictators, to sustain the exploitations of colonialism through a self-colonizing neocolonialism.

In that way and as a psychiatrist, Fanon attended to the psychological condition of internalized racism that allowed colonized

peoples to perpetuate the colonialist and racist myths of their inferiority. He understood why, in reaction against colonialism, colonized peoples often sought to romanticize their precolonial history
and civilization and their racial commonality. After all, the colonizers taught them that they were inferior and had no history or
civilization. But he also saw the distortions in such romanticizing
dreams and believed that the precolonial past could never be recovered, because colonized cultures—like all cultures—change
continuously. Fanon called for the Négritude movement and other
romanticizing visions celebrating a glorious past and collective consciousness to serve as a bridge to a revolutionary practice that would
build a wide range of individual postcolonial nations.

Pursuing the call for decolonization not only of the political system but also of the mind, Kenyan novelist Ngugi wa Thiong'o, noting the close relation between language and thought, argues that
African writers should stop writing in the European languages (such
as English, French, and Portuguese) that the colonizers forced on the
peoples they colonized. Instead, he proposes, they should write in

Ngugi wa Thiong'o (1938–).

their own African languages. Ngugi himself stopped writing novels in English and began to write in Gikuyu, allowing his novels to reach a larger audience among his own people, though he also translates or has others translate his novels into English. Not everyone has accepted Ngugi's argument. Many African or other native writers cannot write in a native language. Some prefer English because it can reach a larger audience, including a larger audience of native peoples. And some, notably the Nigerian novelist Chinua Achebe, have pointed out that the language they write in is not the same as the language of the colonizers. Achebe writes not in British English but in African English, just as many native writers across the world write in their own version of what was once a colonizing language. Sometimes, it is the language or one of the languages of their schooling or their daily lives and the language of the people around them. They have made it their own language.

Chinua Achebe (1930–).

FROM ORIENTALISM TO DECONSTRUCTION: EDWARD SAID, HOMI BHABHA, AND GAYATRI CHAKRAVORTY SPIVAK

In literary studies, the boom in postcolonial criticism began with Edward Said's *Orientalism* (1978). Drawing on the ideas of Michel Foucault (see Chapter 9), the Palestinian American Said (pronounced with two syllables, Sah-eed) argues that the West has constructed a **colonial discourse** (in the Foucauldian sense of the term *discourse*) that produces the ideas about the Orient—the East—that the discourse purports to describe. Said calls that colonial discourse **Orientalism**. Said does not mean the "Orient" in the usual sense the term carries today, to refer to East Asia. Instead he uses it in an older sense to refer to the Indian subcontinent and especially to the Islamic Middle East, though his ideas can be and have been applied to all colonial discourse, including discourse about East Asia, sub-Saharan Africa, racial minorities in the West, and the rest of the colonized world.

In Said's model, and beginning especially in the nineteenth century, Western discourse about the East (travel accounts, journalism, scholarship, literary and political writing, studies of religion and language) constructed the East as sensual, lazy, exotic, irrational, cruel, promiscuous, seductive, inscrutable, dishonest, mystical, superstitious, primitive, ruled by emotion, and as a sink of despotism at the margins of the world where all people are alike and where their actions are determined by the national or racial category they belong to ("the Arabs," "the natives"). Said argues that descriptions of the East in these terms generated a discourse that produced and then continued to reproduce the East in such terms, and that has continued to reproduce the East and the colonized or formerly colonized world in such terms up to the present day. In constructing the East, Orientalist discourse also constructed a West that was everything the East was not: rational, hard-working, kind, democratic, moral, modern, progressive, technological, individualist, and the center of the world, the norm against which everything else was a deviation. The binary that Said observes maps onto a parallel discourse of gender. Orientalist discourse finds qualities in the East that overlap with the qualities that misogynist discourse finds in the feminine (women as supposedly irrational, emotional, promiscuous, seductive, dishonest, lazy), and the qualities it sees in the West overlap with the qualities that it sees in the masculine (men as supposedly rational, dependable, hard-working, and strong). In that sense, colonialism often feminizes the colonized, partly in an effort to masculinize itself. Said argues that the West constructed the East by unconsciously taking qualities that the West feared in itself and projecting them onto the East, allowing Westerners to suppose that the West does not have those qualities and that those qualities define the East, separating it from the West. In that way, Westerners can imagine the East as an Other to the West's self.

To postcolonial scholars, the Orientalism that Said describes continues to shape economic, political, and military relations between the Anglo-American West and the East, including the Islamic Middle East. More broadly, it shapes relations between the colonialist or neocolonialist world and the colonized or formerly colonized world. In the process, it shapes each side's inability to understand or think through the perspectives of the other side. Culturally, the binary between colonizer and colonized reproduces itself by allowing the West to treat its own ways of thinking as universal truths. The ruling assumption is that since the colonizing powers had the means of conquering the rest of the world, the colonizing cultures are therefore superior and the colonized cultures inferior, as if the means of conquest were a measure of all other values. Aesthetically and literarily, the colonizing world treats its own standards for art and literature as if they were universal and simply natural rather than culturally specific and constructed, blinding metropolitan cultures to the value and specificity of art, literature, and ways of thinking in colonized cultures.

Later postcolonial critics, while finding Said's account broadly convincing, often see it as overly binarized, too confidently separating the discourses of the East and the West without attending to the cultural or even deconstructive blur between cultures and the internal differences within cultures, including differences of class and gender. After all, Westerners, even colonizers, sometimes recognize difference and variety within the East. Western people of color, for example, often see the East more sympathetically than white Westerners. While the binary between colonizers and colonized that Said's *Orientalism* exposes has shaped the questions and issues of later postcolonial criticism, the discussion of that binary has often questioned its rigidity. Such questions typically arise either from a historicist sense of cultural complexity or from a characteristically deconstructionist impulse to break down binaries in favor of multiplicity.

Edward Said (1935–
2003).

In that vein, Bhabha and Spivak take a more deconstructive perspective than Said. Their highly theorized, densely jargoned, arcane writings have provoked a storm of interest for the challenges they pose and a storm of resentment for what some readers see as pretentious and impenetrable elitism.

Homi Bhabha (not to be confused with the famous physicist of the same name) joins the critique of Said's *Orientalism* as overly binarized. Drawing on language and ideas from structuralism, deconstruction, psychoanalysis, and Foucault, Bhabha asks us to consider the psychological ambivalence, the struggle of opposite and contradictory feelings, in the colonized or formerly colonized world and in colonial and postcolonial discourse. He describes the colonized and colonizing worlds as **hybrid**, as against Said's sense of one culture thinking about its opposite culture. Popularized by Bhabha, Stuart

Homi K. Bhabha
(1949–).

Hall, and others, the term *hybrid* has emerged as a widely used syn-
onym for cultural multiplicity, though to some critics (myself included), its history as a term for crossbreeding two different species
can carry inappropriately biological connotations and seem to re-
install the binary that the term supposedly undermines. Regardless,
the cultural multiplicity suggested by the term expresses a sense of
continuous cultural change across history that colonialists and some
anticolonial movements might seem to deny.

From Fanon's perspective, for example, the movements celebrating a collective consciousness or a return to a precolonial past seem
blind to the hybridity or cross-cultural multiplicity of contemporary
culture, merely putting a better-intentioned spin on the colonialist
sense that colonized peoples are locked in an unchanging past and
usually locked in a distorted vision of that past as well, as in the stereotypes of Africans (jungle, spear, etc.), American Indians (feathered war bonnet, face paint, etc.), and Arabs (scimitar, camel, etc.).

Just as Westerners no longer typically ride a horse or carry a flintlock, though some Westerners do, especially at ceremonial times, so Africans, American Indians, and Arabs live in a multicultural modernity that often looks like contemporary London, Paris, or New York. And the multicultural modernity of Nairobi, Window Rock (the capitol of the Navajo Nation), and Beirut or of Mumbai (formerly called Bombay), Manila, and Jakarta often *is* the multicultural modernity of London, Paris, and New York, because the same people and goods routinely migrate across political and cultural borders. Rather than seeing borders as dividing utterly different peoples, we might therefore think of borders—such as the southern and northern borders of the United States and the borders between members of the European Union—as porous transit points that sift and sort people as much as they separate them. A large proportion of the world's population now lives in more than one supposedly but not actually separate culture or lives in a country or region other than where they or their near ancestors were born. People sustain and change the cultures they bring with them, and they sustain and change the places where they live, so that those places are no longer culturally separate and distinct (if they ever were). Instead they are hybrid and multiple.

Nevertheless, the pressure to essentialize identity continually invites us to deny the hybridity around us and within us. One form such denial takes is the literary and cultural stereotype, from the warlike images of spear, war bonnet, and scimitar that a conquering culture imposes, ironically, on those it conquers to the full panoply of racial, gender, regional, and national stereotypes, including those that Said exposed as produced by the colonial discourse that purports to describe them. Against our familiar way of critiquing stereotypes, Bhabha argues, deconstructively, that the problem with stereotypes is not their inaccuracy but instead their fixity, their denial of the play of signifiers. Perhaps that amounts to the same thing. But for Bhabha the point lies in the way that the fixity of stereotypes denies variation and change, as if variety and history were the privilege of those who impose stereotypes but are not available for those who have stereotypes imposed on them. He tries to shift the critique of stereotype from saying that one image is positive and another negative to the work of looking at the ambivalent process of stereotyping, the way that stereotypes deny something about the self while they assert something about the other. In that sense, Bhabha's challenge echoes the feminist critique of "images of women" feminism (as discussed in

Chapter 6). He sees stereotypes not so much as false as he sees them as projections of what the stereotyping culture fears about itself onto an "other" that it can delude itself into supposing is separate from the stereotyping self. (In that sense, Bhabha also echoes Said's argument about Orientalism, but Bhabha intensifies the psychoanalytic lingo of projection, introjection, ambivalence, and displacement.) He also sees the discourse of stereotypes, in its ambivalent effort to fix representation, as characteristic of literary realism's denial of those desires and cultures that, despite literary realism's devotion to presenting the truth, it typically runs away from representing. Supposedly realistic novels such as *A Passage to India; The Moon and Sixpence; The Immoralist; Native Son; Cry, the Beloved Country;* and *Goodbye, Columbus,* for example, even as they undermine some stereotypes, still trade on other stereotypes of gender, sexual orientation, race, religion, ethnicity, or nationality. The usual objection is to say that the stereotypes are unrealistic because they are inaccurate. But from Bhabha's perspective, the problem lies less in the misleading inaccuracy than in what the desire to represent fixed, static patterns says about the representing cultures and about readers who go along, passively taking the static patterns for granted.

Bhabha describes cultural ambivalence as dramatized in what he calls **mimicry**. Inevitably, in a world of cultural mixing and differences of power, colonized people often end up mimicking their colonizers, adopting the colonizers' language, educational systems, governmental systems (parliament or congress, courts, constitution, laws), clothing, music, and so on. While some might see such mimicry as a form of internalized colonization or self-colonization, as in Ngugi's critique of African writing in European languages, Bhabha calls attention to the way that the colonized's mimicry of the colonizers can express the colonized's ambivalence and, in turn, can provoke ambivalence and doubt in the colonizers. When the colonizers gaze in the mirror of the colonized's mimicry, the image they see looks, as Bhabha puts it, "*almost the same, but not quite.*" The blend of repetition and difference can threaten the colonizers' sense of their own power and superiority. It can even threaten their sense of racial privilege when they begin to recognize that the mimicry is also, as Bhabha puts it, "*almost the same but not white*" (Bhabha 86, 89). The signifiers slip far enough away from what they supposedly signify that they tilt the mimicry into mockery. The colonizers may suppose that their surveillance of the colonized, in Foucauldian terms, disciplines the colonized. But when the colonizers gaze at the colonized and see the mimicking colonized's displacement of the colonizers' gaze turned back on the colonizers, it alienates the colonizers from their confidence in their own essence, thus destabilizing colonialism itself.

On the other hand, though Bhabha does not say so, mimicry and the mockery that it can verge toward are equal-opportunity employers. The colonized mimic the colonizers, as Bhabha argues, but the colonizers can also mimic the colonized—and they do. Almost any example we might give will spark controversy and disagreement, and, because the binary between colonized and colonizer has multiplied so profusely, some examples can raise questions about who, if anyone, is or resembles the colonized and who, if anyone, is or resembles the colonized. White musicians have often imitated the music of black musicians, and historically many white musicians, like good colonialists, manipulated contracts so that the white imitators and not the black composers got the profits. This is not to say that white imitations or variations on music composed by blacks are necessarily a bad thing, but it is to say that they have a long history of abuse. Similarly, the world music movement could be read as mimicry, as could tanning parlors, or the practice of curling, straightening, or otherwise arranging hair in ways that make it look more like the hair that, however simplistically, many people associate with another race than what they think of as their own race, or whites imitating clothing styles or speech patterns that they associate, however stereotypically, with blacks, or the scandal over college "ghetto parties" where white students dress up like stereotypes of African Americans or "taco and tequila" parties where they dress up like stereotypes of Mexicans. On my own campus, until recently, and amidst enormous controversy, a white student dressed up like a stereotype of an American Indian and performed a callisthenic "dance" at halftime of football and basketball games, to the cheers of a roaring crowd and the horror of most Indian students. Different people will usually interpret provocative examples like this in different ways, and many of our interpretations will vary with the context, with whether one group acts in some way like another group out of envy, respect, scorn, or parallel responses to similar patterns in style, or out of mockery. Even then we will often debate whether imitations intended as respectful can nevertheless come across—given the intentional fallacy—as disrespectful.

Neither side, colonizers or colonized—if we can still speak, for convenience, of two sides and a binary amidst the circulation of so much deconstructive imitation and instability—can hold a monopoly on mockery. And neither side can hold a monopoly on in-stability or on the capacity to expose the other side's instability. The two directions of mimicry, however, do not disrupt in the same ways. When less powerful people mimic more powerful people, they can menace the power structure, as Bhabha argues. But when more powerful people mimic less powerful people, they can reinforce the power structure. Even so, when colonizing people mimic colo-nized people, the mimicry can suggest the colonizers' vulnerability, expressed as a desire for what they also suppress, both when that means suppressing other people and when it means suppressing something within themselves. That sense of ambivalent vulnerabil-ity and desire makes mimicry a potent force in any cultural repeti-tion, lying in wait to shake up dominant discourses and ideologies.

Gayatri Chakravorty Spivak first attracted wide notice by trans-lating into English Derrida's most influential book, *Of Grammatol-ogy*. Her own work brings deconstruction together with feminism, Marxism, and postcolonial theory, and her interest in feminism and gender helped expand and deepen postcolonial criticism. Spivak notes that imperialism is central to British history and culture, and yet the study of British literature (before the growth of postcolonial studies) largely ignored it, colluding in the ideological suppression of one of the motors of British culture. She contends that to study the role of imperialism in the literature of colonizing countries can help make visible the **worlding** of the so-called Third World. By that she means that it is not enough to see Third World writing as a sepa-rate thing out on the margins of metropolitan culture. Instead, given the hybridity or interconnectedness of cultures, the Third World is part of the metropolitan world, just as the metropolitan world is part of the Third World.

Spivak has chided early Anglo-American feminist literary criti-cism for concentrating on how female characters heroically consol-idate their subjectivity. In effect, she criticizes "images of women" feminism (see Chapter 6) for a narcissistic obsession with the indi-vidualism of "strong women" and an obliviousness to imperialism and colonialism, an obliviousness that Spivak's work helps to change. To Spivak, the "feminist individualist heroine" offers "an allegory of the general epistemic violence of imperialism, the construction of a self-immolating subject for the glorification of the social mission of the colonizer" (Spivak, "Three Women's Texts and a Critique of Imperialism" 251). That is, she sees the ideology of individualism, including bourgeois feminist individualism, as part of the suppressed logic of colonialism, as something to be criticized, not, as traditional feminists supposed, something to be celebrated. For metropolitan women, bourgeois individualism offers a false freedom earned partly on the backs of women and men in the Third World, whose labor and subjugation pays for metropolitan privilege. To Spivak's thinking, metropolitan women see Third World women as disrespectful of themselves, as "self-immolating," as compared to metropolitan women, who are in love with their own newly achieved feminist selfhood. By seeing Third World women as persecuted and as submitting to their own persecution, metropolitan feminists put themselves in a self-glorifying position of superiority that allows them to tell Third World women how to do things better.

In this context, Spivak's influential article "Can the Subaltern Speak?" (1985) raises reverberating questions for postcolonial theory, feminist theory, and minority, or *subaltern*, studies. But Spivak's writing is notoriously dense, and "Can the Subaltern Speak?," like much of her writing, often verges on the unreadable. Because it is so provocative, however, I will try to summarize the article's key argument.

To understand Spivak's argument, you need to know that the term *subaltern*, which she takes from Antonio Gramsci, refers to people

Gayatri Chakravorty Spivak (1942–).

with less power. (For Gramsci, see Chapter 8.) Spivak's examples of subalterns are women, Indians (South Asian Indians), and Indian women in particular. You also need to know about the history of "sati," the controversial Hindu practice of widow burning. (Sometimes spelled suttee, it rhymes with "What, me?")

British colonialists had their ways of rationalizing the British empire, and they often saw themselves not just as conquerors but as good liberal conquerors. As supposedly good conquerors, they often sought to let Indians rule themselves according to Indian practices. But the British ran into a problem following that principle when it came to sati. On the one hand, their liberalism told them not to interfere with Indian practices. On the other hand, it told them that widow-burning was abhorrent and had to be halted. The conflict seemed irresolvable. Their solution was to say that widows could only be burned if they first agreed to be burned. To complicate matters, the literal meaning of "sati" is not "widow burning" but "good wife." To some Hindus, for a widow to be a good wife meant that she must want to be burned. You can imagine the dilemma, then, in the British colonial authorities asking a woman to say that she did not want to be a sati, since a widow and others could see that as meaning that she did not want to be a good wife. By contrast, the British and many others—including many Hindus—who opposed sati argued that to be a good wife did not require widows to commit fiery suicide.

All this raises thorny issues for a postcolonialist, Derridean, Marxist feminist like Spivak. When a widow says that, yes, she wants to be burned, who is speaking? Is she choosing for herself, Spivak asks, or is that impossible, because she has been interpellated into a misogynist set of expectations for feminine behavior? Is she speaking for herself, or has she been so absorbed into patriarchal culture that she speaks for the patriarchy, even if she believes that she speaks for herself? Can we even tell whether it is one or the other, and, if so, how can we tell? Can people who oppose or support sati speak for the sati better than she can speak for herself?

As a Derridean, Spivak is skeptical of what she sees as the romanticizing notion that anyone can voice an inner, true, and complete self, an essence. As a Marxist, she believes that we often exaggerate our individuality and do not realize how much we speak for larger, often oppressive ideologies—like sexism and patriarchy—that we have been interpellated into believing are our own. As a feminist, she is suspicious that women who say they want to be burned to death because their husband has died are speaking for the patriarchy, not for themselves, even if they think that they speak for themselves. And yet, as a feminist, she also wants to take seriously what women say and think. She fears that it is terribly presumptuous to tell a woman that what that woman says she thinks is not really what she thinks but is only what the patriarchy wants her to think. Putting all this together, Spivak finds the question of whether the subaltern can speak for herself or even for a larger subaltern group, such as women or colonized Indians or Indian women, an aporia. As you may recall from Chapter 4, *aporia* is the term Derrida uses for an undecidable impasse, a question that, no matter how urgent, cannot be answered.

And Spivak's question is enormously urgent. It is not just an arid calculation or empty philosophical puzzle. Let us think about the implications of the issue by looking at some common places where it might turn up. Think of the innumerable times you have heard someone (perhaps yourself) say something like: I want to study African American literature (or queer studies or women's literature or some particular subaltern topic) so that I can see what African Americans (or women or Asian American women or Latinas and Latinos) *really think*, so that I can hear their true voice. You have probably heard politicians and cultural commentators say they want to find out what a given group of people really thinks, want to hear the voice of the people or of some particular group of people. But you may also notice that some people from a given group—say, African American women—will say one thing, and others will say something else, sometimes something dramatically different. Which of them speaks in the true voice of African American women? Spivak's argument suggests that there is no true voice, no essence, of African American women or Indian women or any subaltern group (or any group at all) and that whenever we say there is, we demeaningly oversimplify and essentialize Indian women, African American women, or whatever group we are addressing.

As you can imagine, Spivak's approach has set off a good deal of controversy. It challenges ideas that many people take for granted, unsettling common assumptions in minority studies, postcolonial studies, and women's studies. On the other hand, many people in minority studies, postcolonial studies, and women's studies welcome Spivak's nonessentialist approach. They see it as helping us do minority studies, postcolonial studies, and women's studies by helping us respect the variety of opinions and voices in any group. It can make us more alert to how, when we think that people speak for a particular group or when people claim to speak for a particular group or even claim to speak for themselves, they may be speaking for another group whose interests they have been interpellated into mistaking for their own. This leads to a crucial point of clarification. Spivak does not answer "No" to the question "Can the subaltern speak?" She does not argue that subalterns cannot speak. She sees the question as open, continuous, and unanswerable. After all, she says in a later piece, she is a subaltern and she speaks perfectly well (Spivak, *Outside* 59). (People who dislike her prose style might say that she doesn't speak so well after all.) But at the end of her article, in a regrettable moment that caused widespread confusion, she does say, "The subaltern cannot speak" (Spivak, "Can the Subaltern Speak?" 130). People who follow her argument have always understood that she did not mean that sentence as a conclusion and that in context that sentence only names a tempting conclusion she is not ready to accept. But other people who succumbed to the near-impenetrability of Spivak's prose seized on that one sentence, took it out of context, and used it to represent the whole argument. (Does all this, ironically, back up Spivak's point that we cannot take someone's words as representing their true belief?) Thus some people roundly attacked Spivak for saying that subalterns cannot speak, wondering how she could possibly say that, as a speaking subaltern herself. In the latest version of her article, Spivak regrets that she ever wrote that sentence, clarifying that she did not mean it as a conclusion (Spivak, *Critique* 308).

Spivak's argument encourages us not to oversimplify the opinions and writing of individual speakers and writers or of groups of people. It encourages us to see the range of views in any group and even within a single person. It can also help make us more alert to the internal contradictions in any speaking, writing, set of opinions, individual, or group of people, for it reminds us that even when we think we speak for ourselves, we might be a mouthpiece for ideas that come from somewhere else. In that way it challenges the generalizations we make or witness day after day—the claims that this group of people believes this or that group believes something else, that this group is like that or that group is like this. But like Bhabha's argument about ambivalence, Spivak leaves us hanging. Rather than telling us that people do speak for themselves or that they only think they speak for themselves while they actually speak for ideas imposed on them, she audaciously casts aside essentialist conclusions about individuals and groups and leaves the question both urgent and unanswerable.

Known for her resistance to essentialism, Spivak has also invited cultural critics, who usually look skeptically at essentialism, to experiment by making their resistance to essentialism more flexible. In a world that often takes essentialist beliefs for granted, essentialist arguments, she notes, sometimes inspire people to seek political change, including people who would not find inspiration in the nonessentialist arguments of literary and cultural critics. In some of her writings, Spivak suggests that in such circumstances, it might not betray our principles to try out essentialist claims, in a temporary way, to help inspire change for the better. She calls that kind of provisional essentialism **strategic essentialism**. While Spivak never makes much of this argument and has not even stuck to it, others—eager to license essentialism—have seized on the idea of strategic essentialism.

The question might hinge on whether an expression of strategic essentialism does more harm in the long run than good in the short run. If we say, for example, that children are worse off in households headed by women, do we do more good by encouraging men to stay with the mothers of their children or more harm by suggesting that households must have a head, that only one person can be the head, and that it is best for men and not women to be that one person and suggesting as well (less directly) that women need to pair off with men, that heterosexual couples are preferable to same-sex couples, and that lesbians and single women make bad mothers? Similar questions arise in the controversy over racial gerrymandering (separate electoral districts based on race), profiling for security at airports (who "looks" like a terrorist?), or claims about literary style according to gender, race, or nationality (do female and male writers, or German and French writers, or indigenous and European writers, have distinct styles?). To some critics and theorists, such questions—or questions about other essentialist claims designed to encourage people to improve their lives—lead to yet another aporia. Many other critics and theorists, however, believe that essentialist claims can help out in practical ways that matter more than the sometimes demeaning implications they carry. And others argue that the demeaning implications magnify over time and end up hurting people more than they help people.

Some readers resent the high-theoretical approach of Bhabha, Spivak, and the many less well-known critics who roughly work in or follow their manner. Critics who think that Spivak says that the subaltern cannot speak wonder how she could let her deconstructive sense of play lead her away from practical politics, but Spivak pays considerable attention to practical politics, far more than Bhabha. Bhabha's critics, especially, sometimes prefer less abstract talk of ambivalence and mimicry and more attention to material politics. It is one thing to destabilize colonialism by a little mimicry that exposes colonial ambivalence and another thing to destabilize it by blowing up a bridge or, without violence, by nationalizing the assets of colonialist foreign corporations, unionizing exploited laborers, building schools, or redistributing land monopolized by colonialist and neocolonialist overlords. Skeptics sometimes see Bhabha and Spivak, both originally from India, as betraying their postcolonial status and perspective by studying and teaching in Britain (Bhabha) and the United States (Spivak, and now also Bhabha). Or at least they resent that Western critics have celebrated postcolonial critics who live in the West, not in the East. Some critics also resent that Bhabha, Spivak, and many other postcolonial critics rely on what skeptics describe as European theory. Such doubts oversimplify the picture by a good deal. Derrida, to take just one notable example, was African as well as European. He was born and raised in Algeria, not Paris, and he dedicated his career to overturning the truisms of European philosophy. While he did not develop his ideas independently of European thinking and cultural practices, it would turn his writing inside out to reduce it to a representative product of European thought and culture. Spivak especially relies on Indian bodies of thought as well as on figures like Derrida, Marx, and Freud, and she insists that no one has the right to limit what ideas she can think with.

Spivak and others have especially encouraged postcolonial thinkers to bring feminism to postcolonialism. Some postcolonial cultural critics, determined to address Third World cultures respectfully, close their eyes to Third World misogyny or even defend it as part of local cultural practices. From such a perspective, outsiders and feminists are asked to refrain from criticizing not only historical practices that abuse women, such as sati, but also such locally common contemporary practices as domestic violence, rape, limited rights to own property, limited educational opportunity, lack of voting rights, restrictions on the right to work outside the home, restrictions on dress or movement, female genital mutilation (even the name for that practice provokes controversy), and restrictions on choice about whether to marry or when or whom to marry. Such requests to hold off criticism come from a fear that misogynist practices like these might be misconstrued as specific to the colonized world or specific to one particular colonized people. They often get called on to prop up colonialist fantasies about the supposedly primitive practices of colonized peoples. By publicizing misogynist practices in the Third World, people from the colonizing metropole can help blind themselves to their own culture's abuse of women, and they can help blind themselves, as well, to the ways that colonization has encouraged the abuse of women.

Nevertheless (and to be open about my own perspective), to refrain from criticizing such abuses is to suppress the variety in the history and traditions of the so-called Third World, for just as such practices have their supporters among colonized peoples, so do they also have their opponents. An unwillingness to criticize Third World practices essentializes formerly colonized cultures as unchanging and internally consistent, condescending to the Third World as an exotic, precious land fenced off from cultural debate, a land where neocolonialist demagogues can twist postcolonialism into an excuse for naturalizing and essentializing the abuse of women. Instead of separating feminism from postcolonial studies, as if they were opposites, many feminists argue, therefore, that it is dangerous to pursue postcolonial studies and postcolonial politics without feminism. Often, they argue that feminism and postcolonialism must depend on each other in their mutual commitments to recognition and justice.

RACE STUDIES: POSTCOLONIAL THEORY AND THE CONSTRUCTION OF RACE

As postcolonial studies has grown, so has the study of race and ethnicity, which both draws on and contributes to postcolonial studies. That study comes under many names and in many varieties. In its more specific dimensions, it overlaps with area studies, such as South Asian studies, African studies, Latin American studies, and Pacific studies, and in the United States it overlaps with such areas as Asian American studies, Latina/Latino studies, Chicana/Chicano studies, American Indian studies, Hawaiian studies, indigenous studies, whiteness studies, and, the most established of these undertakings, African American studies. In its broader dimensions, the study of race and ethnicity is sometimes simply called *race studies* or *ethnic studies*. In contemporary practice, it also includes what has come to be called *critical race studies* or *critical race theory*, which considers these topics in light of the many ways of thinking addressed in this book. Each of these movements has its own nuanced and elaborate history, and often a much longer history than postcolonial studies. Rather than trying to recount those many long histories here, then, I will briefly review patterns of thought and directions of inquiry in contemporary critical race theory that have done the most to draw on and contribute to postcolonial, literary, and cultural studies.

Contemporary studies of race, region, and ethnicity, like feminism and queer studies, often join with postcolonial studies to rethink essentialist assumptions about identity, history, politics, and literature. In United States Latina/Latino and Chicana/Chicano studies (more traditionally known, in ways that assume a masculine norm, as Latino, Chicano, Latino/Latina, or Chicano/Chicana studies), the political and cultural border between Mexico and the United States has emerged as a figure of the irrepressible yet contested mobility of Latina/Latino peoples and cultures. In the influential *Borderlands/ La Frontera: The New Mestiza* (1987, 1999), Gloria Anzaldúa evokes the **borderlands** in her bilingual title and through a feminist and queer blend of autobiography, history, and advocacy, written in a mixture of prose and poetry. Writing in English, Spanish, Spanglish, and Nahuatl, Anzaldúa insists on a mixing of national, racial, sexual, and gendered cultures and identities—Mexican, Chicana, Indian, mestiza (racially "mixed"), lesbian, working class, Tejana—that colonialist and patriarchal assumptions have denied and that the porous border can evoke but cannot suppress. She calls for crossing the borders of multiple identities instead of supposing that different identities can continue along separate paths. Anzaldúa helped popularize the notion of *mestizaje*, or racial mixing, as a representative figure for Latina/Latino people and cultures. The term *mestizaje* has a diverse history. Its connotations vary across the many different countries of Latin America, where it can sometimes suggest romantic and patriarchal celebrations of a mythically unified national identity. But for Latinas and Latinos in the United States, Anzaldúa helped reshape the term to figure resistance to assimilation and to figure pride in the mobility and multiplicity of identity, both politically and artistically.

Similarly, Caribbean writers and cultural critics have theorized *métissage* (mixing, or **creolization**), led especially by the Martinican writer Edouard Glissant, a student of Césaire and associate of Fanon. Glissant describes what he calls *antillanité* (after the Antilles, the Caribbean islands), translated from French into English as "Caribbeanness." Acknowledging the influence of Césaire's belief in a singular black identity based in Africa, Glissant sets his vision of Caribbean culture and art in a multiplicity that defies Négritude through the Caribbean model of many cultures, languages, and peoples mixed together. He sees Caribbean peoples, with their mixture of African, French, English, Spanish, indigenous, and South Asian origins, as producing a *métissage* that never settles into what he sees as the stable sameness of Négritude or of conventional European models of identity. For Glissant, *antillanité* and *métissage* represent a *"poétique de la relation,"* rendered in English as a "cross-cultural poetics," based in a continuous changing within and between languages, such as the Creole French of Martinique and the European French also spoken in Martinique. While *antillanité* and *métissage* represent roughly the same thing as hybridity or borderlands, borders take a distinct form in the Caribbean, with its island nations and their in-some-ways-parallel histories, and with Martinique and Guadeloupe now recognized as provinces of France. Hybridity can suggest a completed combination of separate histories, whereas for Glissant, *antillanité* and *métissage* suggest a combination that produces something different from its contributing parts, fluidly recombining in a process of continuous change.

Glissant does not set creolized cultures against noncreolized or "pure" cultures. He does not see creolization as a way to glorify the Caribbean world compared to the rest of the world. For all peoples, he argues, are cross-cultural. Instead, he poses creolization against the idea that cultures ground their identity on an inherited and unique history and then hold to that identity without change, exiling people who do not live up to the inherited model. "To assert peoples are creolized, that creolization has value," he argues, "is to deconstruct in this way the category of 'creolized' that is considered as halfway between two 'pure' extremes." He objects, for example, to the category of "Colored" in apartheid South Africa, calling it "barbaric... that this intermediary category has been officially recognized." "Composite peoples," Glissant believes, cannot "deny or mask their hybrid composition, nor sublimate it in the notion of a mythical pedigree, ... because they do not need the myth of pure lineage" (Glissant 140–41). Glissant's work has helped inspire a younger generation of Martinican writers, notably Patrick Chamoiseau, to call on *Créolité* (creolization) as a figure for Caribbean language and literature.

Yet another similar pattern of thinking has emerged in the discussion of American Indian literature, where the Anishinaabe (Ojibwe,

Chippewa) writer Gerald Vizenor has tried to undermine notions of racial purity and fixed ideas of Indianness by seeing the performance of Indian identity as under pressure to live up to the colonialist culture's fantasies of Indianness: the stoic wooden Indian, the savage warrior in a feathered headdress, the romantic Indian princess, the natural ecologist, and so on. Vizenor refers to such fixed beliefs about Indianness as "terminal creeds," and he makes fun of their power over people's imaginations. Instead of essentializing racial or genetic purity, Vizenor values tribal history and heritage. Thinking through humor and satire, Vizenor models many of his writings on the irrepressible playfulness of tribal trickster stories, and he revalorizes the sometimes-derogatory terms *mixedblood* and *crossblood* as models for the unpredictable combinations of ideas and histories in contemporary "postindian" life and writing. For Vizenor the terms *mixedblood* and *crossblood*—his rewriting of mixed blood or half breed—evoke a cultural, not a biological identity, though for some later critics the terms carry uncomfortably biological connotations. Some critics also fear that Vizenor's skepticism about stable identities can threaten indigenous sovereignty and practical, tribally rooted politics. To Vizenor, however, the terms *mixedblood* and *crossblood* represent not a biological essence passively received by those who carry it but instead a cultural heritage passed down by Indian people and to Indian people across a long and steadily changing history.

Notions such as the borderlands, the new mestiza, Caribbeanness, *métissage*, creolization, Créolité, and trickster mixedbloods echo the model of double-consciousness that W. E. B. Du Bois chose to describe African Americans in *The Souls of Black Folk* (1903). In Du Bois's famous words,

> the Negro is a sort of seventh son, born with a veil, and gifted with second-sight in this American world,—a world which yields him no true self-consciousness, but only lets him see himself through the revelation of the other world. It is a peculiar sensation, this double-consciousness, this sense of always looking at one's self through the eyes of others, of measuring one's soul by the tape of a world that looks on in amused contempt and pity. One ever feels his twoness,—an American, a Negro; two souls, two thoughts, two unreconciled strivings; two warring ideals in one dark body, whose dogged strength alone keeps it from being torn asunder. (Du Bois 16–17)

Du Bois's words can help relieve a burdensome pressure by exposing that pressure's causes and logic. At the same time, they can suggest a muted, sympathetic self-criticism. They can help caution us against the temptation that some critics feel to celebrate the mixing of cultures and races, as if more conspicuously mixed people were somehow better than less conspicuously mixed people. As Glissant is at pains to argue, that would miss the point. *Métissage* does not mean that mixed people are better than unmixed people. It means that everyone is mixed and that we do better to acknowledge the ceaseless mixing than to fantasize that any one people somehow is or should be pure and separate from other peoples.

Scholars of indigenous studies often note with dismay that postcolonial studies and race and ethnicity studies usually ignore or give little heed to indigenous peoples, even though indigenous peoples are central to their concerns. From the perspective of indigenous peoples, we still live in colonial times, not postcolonial times, and so indigenous studies has much to contribute to postcolonial studies. Increasingly, indigenous studies scholars address the problem of internalized colonization, or self-colonization, what Ngugi calls "the colonization of the mind." That is to say that, though indigenous and other colonized peoples have often resisted the colonizers, they have also often had to go along with the colonizers, and as a consequence they have often absorbed colonialist values as their own. Indigenous studies scholars, therefore, increasingly seek out strategies of decolonization.

The Maori scholar Linda Tuhiwai Smith, for example, writes about the ways that researchers studying indigenous peoples typically focus on the researchers' needs, not on the needs of the colonized, indigenous peoples. Much as colonizers exploit colonized and indigenous peoples and their natural resources for the colonizers' own purposes, so researchers studying indigenous peoples often treat the people they study like natural resources waiting to be exploited. Researchers typically ask what indigenous people can do for them, not what they can do for the indigenous people they study. In *Decolonizing Methodologies: Research and Indigenous Peoples* (1999), Smith proposes strategies for indigenous peoples to help shape their own futures by decolonizing the ways they think about themselves and the ways that they work with professionals who study them, both outside researchers and indigenous researchers. Some scholars and indigenous leaders believe that all research about an indigenous community should first receive approval from the community. Other scholars see that as an infringement on the academic and intellectual freedom of the researchers and challenge the ability of a given group of community members, even elected officials, to speak for the community at large. Such debates have revolved around social science research, which can have large and direct social consequences—helpful or damaging—for indigenous communities.

It is harder to anticipate how such debates will shape out in the humanities. Euroamerican poets and novelists, for example, working without a community's permission, have often rewritten sacred indigenous ceremonies as poetry or mined them as atmosphere for fiction. From one perspective, such writers are exercising their creative imagination and showing their appreciation for native cultures. From another perspective, they are treating indigenous rituals as "material" for their own purposes, much as other people have stolen indigenous natural resources or stolen or occupied indigenous lands. Should a tribal poet or a poet from outside the tribal community receive permission to write a poem about a flower that grows on tribal land? Perhaps not. But what if the poem describes a custom? What if it describes a sacred ceremony that depends on specialized knowledge, perhaps knowledge that, according to custom and belief, would be compromised if outsiders learned about it or commercialized it? What if the poem criticizes the community's leaders or governing council or its traditional beliefs?

Such questions partly have to do with the vexed issue of indigenous sovereignty. When people have survived a history of direct and indirect genocide, had their lands stolen, their governments and customs displaced, their children taken away, their languages and religious ceremonies banned, and their cultures trivialized as the playthings and entertainment of the colonizing culture (think cowboys and Indians in toy stores and on the screen or Indian sports mascots like the Cleveland Indians' "Chief Wahoo"), they sometimes take a special interest in asserting their right to run their own lives, including their governments, lands, schools, religious practices, laws, and so on. What, then, about their intellectual life, art, and literature and the intellectual life, art, and literature of people from the colonizers' world when they visit or trespass on indigenous lands or use indigenous cultures for their own purposes? Perhaps different questions of this kind call for different answers. Indigenous, anticolonialist scholars are beginning to raise such questions, and the responses to many of the questions are still emerging and hard to codify.

All these notions contribute to or overlap with critical race theory. Critical race theory emerged in legal studies in the 1970s and 1980s as an outgrowth of and response to critical legal studies, a left-influenced rethinking of rights discourse. For critical legal scholars, the institutions of law are not neutral, as they believe that liberals have traditionally supposed. The discourse of rights is not something that simply needs opening up to all populations. Instead, critical legal scholars see the discourse of law and rights as committed to upholding traditional power relations, even if indirectly. For example, a traditionally liberal, rights-based perspective might say that all people should have the right to own a radio or TV station or contribute as much as they like to a political candidate. By contrast, a position more skeptical of rights-based thinking might say that we need to put limits on rights, in this case the right to own media outlets or contribute to political candidates, or else the rich will use their radio and TV stations and their paid-for politicians to drive out the competition, so that all the mass media and all the politicians will end up in the hands of the wealthy few.

Building from such perspectives, Derrick Bell, a founding figure for critical race theory, argues that in the United States, white jurists and leaders began to support civil rights not so much from a commitment to people of color as from a desire to protect entrenched white interests. For example, in the famous 1954 Brown vs. Board of Education case that declared school segregation illegal, the United States Supreme Court palliated restive African Americans and burnished the United States's image for the Cold War, but the court did little to enforce desegregation. Segregation not only continued but actually increased. Instead of threatening white privilege, therefore, such decisions, based on abstract rights rather than actual power relations, end up propping up white privilege. According to critical race theory, then, racism is not merely a removable blemish on an otherwise sound system. It is integral to the system itself. And those in power will rarely join in changing the system unless they see change as serving their own interests.

In this view, power relations produce racial difference. Hegemonic power relations (see Chapter 9 on Marxism) would have us believe that racial difference comes from biology, but the biology of race is a cultural fiction. As a hegemonic cultural fiction, the idea that race is biological is so deeply entrenched that most people take it for granted as unquestioned fact. But biologists say exactly the opposite, that people of "different" races usually have more in common genetically than people of the "same" race. The markers of race, such as skin color and hair texture, have a visual convenience but otherwise hold little biological meaning compared to other genetic variables. Historical and cultural conventions attribute vast significance to those markers, but nothing requires us to see them as so meaningful. Still, the superficial markers of race offer a convenient tool for colonialism and racism, which desperately seek to naturalize abusive power relations, pretending to discover differences between peoples that they actually impose.

Following this logic that sees race as a construction rather than an essence, critical race theory, in legal studies and the social sciences and in the humanities as well, pays special heed to rethinking race as a cultural category rather than a biological category. With its history of critiquing rights discourse, including the discourse of civil rights, critical race studies invites us to include but also to move beyond the politics of recognition and inclusion or the mere exposure of inequity and oppression, the traditional goals of civil rights advocates. For example, critical race scholars look skeptically on what they call **race-blind racism** (also called *color-blind* or *race-neutral racism*). A rights discourse supposes that we can decide policy most fairly by ignoring race and basing policy on other concerns, such as merit. But from the perspective of critical race theory, racial prejudice is always already embedded in the system, so that to be blind to race is to allow deeply ingrained racism to continue unchallenged. Even supposedly neutral notions such as merit are not always neutral, for they often carry within them racial preconceptions that favor certain kinds of merit over other kinds. The advocates of racial neutrality can see the same behavior from people of different races and judge its merit differently. Or they can see members of another racial group, for example, as too quiet or too vocal or keeping too much to themselves or mixing too much with others while seeing their own ways as if they represented a universal, merit-based norm rather than a cultural pattern.

Such considerations can have everything to do with how we interpret literary characters or variations in literary style. Japaneseinfluenced literary understatement in such writers as the American Hisaye Yamamoto and the Canadian Joy Kogawa, for example, while not representative of all Asian American and Asian Canadian writers (far from it), can get misread as blandness or as feminine timidity, whereas understatement in the prose of Ernest Hemingway can be taken to evoke a profoundly understated universal insight into human character and the suggestive power of literary language. That is why race-blindness can foster unwitting racism and why claims for objectivity, however well meant, can end up reinforcing white privilege. Cultural institutions, therefore, such as the legal system and the systems of literary taste, may see themselves as objective but always include bias. As Fanon put it, "For the native, objectivity is always directed against him" (Fanon 77).

In the process of reevaluating how the dominant culture presupposes its own ways as timeless and universal, critical race studies has taken up the study of whiteness, often impelled by African American scholars and other scholars of color. Just as the broad category of race takes on new dimensions once we think of it as a construction rather than an essence, so any particular race takes on new dimensions when looked at with an awareness of its constructedness. Historians, sometimes influenced by deconstruction and poststructuralism, have asked how whites became white, a question that would be impossible if whiteness were an unchanging essence. From the perspective of whiteness studies, whiteness is a position of power masked as a position of biology. For example, in a controversial and influential argument, historians such as Noel Ignatiev have claimed that in the United States, Irish immigrants were not initially understood as white people and indeed were often seen in the same light as supposedly degraded African Americans. Irish Americans then became white by joining whites in looking down on African Americans. The process of looking down on African Americans became a ladder that European immigrants climbed to reach the social and racial position of white privilege. In that way, European immigrants and their descendents exploited the visual markers of difference between African and white Americans. Inspired in part by the novelist Toni Morrison's *Playing in the Dark: Whiteness and the Literary Imagination* (1992), whiteness studies undermines the cultural habit of seeing whiteness as a natural and universal standard from which everything else is a deviation. Whiteness studies notes the many differences among white people and the pressure that whites often feel or cultivate to suppress their differences so as to construct an imaginary unity among whites that makes it possible for whites to exclude nonwhites.

At the same time, whiteness studies carries its own dangers. After all, scholars and students of literature have been studying whiteness for a long time, without calling it whiteness. Wherever race may seem absent—perhaps in novels by Jane Austen, Edith Wharton, and Henry James, in poems by Alexander Pope and Emily Dickinson, in films by Alfred Hitchcock and stories by Edgar Allan Poe—it is nevertheless always there. Scholars and students might not recognize race when it comes masked in the false neutrality of invisible whiteness, but the study of whiteness and race is one of the unspoken topics of the study of writing by white writers, just as the study of blackness is one of the frequently spoken topics of the study of writing by black writers. The danger looms, then, that whiteness studies can slide into the same old thing under an updated name. But that might not happen if whiteness gets seen as a constructed position of privilege and power that, like a colonizing culture, trades on power and trades on false notions of universality to sustain its power.

Still, the idea that whiteness is a construction may not come across as terribly threatening to white people, whose position of power is secure enough for them to continue enjoying its privileges. But the idea that racial categories are culturally constructed can come across as threatening to some people of color if, out of newness to poststructuralism, they misconstrue the deconstruction of race to mean that race in general or any particular race does not exist. But as many scholars of color, along with Euroamerican scholars, have pointed out, to say that race or any particular race is not a biological or essential category does not mean that race does not exist. Instead, it changes our understanding of how race exists. It changes race from something biological and essential to something historical. In that sense, the idea that racial categories are constructed can help us resist racist ideas, understand race itself, and understand individual races. For example, it can help us recognize the wide range of ways of being black for black cultures across Africa and across the African diaspora as well as within any individual black person. That, in turn, can help individual black people resist essentializing pressures to conform to one particular model of blackness rather than other models that they may prefer. It can help us understand how "black" in Great Britain can refer both to people with African ancestors and to people with South Asian ancestors, while "black" in the United States refers only to people with African ancestors. Similarly, the notion of race as a construction can help us understand Anzaldúa's ideas about the borderlands, and it can help us understand the international and cross-border alliances and histories that have yoked so many different people together under the umbrella concept of "Asian American."

Because race is a cultural category, it has a cultural history, and scholars can trace the cultural history of racial and ethnic groups and the ways they express that history in literature. For example,

Houston A. Baker, Henry Louis Gates, and Hortense J. Spillers have proposed specific cultural histories, traditions, and rhetorical patterns from African, African diasporic, and specifically African American culture that shape the continuing history of African American literature. Spillers plots African American cultural studies and structures of gender through an intricate web of poststructuralism and psychoanalysis, while Baker uncovers what he calls a "vernacular theory," finding patterns in African American literature that emerge from the blues and its grounding in economic strife. Working concurrently with Baker, Gates proposes a "vernacular theory" of African American literature that evokes a tradition of theorizing in black speech and oral storytelling. He considers West African trickster traditions of "double-voiced discourse"—figurative language—as African Americans have shaped and reshaped them through the oral practice of signifying, or—as Gates more playfully evokes the spoken word—Signifyin(g).

For Gates, Signifyin(g) suggests not only the ceaseless proliferation of signifiers in Derrida's expansion of Saussure's ideas, but also an African American tradition of language play through repetition with difference. Through repeating the language of both African Americans and non-African Americans—yet repeating it with a difference—African American speech often delights in figurative language, sometimes in a playfully competitive way and sometimes as an homage to community and tradition. Gates sees examples of such Signifyin(g) and repetition with a difference in everyday talk and in art that ranges from playing the dozens to jazz musicians playing each other's standards, not for "critique and difference," but for "unity and resemblance" (Gates xxvii). He also sees it in the way that African American novelists signify on their mainstream literary predecessors, on African American oral traditions, and on the Signifyin(g) of earlier African American novels, thus signifying an African American literary tradition.

For example, Gates argues that in her novel *Their Eyes Were Watching God*, Zora Neale Hurston mixes together the English of traditional novelists with the English associated with African American speech, often twining the two together in free indirect discourse, a form that, as we saw in Chapter 3, mixes the voices of an exterior narrator and an interior character. In that way, Hurston signifies on the mainstream tradition of self-consciously focalizing narration represented, for example, by Henry James. At the same time, in a double voicing that signifies on Du Bois's theory of double-consciousness, Hurston's free indirect discourse also signifies on the controversial tradition of African American writers, such as Paul Laurence Dunbar, writing in language associated with specially African American speech. Then, over a generation later, Gates argues, in *The Color Purple* Alice Walker—who did much to return attention to Hurston's forgotten writing—signifies on Hurston by having her characters *write* in a language that echoes the way Hurston's characters *speak*. The ongoing dialogue of books talking to other books and talking about talk as well as about books builds what Gates calls "the black tradition's own theory of itself" (Gates xxiii).

HOW TO INTERPRET: POSTCOLONIAL AND RACE STUDIES EXAMPLES

Let us look at some examples. Hemingway's famous stories "The Snows of Kilimanjaro" and "The Short Happy Life of Francis Macomber" take for granted a colonialist way of thinking. They purport to portray what they call "Africa," as if their little space in British-ruled Kenya could represent the vast variety of peoples and places from Casablanca to Nairobi, Addis Ababa to Accra, and Cairo to Capetown. The whites on safari in Hemingway's stories depend utterly on their black servants, but the stories reduce their servants to the background. As exotic local color, like part of the scenery, the servants have no names, though now and then they step forth from the shadows to receive a command from the great white hunters who cannot admit that they depend on Africans. The white hunters call their African servants "boy," with the usual contortions of colonizers trying to prop up their power and masculinity by feminizing and infantilizing the colonized. Conveniently for colonialist fantasy, the colonized Africans never talk back, and they never have their interiority represented or even acknowledged, beyond a vague romanticizing sense that they know the secrets of the bush, secrets that the great white hunters know too but that tenderfoot white tourists like the Macombers must have explained to them.

Hemingway published those stories in 1936, two years before the birth of Ngugi wa Thiong'o, black Kenya's first novelist. Ngugi's first novel, *Weep Not, Child* (1964), offers another perspective. It is not entirely an opposite portrait, because Ngugi especially concerns himself with internalized colonialism and neocolonialism, and thus many of Ngugi's African characters naturalize European power as much as do Hemingway's white characters. In the opening pages of *Weep Not, Child*, the young boy Njoroge, who wants desperately to go to school and perhaps eventually to study overseas, talks with his older brother, trying to understand the local white settler who has taken over their family's land. "I wonder why he left England, the home of learning, and came here. He must be foolish," Njoroge says. "I don't know," his brother replies. "You cannot understand a white man" (Ngugi 23). Not surprisingly, Ngugi takes for granted the black interiority that is unimaginable to Hemingway. But if Hemingway's white characters do not think to speculate about black interiority, Ngugi's black characters think hard about white interiority, though they do not claim to understand it. Indeed, because they are subject to white rulers, they have little choice but to think about it. They cannot afford the denial of the other that the white settlers luxuriate in and that the white settlers depend on to uphold and rationalize their colonialism. Nevertheless, Njoroge has absorbed the colonialist belief system that makes a European education seem superior to a Kenyan education. And in material ways, it is superior, because the exchange between cultures, the worlding of Kenya as shaped by colonialism, makes the colonizers' knowledge hold special value for the colonized, even apart from the way that internalized colonialism exaggerates that value. Yet even as Njoroge admires white knowledge, he also looks at it with comical but insightful skepticism. To Njoroge, only a fool would leave the England that Njoroge aspires to and trade it for the Kenya that Njoroge wants to escape. He cannot understand what Kenya has for the white man, whose ancestors lived on another land, because, as a young boy, he does not understand the economics of colonialism. Nevertheless, Nguki implies, Njoroge understands more than he realizes when he decides that the project of colonialism must be foolish.

The movie *Dirty Pretty Things* (2002) shows colonialism and neocolonialism as they continue to evolve, this time in the London metropole, now worlded by legal and illegal immigrants from across the globe, whose mere presence reshapes empire and challenges the idea of borders. Or maybe their presence does not reshape and change so much after all, for neocolonialism does not do much to transform colonialism. Okwe, a Nigerian doctor and illegal immigrant, works in London by day as a taxi driver and by night as a hotel clerk. As he stares down into a hotel toilet that overflows because someone has stuffed it with a human heart and as we stare back up at

Okwe through a camera that looks from the perspective of the heart in the toilet, *Dirty Pretty Things* gives new meaning to the expression "heart of darkness," the colonialist phrase for Africa made unforgettable by Joseph Conrad, another immigrant who wrote in Britain at the peak of colonialism. In this heart of darkness of nighttime London, illegal immigrants sell their organs to a legal immigrant who sells them to a Briton. In return, the illegals get forged documents that recast them as legal. Their organs and prostituted bodies become objects and metaphors of colonialist appropriation, the new exploited natural resources of neocolonialism. The immigrants participate, however reluctantly, in their own colonization by agreeing to sell their organs and by submitting to the sexual abuse that other immigrants—a South Asian sweatshop boss and the movie's villain, "Sneaky" the Spanish organ merchant—charge to keep from turning them in to the authorities. The movie itself self-colonizes, and tries to colonize its audience, through a tawdry resort to frozen stereotype in its only extended portrayal of a black woman, Juliette. Surprise of surprises, Juliette turns out to be the familiar whore that Western movies have such difficulty escaping when they imagine black women. In yet another nonsurprise, Juliette is—if you'll excuse the expression—a whore with a heart.

When Okwe, Juliette, and the sexually abused Turkish hotel maid Senay turn the tables on Sneaky the organ merchant by drugging him to cut out and sell his kidney, the British organ buyer gets suspicious. Used to dealing with Sneaky, not Okwe, he asks, "How come I've never seen you people before?" Okwe responds, in a set piece for the movie, "Because we are the people you do not see. We are the ones who drive your cabs. We clean your rooms. And suck your cocks." The last sentence throws in a dash of half-gratuitous sex for the trailer to help market the film. Abusive and self-colonizing though that may be, it can also draw the neocolonialist market to see a movie that chastises neocolonialism. In some ways, in the eyes of the colonizers, the immigrants of London are not all that different from the nearly invisible African "boys" of Hemingway's stories. They are the workers—here represented by taxi drivers, maids, and sex workers—whose colonized labor makes the empire possible. Yet the colonizers suppose that the colonialist world is self-supporting and that its international workforce does not exist. Or at least, when they can no longer suppose that, they try to keep supposing it, in the form of immigration restrictions and enforcement. Meanwhile, desperate to escape the corrupt neocolonialism that Okwe runs from in

Nigeria, the worlded refugees of colonized and formerly colonized lands join with the colonizers in the London metropole. Together, they break the colonizer/colonized binary, and, with whatever anguish, the colonized and formerly colonized find themselves complicit in their own continuing colonization. It may sometimes be a pretty thing, with the colonialist exoticizing of the colonial world and with the colonized people's attraction to the enticements of the West, but it is also a dirty thing.

*   *   *   *   *

Race studies has influenced literary studies by inviting readers to expand beyond the traditional range of white-written works and to read race in nonessentialist ways. By unveiling the central role of race, it has given critics ways to understand power relations across literary history. In that light, critical race theory, as a more specific dimension of race studies, contributes to the nonessentialist momentum of race studies, encouraging critics to think about racial difference as rooted in the distribution of power, much like colonialism.

Meanwhile, postcolonial studies, combined with race studies, has also changed literary studies. In English departments, we increasingly read writing from formerly colonized countries beyond Great Britain, Ireland, and the United States. We continue to read Shakespeare, Jane Austen, and Virginia Woolf, for example, but we also read Achebe, Ngugi, Soyinka, Jean Rhys, V. S. Naipaul, R. K. Narayan, Anita Desai, Buchi Emecheta, Salman Rushdie, and many other writers from formerly colonized lands.

Moreover, postcolonial studies has changed the way that we read British, Irish, and American writing. In an economy and cultural life that depend on colonial and neocolonial exploitation, colonialism is woven through the literary self-portrait of imperialist nations, sometimes explicitly, as in Conrad's *Heart of Darkness,* and sometimes surreptitiously. In the wake of postcolonial studies, even Shakespeare's *The Tempest,* for example, often emerges as a parable of the colonized and the colonizer. For contemporary criticism, *The Tempest*'s Prospero and Miranda often represent the characteristically masculine and feminine roles of European colonizers. Ariel stands in for the colonized elite, and Caliban dramatizes the fate of the colonized masses. In Austen's *Mansfield Park,* Said argues, Sir Thomas Bertram's rule at home follows principles of order that echo and, by implication, partly depend on his rule over his barely mentioned sugar plantations in Antigua (in the Caribbean). From that observation, Said unearths the suppressed reliance of Austen's refined novel and its social world on the unmentioned but sordid economics and cultural violence of slavery and colonialism. Similarly, Spivak—and many critics following her—interpret Charlotte Brontë's *Jane Eyre* (as we saw in Chapter 6) as resting on and struggling to deny its Jamaican Creole backstory. Achebe himself has famously proposed what we might call an African postcolonial re-reading of Conrad's *Heart of Darkness*. He recognizes that Conrad's novel bemoans colonial violence. Even so, Achebe argues, *Heart of Darkness* reduces African people to a foil for the horrors that Europeans fear in themselves, thus leaving Conrad and his European characters unable to see Africans as full-fledged people with their own languages, cultures, thinking, and psychological interiority. Rather than seeing Africans as people, Conrad sees them as a mere stage for the playing out of a drama about Europeans. In these ways, whether or not literary writing dwells explicitly on colonialism and racial conflict, it often depends on them, for colonialism and racial conflict are part of the economic and cultural foundation of Europe, the United States, and the many lands that they have conquered militarily, politically, or economically. From Shakespeare to the present, colonialism and racial conflict have helped to shape English-language culture and literature.

✻ 11 ✻

Reader Response

In the late 1960s and the 1970s, a good deal of excitement arose about what often came to be called *reader-response criticism* or *reader-response theory*. The idea of basing our critical perspective on what reader-response critics usually call "the reader" held a special appeal to critics and has continued to hold a special appeal to students, because most of us feel intensely aware of ourselves as readers, and so reader-response criticism can seem to speak directly to who we are and what we do. In that light, most critical theory surveys began to include a separate section on reader-response criticism.

Nevertheless, the hodgepodge of formalist, philosophical, psychological, and historicist activities loosely netted together under the label of *reader-response criticism* (and similar terms) have little to do with each other beyond their interest in "the reader," in readers in general, or in actual, historical readers. We might go so far as to say that there is no separate category of "reader-response criticism," because all criticism is reader-response criticism. As critics have increasingly recognized that all criticism is reader-response criticism, the once seemingly sharp cutting edge of reader-response criticism and theory has blunted over the years, and its influence has faded. It seems best to me, therefore, to integrate reader-response criticism into all the other kinds of criticism that we do, and I have tried to live up to that goal throughout this book. We see reader-response criticism at work in the discussion of how readers project unity onto a text in Chapter 2, on new criticism. We also see versions of reader-response criticism in the discussion of how audiences read situation comedies, detective novels, and other genres in Chapter 3, on structuralism, in deconstructionist double readings of a text in Chapter 4, on deconstruction, in Lacan's view of how we project our own desires onto the space of the other in Chapter 5, on psycho-analysis, or in how film spectators view gender in Chapter 6, on feminism. Chapter 7, on queer studies, sees homosexual panic as certain readers' response to the discourse of homophobia. Reader response continues to influence key concepts in Chapter 8, on Marxism, in the discussion of how a text can interpellate readers or—as Brecht argued—can jar readers out of their interpellations, and in Chapter 9, on historicism and cultural studies, in the discussion of how fans interpret popular culture and readers approach a Shake-speare sonnet. In Chapter 10, on postcolonialism and race studies, we can see mimicry and the construction of race as sociocultural forms of reader response. With so much address to reader-response criticism in the other chapters, then, this chapter, which focuses on reader-response criticism in itself, is the shortest chapter in the book. Still, reader-response criticism has struck a nerve and raised fundamental questions about how we read and what reading is in the first place. For that reason, it deserves separate treatment as well as integration into the rest of the book.

Reader-response critics oppose themselves to the new criticism. As we have seen in Chapter 2, the new critics believed in inter-preting a literary text as a relatively intrinsic object, minimizing the role of the history and culture that surround a text. Working from that principle, William K. Wimsatt and Monroe C. Beardsley de-cided that to interpret the meaning of a text based on our affective response to the text was a fallacy, an error in interpretive logic. The entire concept of reader-response criticism and theory opposes itself to Wimsatt and Beardsley's dismissal of affective responses. But if we reject Wimsatt and Beardsley's principle and declare that interpre-tation based on responses is not fallacious, then we can oppose our way of interpreting to their theory but not really to their methods, because even Wimsatt and Beardsley and the other new critics, in interpreting a text, are responding to it. They may believe that their interpretations depend on the intrinsic meaning of a text, but they still derive their sense of intrinsic meaning from their own responses. They may include other readers' responses as well, but even then they depend on their responses to other responses. There is no es-cape from readers' responses. It is, so to speak, responses all the way down. Every method in this book is a reader-response method, whether or not it chooses to focus on that dimension of its own method. If there is anything specific to reader-response criticism, then, it is not the use of readers' responses. It is the focus on the use of readers' responses.

The brief flame of the vogue for reader-response criticism first burned brightly in the early work of Stanley Fish, who set his procedure directly against the new criticism by calling it *affective stylistics*. He concentrated on following the zigs and zags of the reader's response as it unrolls sequentially, word by word, while reading a text. The text raises certain expectations in the reader and then frustrates or fulfills them as it proceeds along. For example, Virginia Woolf's novel *Mrs. Dalloway* begins with the following one-sentence paragraph: "Mrs. Dalloway said she would buy the flowers herself." That sentence raises a variety of expectations from readers. We expect that, as we read on, we will find more about who Mrs. Dalloway is, whom she says this to, why she might or—perhaps still more— might not have bought them herself, and why she or someone else wants flowers in the first place. Something is up, we expect, and we expect to find out what. How and when we find the answers to those questions and even whether we find them will influence our gradually building understanding and interpretation of the novel. We might even expect that, as the novel goes on, its opening words will end up carrying extra importance. Fish's reader is not just any reader, however, but an "informed reader" or even, because informed, an "ideal reader." The **ideal reader** is not the sort who says go hang Mrs. Dalloway and her flowers and has no patience for an opening sentence that does not explain itself. Instead, the ideal reader responds to challenges and mysteries with relish. Because of his dependence on an ideal reader, Fish ends up basing his suppositions about how readers respond on his own understanding of how he himself responds. Regardless, the key thing is the reader's response, so that the meaning of a text lies not in what readers find in a text, as if it existed there before and independently of a reading. Instead, the meaning lies in what readers do as they read.

Similarly, the German critic Wolfgang Iser, drawing on German phenomenological philosophy, follows the way a text sets up an **implied reader**. As we read a text, we can sort out implicit assumptions that it makes about its readers, what they know and believe or do not know and believe. But a text always remains incomplete, all the more obviously while readers find themselves in the middle of its sequence of words and implications. In that way, a text sets up "gaps," inviting readers to fill in the gaps and inviting readers then to compare how they fill in the gaps to the way that the text itself eventually fills or does not fill in the same gaps.

For both Fish and Iser, reading a text is a continuous dialogue between expectations that a text provokes in the reader and how readers respond to those expectations, forming hypotheses about the text and then testing those hypotheses against the continuing sequence of text. In a more extreme reader-response model, there is no text except in the mind of the reader, for we only know a text by how readers respond to it. But for Fish and Iser, the text guides readers' responses, so that reading enacts a continuous dialogue between the shifting directions of a text and the shifting responses of a reader.

Less influentially than Fish and Iser, the work of Norman Holland and David Bleich has called attention to the psychological process of readers. Both Holland and Bleich study actual readers, as opposed to the hypothetical informed and implied readers of Fish and Iser. Holland draws on *ego psychology,* a mostly American branch of psychoanalysis that, in literary and cultural criticism, has never achieved anything like the prominence of more deconstructive psychoanalytic approaches. From the perspective of more contemporary deconstructive psychoanalytic criticism, ego psychology suggests too confident a sense of a singular, stable subject, of a secure self or ego, which probably accounts for the limited interest that Holland's work has attracted except as a representative example of psychologically based reader-response criticism. Holland supposes that each reader forms a particular ego or "primary identity" based on early childhood and then projects the concerns of that identity onto a literary text. In his model, the text almost disappears in favor of different readers' more or less idiosyncratic responses to the text. Bleich takes Holland's model to its logical conclusion by calling forthrightly for a full-scale focus on the readers' subjectivity, calling for readers to write out their responses, grounding their view of a text in the ways that it connects to their personal experience. For Bleich, more objective interpretations of a text merely mask interpretations that grow out of our personal quirks and histories. Bleich's method may tell us a great deal about individual readers, but it does not try to tell us much about the texts they read. It might not even tell us much about readers, for if we follow its logic, then when we read about readers' responses, we project our own personal interests onto our reading of the other readers, making them yet another text that all but disappears under the veil of our own subjective concerns.

The method has a logic to it, therefore, but not a very communal logic.

Structuralists and historicists, along with the later work of Fish, have taken reader-response criticism in more communal directions. Fish proposes that our readings of literary texts depend not so much on what the texts say in some intrinsic way as on what he calls **interpretive communities**, with their own interpretive strategies and conventions. Critics like to think that they propose original interpretations, but from the perspective of Fish's model of interpretive communities, the very idea of originality is part of the anything-but-original form that interpretive communities dictate for our interpretations. When the expectations of the interpretive community require all critics to claim originality, then the process of claiming originality is itself an unoriginal act, a rote submission to preexisting conventions of interpretation. After all, to claim originality, critics and students go through the same unoriginal motions that others who claim originality have already gone through before. That is, they say how previous critics got it wrong, how, perhaps, the previous critics "failed" to account for this or that (often something they were not even trying to account for), and how their own approach will show something that previous critics missed. And then the next critic will do the same thing to them, repeating the same formula of bogus originality. Fish's model has much in common with the structuralist notion that language produces the world it describes rather than merely reflecting that world. Though we might see Fish's model as a critique of interpretive communities, he does not see it that way. He sees it as describing a routine part of the way things work. When we judge the quality of our interpretations, for Fish, we are not judging their degree of truth about the text so much as their ability to understand the protocols of our interpretive communities. Nevertheless, Fish's model gets astutely at the numbing, thumb-twiddling routine of much professional and daily life. It can help students, for example, to understand that whether or not they write insightful interpretations for their classes, they need to learn the form of writing insightful interpretations. If they learn the form, that will go at least a long way to carrying the day, whether or not their interpretations have all that much insight.

The problem with Fish's view of interpretive communities, however, is that it gives us little reason to care, little reason to favor one interpretation over another, if they both live up to the expectations of an interpretive community. But if you care about feminism, for example, or about aesthetic ingenuity, then you might give special value to a feminist interpretation or an interpretation that has an eye for aesthetic playfulness. While Fish could respond that such caring only defines your interpretive community, the broader interpretive community of literary and cultural criticism does not always pay heed to questions of aesthetics and certainly has not usually favored feminism. Indeed, interpretive communities have often sought to exile feminism. Fish acknowledges differences within interpretive communities (arguing over differences is itself one of the principles of the broader interpretive community), but to most other critics' way of thinking, interpretive communities themselves are less stable entities than Fish's model allows for, and the things we care about most often come at least partly from motives that the uninspiring model of interpretive communities cannot capture.

In a structuralist mode that can bear comparison to Fish's sense of interpretive communities, Jonathan Culler, as we have seen in Chapter 3, argues that readers bring a specific competence to the process of reading specific genres of literature. Readers who are not competent in the rules of reading a novel, for example, could mistake a novel for a history or a biography, just as a reader not competent in colloquial speech will misunderstand such expressions as "Hold your horses" and "Don't go off your rocker." For Culler, as a structuralist, then, the goal of structuralist interpretation, or structuralist poetics, is not to interpret an individual literary text but instead to describe the competence that readers depend on and expect for any particular genre, from sonnets to film noir, from stage comedies to high school movies or detective novels. More skeptical poststructuralists respond by asking "Whose competence is the right competence? And what if two readers disagree over the competence required to read a particular genre?" As Culler himself recognizes more in his later, deconstructive writing, where he explores the question of what it would mean to read specifically as a woman, different readers and different groups of readers—we might even say different interpretive communities—bring different perspectives.

Judith Fetterley calls for a specifically feminist approach to reader-response criticism. A key though often-underrecognized contributor to the early years of feminist criticism, Fetterley proposes, in *The Resisting Reader: A Feminist Approach to American Fiction* (1978), that critics traditionally did not see how the most frequently studied American writing takes patriarchal assumptions for granted, as if making everything hinge on how a story turns out for its male characters, whatever the cost to its female characters, were the natural and universal way to read. Fetterley seeks a reader-response criticism that does not merely trace a neutral process of reading the formalist strategies of a literary text. For in a patriarchal setting, strategies that present themselves as neutral have a way of ending up as patriarchal. Such strategies ask even women readers to read as if they were patriarchal men. Instead, Fetterley asks critics to challenge patriarchal ideology by seeing how it shapes characters and readers. She invites critics to see how literary texts and literary criticism can choose between joining patriarchal assumptions and exposing and criticizing them. To Fetterley, classic American fiction and much of the criticism of that fiction, from Washington Irving's "Rip Van Winkle," Nathaniel Hawthorne's "The Birthmark," and Ernest Hemingway's *A Farewell to Arms* to Norman Mailer's *An American Dream,* sees women and women characters as problems, unless they die. If we allow such guiding patterns and beliefs to fade into the unnoticed wallpaper in the literary background, then they hurt readers, especially women readers. Her approach has much in common with Althusser's description of the way that ideology recruits subjects to go along with the system that hurts them (as we saw in Chapter 8, on Marxism), except that Fetterley insists that through feminist reading we can recognize patriarchal ideology and that by recognizing it we can begin to change it.

In more explicitly historicist terms than Fish or Iser, and in terms that can be combined with Fetterley's call to change our way of reading, the phenomenological critic Hans Robert Jauss, the leading figure in a German version of reader-response theory known as *reception aesthetics* or *reception theory,* has called for interpreting the history of the ways people read a literary work by studying the **horizon of expectations** that surrounds that work. Jauss asks what was possible for writers to expect when and where a work was written, and he compares that range of possible expectations to the range of possible expectations for a work's readers, both when the work was written and as those expectations change over time. Carson McCullers' novel *The Heart Is a Lonely Hunter,* for example, trades on the expectations that readers in 1940 brought to a potentially popular new novel. Though from the perspective of today's horizon of expectations, McCullers' novel seems fascinated with unfulfilled, even unrecognized queer sexualities, there is little address to queer concerns in recorded responses from the novel's first readers or even from the next generation of readers. In the 1960s, high school English teachers frequently assigned *The Heart Is a Lonely Hunter,* even though those same teachers would not think of bringing, or at least would not dare to bring, queer questions explicitly into the high school classroom, if for no other reason than fear for their jobs in a queer-hostile world. Given the horizon of expectations in the 1940s, McCullers could closet the novel's queerness, making it at once highly visible and highly invisible, according to different readers' varying familiarity with horizons of expectations that included or excluded queerness. Today, the horizon of queer expectations has enlarged, and though the novel has no unequivocal gay or lesbian acts or characters, its queerness seems poignantly visible.

Similarly, when I first taught Hemingway's *The Sun Also Rises* and referred to the scene where Brett arrives at a bar with a group of gay friends, students insisted that they remembered no such scene. Or if any students did notice it, they felt that they needed to keep silent. When I then pointed the scene out, the vocal students were shocked that Hemingway could write with what they saw as such subtlety, that he could signal gayness with clarity and yet code it in ways that kept them from noticing it, that trapped them in their naturalization of heterosexuality. Today, the horizon of expectations has changed. The words on the page may be the same, but their meaning has shifted, for the same passage needs no explanation. Students pick up on it so easily that the same words that my earlier students found subtle now look heavy-handed.

Inspired partly by German reception theory, Anglo-American critics have developed what they call **reception history**. Reception history studies the history of how readers have responded to a given film or literary work, writer, or movement in literature or film. It is not easy to uncover the reception history of older works in their own time. Few of Chaucer's or Shakespeare's contemporaries wrote down their responses; even if they did write them down, in most cases what they wrote did not survive. But we can more easily study the history of responses to Chaucer or Shakespeare in later times as well as study the responses to later works. With the growth of the printing press, the emergence of newspapers, magazines, and book reviews, the increasing proliferation and survival of books that readers have scribbled on, and of letters, diaries, and the Internet, critics can uncover a vast history of responses to literature and film by actual readers and audiences, as opposed to the hypothetical and abstract readers of most reader-response theory. Critics can even follow how responses to a work have changed as each new wave of critical theory discussed in this book emerges and joins the conversation.

Sometimes scholars compare the reception of different works or writers. Michael Bérubé has compared the reception of the white novelist Thomas Pynchon, who tried to hide from the public yet instantly achieved enormous fame, to the reception of the African American poet Melvin Tolson, who did every thing he could think of to build his reputation and yet was forgotten as remarkably as Pynchon was lionized. Jacqueline Bobo has studied African American women's responses to films about black women, such as *The Color Purple* and *Daughters of the Dust*. Besides the many reception histories of individual writers or books, some scholars take a more cultural studies or sociohistorical approach. Janice Radway, for example, joined a group of women romance readers and wrote about their patterns of reading as an anthropologist might write an ethnography based on participant observation. Her work has contributed to the growth of audience studies in cultural studies, as in the cultural studies interpretations of popular culture and its fans discussed in Chapter 9. Elizabeth McHenry has researched the history of African American readers by studying African American literary societies in the nineteenth and early twentieth centuries. Work such as Bobo's and McHenry's can help deter critics from the common practice of assuming, without realizing it, that readers are white, in a world where cultural ideologies of race encourage people to naturalize whiteness just as they naturalize heterosexuality. Similarly, works such as Fetterley's, Radway's, and Bobo's speak critically to the unconscious but common assumption that readers are men or are privileged students and academics. As we study the history of readers and reading, therefore, we do well to keep in mind the multiplicity of readers and the ways that each writer's audience differs from the audience of another writer.

Let me return, then, to the idea that texts do not make meaning by themselves. Readers make meaning. Scholars disagree about whether readers make meaning in collaboration with texts, such that texts shape and limit how readers can interpret them, or whether, as the tree might not fall in the forest if no one hears or sees it, readers bear sole responsibility for their interpretations. But either way, reading is not merely a passive process. Just as we discussed critical spectators in our consideration of feminist film theory, so readers are spectators and, like all audiences, read with varying degrees of passivity and criticism. One goal of this book is to encourage our dialogue about how, as readers, we can respond less passively and more critically.

✻ Afterword ✻

In the years when critical theory moved to the center of literary studies and provoked a good deal of resistance from skeptics, the scholars, teachers, and journalists who resisted critical theory sometimes saw it as dangerous. They argued that critical theory made literature and literary study too abstract. And the abstraction of critical theory, they believed, made it less relevant to students and other readers and more distant from students' and readers' everyday lives. By now you can see, I hope, that critical theory can work in exactly the opposite way. It can make the study of literature more concrete, because critical theory is about the connections between literature and our everyday lives. Critical theory makes literary study more relevant to our lives, not less relevant.

As our lives change and the generations shift, so do the strategies of interpretation that we bring to interpreting literature and culture. While the pace of change in literary and cultural criticism may have slowed down over the last fifteen or twenty years, after the early boom years that marked the first surge of critical and literary theory to the center of literary studies, change will continue. Readers can keep up with the changes simply by continuing to read and perhaps by talking over their interests with other readers. A course can help, but keeping up does not require a course. I never had the chance to take a critical theory course, and most of what I have written about in this book I learned after I finished taking courses. Much of it did not even exist yet while I was taking courses. I had to teach myself. You can teach yourself too.

It might help us understand change if we try to anticipate the future based on what we know about the present. We might guess, for example, that such recently growing interests as disability studies and ecocriticism might continue to grow or might reach a plateau or that the increasing interest in culture will continue to split literary studies into those who care little about aesthetics and art and those who (like myself) persist in merging literary studies with cultural studies, continuing to think about form and aesthetics as they think about culture. But we cannot count on our predictions for the future. We can, however, choose to help make that future by engaging with it, by continuing to read and question.

To encourage your continuing reading and questioning, you might go back and review a part of this book that caught your interest and then read some of the critical writings that it discusses. If we ever suppose that we have already learned what critical theory has to teach us, then we will stop learning. But if we keep reading and questioning, then we will adapt to the future and help shape that future.

⇥ Works Cited and Further Reading ⇤

WORKS CITED

Althusser, Louis. "Ideology and Ideological State Apparatuses (Notes towards an Investigation)." *Lenin and Philosophy and Other Essays*. Trans. Ben Brewster. New York: Monthly Review Press, 1971.

Aristotle. *Poetics*. Trans. S. H. Butcher. New York: Hill and Wang, 1961.

Austen, Jane. *Pride and Prejudice*. 1813. New York: Norton, 2000.

Barthes, Roland. "The Death of the Author." *Image-Music-Text*. Selected and trans. Stephen Heath. New York: Hill and Wang, 1977. 142–48.

Bhabha, Homi K. *The Location of Culture*. London: Routledge, 1994.

Booth, Wayne. *The Rhetoric of Fiction*. Chicago: University of Chicago Press, 1961.

Brooks, Cleanth. *The Well Wrought Urn: Studies in the Structure of Poetry*. New York: Reynal & Hitchcock, 1947.

Chopin, Kate. *The Complete Works of Kate Chopin*. Ed. Per Seyersted. Baton Rouge: Louisiana State University Press, 1969.

Cixous, Hélène. "The Laugh of the Medusa." *New French Feminisms: An Anthology*. Ed. Elaine Marks and Isabelle de Courtivron. Amherst: University of Massachusetts Press, 1980. 245–64.

Coleridge, Samuel Taylor. *Biographia Literaria or Biographical Sketches of My Literary Life and Opinions*. Ed. James Engell and W. Jackson Bate. 2 vols. Princeton, NJ: Princeton University Press, 1983.

Derrida, Jacques. "Différance." *Margins of Philosophy*. Trans. Alan Bass. Chicago: University of Chicago Press, 1982.

Dickinson, Emily. *The Poems of Emily Dickinson: Reading Edition*. Ed. R. W. Franklin. Cambridge, MA: Harvard University Press, 1999.

Donne, John. *The Complete English Poems*. Ed. C. J. Patrides and Robin Hamilton. 2nd ed. London: Dent, 1994.

Doyle, Arthur Conan. "The Adventure of Charles Augustus Milverton." 1904. *The Return of Sherlock Holmes*. Ed. Richard Lancelyn Green. Oxford: Oxford University Press, 1993.

Du Bois, W. E. Burghardt. *The Souls of Black Folk*. 1903. New York: Fawcett, 1961.

Duggan, Lisa. "Queering the State." *Social Text* 39 (1994): 1–14.

Eagleton, Terry. *Literary Theory.* Minneapolis: University of Minnesota Press, 1983.

Fanon, Frantz. *The Wretched of the Earth.* Preface by Jean-Paul Sartre. Trans. Constance Farrington. New York: Grove Press, 1963.

Faulkner, William. *As I Lay Dying.* 1930. Rpt. New York: Vintage International, 1990.

———. *Light in August.* 1932. Rpt. New York: Vintage International, 1990.

Freud, Sigmund. *The Interpretation of Dreams (First Part).* Vol. 4. *The Standard Edition of the Complete Psychological Works of Sigmund Freud.* Ed. and trans. James Strachey. London: Hogarth Press, 1955.

Gates, Henry Louis, Jr. *The Signifying Monkey: A Theory of African-American Literary Criticism.* New York: Oxford University Press, 1988.

Glissant, Edouard. *Caribbean Discourse: Selected Essays.* Trans. J. Michael Dash. Charlottesville: University Press of Virginia, 1989.

Hall, Stuart. "Cultural Identity and Cinematic Representation." *Framework* 36 (1989): 68–81.

Jahn, Janheinz. *Neo-African Literature: A History of Black Writing.* 1966. Trans. Oliver Coburn and Ursula Lehrburger. New York: Grove Press, 1968.

Jameson, Fredric. *The Political Unconscious: Narrative as a Socially Symbolic Act.* Ithaca, NY: Cornell University Press, 1981.

Lacan, Jacques. *Ecrits: A Selection.* Trans. Alan Sheridan. New York: Norton, 1977.

———. *The Four Fundamental Concepts of Psycho-Analysis.* 1973. Ed. Jacques-Alain Miller. Trans. Alan Sheridan. London: Hogarth Press, 1977.

Laqueur, Thomas. *Making Sex: Body and Gender from the Greeks to Freud.* Cambridge, MA: Harvard University Press, 1990.

Mulvey, Laura. "Visual Pleasure and Narrative Cinema." *Visual and Other Pleasures.* Bloomington: Indiana University Press, 1989. 14–26.

Ngugi, James. [Ngugi wa Thiong'o.] *Weep Not, Child.* 1964. Rpt. New York: Collier Books, 1969.

Plato. *The Dialogues of Plato.* Trans. B. Jowett. 4th ed. 4 vols. Oxford: Oxford University Press, 1953.

Pound, Ezra. *Selected Poems.* New York: New Directions, 1949.

Rich, Adrienne. "Compulsory Heterosexuality and Lesbian Existence." *Signs* 5, 4 (Summer 1980): 631–60.

Robinson, Edwin Arlington. *Selected Poems of Edwin Arlington Robinson.* Ed. Morton Dauwen Zabel. New York: Collier, 1965.

Saussure, Ferdinand de. *Course in General Linguistics.* Ed. Charles Bally and Albert Reidlinger. Trans. Wade Baskin. New York: Philosophical Library, 1959.

Shakespeare, William. *The Riverside Shakespeare.* Ed. G. Blakemore Evans et al. 2nd ed. Boston: Houghton, 1997.

Soyinka, Wole. *Myth, Literature and the African World.* Cambridge: Cambridge University Press, 1976.

Spivak, Gayatri Chakravorty. "Can the Subaltern Speak? Speculations on Widow-Sacrifice." *Wedge* 7/8 (Winter/Spring 1985): 120–30. Longer version in *Marxism and the Interpretation of Culture.* Ed. Laurence Grossberg and Cary Nelson. Urbana: University of Illinois Press, 1985. 271–313.

———. *A Critique of Postcolonial Reason: Toward a History of the Vanishing Present.* Cambridge, MA: Harvard University Press, 1999.

———. *Outside in the Teaching Machine.* New York: Routledge, 1993.

———. "Three Women's Texts and a Critique of Imperialism." *Critical Inquiry* 12 (Autumn 1985): 243–61.

Stevens, Wallace. *The Collected Poems of Wallace Stevens.* New York: Knopf, 1982.

Whitman, Walt. *Complete Poetry and Collected Prose.* Ed. Justin Kaplan. New York: Library of America, 1982.

Wordsworth, William. *Poetical Works.* Ed. Thomas Hutchinson and Ernest de Selincourt. Oxford: Oxford University Press, 1969.

FURTHER READING

Though the items listed here are divided according to this book's chapter titles, that division produces distortions, because many items can fit within more than one chapter. Interested readers will therefore want to look beyond the listings for any one chapter. Readers may also wish to consult anthologies of theoretical writing, such as *The Norton Anthology of Theory and Criticism,* ed. Vincent B. Leitch et al. (New York: Norton, 2001), *Modern Literary Theory,* ed. Philip Rice and Patricia Waugh, 4th ed. (New York: Oxford University Press, 2001), and *Literary Theory: An Anthology,* ed. Julie Rivkin and Michael Ryan, 2nd. ed. (Oxford: Blackwell, 2004).

New Criticism

Brooks, Cleanth. "The Language of Paradox." In *The Well Wrought Urn.* New York: Reynal & Hitchcock, 1947.

———. *Modern Poetry and the Tradition.* Chapel Hill: University of North Carolina Press, 1939.

———. *The Well Wrought Urn: Studies in the Structure of Poetry.* New York: Reynal & Hitchcock, 1947.

Brooks, Cleanth, and Robert B. Heilman. *Understanding Drama.* New York: H. Holt, 1945.

Brooks, Cleanth, and Robert Penn Warren. *Understanding Fiction.* New York: F. S. Crofts, 1943.

———. *Understanding Poetry: An Anthology for College Students.* New York: H. Holt, 1938.

Empson, William. *Seven Types of Ambiguity.* London: Chatto and Windus, 1930.

Ransom, John Crowe. *The New Criticism.* Norfolk, CT: New Directions, 1941.

———. *The World's Body.* New York: Charles Scribner's Sons, 1938.

Richards, I. A. *Practical Criticism: A Study of Literary Judgment*. London: K. Paul, Trench, Trubner, 1929.

――――. *Principles of Literary Criticism*. London: K. Paul, Trench, Trubner, 1925.

Wellek, René, and Austin Warren. *Theory of Literature*. New York: Harcourt, Brace, 1949.

Wimsatt, William K., with Monroe C. Beardsley. *The Verbal Icon: Studies in the Meaning of Poetry*. Lexington: University of Kentucky Press, 1954.

Structuralism

Barthes, Roland. "The Death of the Author." In *Image-Music-Text*. Selected and trans. Stephen Heath. New York: Hill and Wang, 1977.

――――. *Elements of Semiology*. Trans. Annette Lavers and Colin Smith. London: Cape, 1967.

――――. *Image-Music-Text*. Selected and trans. Stephen Heath. New York: Hill and Wang, 1977.

――――. *Mythologies*. 1957. Selected and trans. Annette Lavers. New York: Hill and Wang, 1972.

――――. *S/Z*. 1970. Trans. Richard Miller. New York: Hill and Wang, 1974.

Benveniste, Émile. *Problems in General Linguistics*. 1966. Trans. Mary Elizabeth Meek. Coral Gables, FL: University of Miami Press, 1971.

Chatman, Seymour. *Story and Discourse: Narrative Structure in Fiction and Film*. Ithaca, NY: Cornell University Press, 1978.

Culler, Jonathan. *Structuralist Poetics: Structuralism, Linguistics, and the Study of Literature*. Ithaca, NY: Cornell University Press, 1975. An excellent overview.

Eco, Umberto. *A Theory of Semiotics*. Bloomington: Indiana University Press, 1976.

Erlich, Victor. *Russian Formalism: History, Doctrine*. 4th ed. The Hague: Mouton, 1980.

Genette, Gérard. *Figures of Literary Discourse*. 1966–72. Trans. Alan Sheridan. New York: Columbia University Press, 1982.

――――. *Narrative Discourse: An Essay in Method*. 1972. Trans. Jane E. Lewin. Ithaca, NY: Cornell University Press, 1980.

――――. *Narrative Discourse Revisited*. 1983. Trans. Jane E. Lewin. Ithaca, NY: Cornell University Press, 1988.

Greimas, A. J. *On Meaning: Selected Writings in Semiotic Theory*. 1970–83. Trans. Paul J. Perron and Frank Collins. Minneapolis: University of Minnesota Press, 1987.

――――. *Structural Semantics: An Attempt at a Method*. 1966. Trans. Daniele McDowell, Ronald Schleifer, and Alan Velie. Lincoln: University of Nebraska Press, 1983.

Hawkes, Terence. *Structuralism and Semiotics*. Berkeley: University of California Press, 1977. An excellent introduction.

Jakobson, Roman. "Closing Statement: Linguistics and Poetics." *Style in Language*. Ed. Thomas A. Sebeok. Cambridge, MA: MIT Press, 1960. 350–77.

Jameson, Fredric. *The Prison-House of Language: A Critical Account of Structuralism and Russian Formalism*. Princeton, NJ: Princeton University Press, 1972.

Lemon, Lee T., and Marion J. Reis, trans. *Russian Formalist Criticism: Four Essays*. Lincoln: University of Nebraska Press, 1965.

Lévi-Strauss, Claude. *Structural Anthropology*. 1958. Trans. Claire Jacobson and Brooke Grundfest Schoepf. New York: Basic Books, 1963.

———. *Tristes Tropiques*. 1955. Trans. John and Doreen Weightman. New York: Atheneum Press, 1974.

McHale, Brian. "Free Indirect Discourse: A Survey of Recent Accounts." *PTL: A Journal for Descriptive Poetics and the Theory of Literature* 3 (1978): 249–87.

Prince, Gerald. *A Dictionary of Narratology*. Rev. ed. Lincoln: University of Nebraska Press, 2003.

Propp, V. *Morphology of the Folktale*. 1928. Trans. Laurence Scott. 2nd ed. Austin: University of Texas Press, 1968.

Rimmon-Kenan, Shlomith. *Narrative Fiction: Contemporary Poetics*. 2nd. ed. London: Routledge, 2002.

Saussure, Ferdinand de. *Course in General Linguistics*. 1916. Ed. Charles Bally and Albert Reidlinger. Trans. Wade Baskin. New York: Philosophical Library, 1959.

Todorov, Tzvetan. *The Poetics of Prose*. Trans. Richard Howard. Ithaca, NY: Cornell University Press, 1977.

Deconstruction

Barthes, Roland. *The Pleasure of the Text*. 1973. Trans. Richard Miller. New York: Hill and Wang, 1975.

Culler, Jonathan. *On Deconstruction: Theory and Criticism After Structuralism*. Ithaca, NY: Cornell University Press, 1982.

De Man, Paul. *Allegories of Reading: Figural Language in Rousseau, Nietzsche, Rilke, and Proust*. New Haven, CT: Yale University Press, 1979.

———. *Blindness and Insight: Essays in the Rhetoric of Contemporary Criticism*. New York: Oxford University Press, 1971.

Derrida, Jacques. *A Derrida Reader: Between the Blinds*. Ed. Peggy Kamuf. New York: Columbia University Press, 1991.

———. *Of Grammatology*. 1967. Trans. Gayatri Chakravorty Spivak. 2nd ed. Baltimore: Johns Hopkins University Press, 1998.

———. *Writing and Difference*. 1967. Trans. Alan Bass. Chicago: University of Chicago Press, 1978.

Hartman, Geoffrey H. *Criticism in the Wilderness: The Study of Literature Today*. New Haven, CT: Yale University Press, 1980.

―――. *Saving the Text: Literature, Derrida, Philosophy*. Baltimore: Johns Hopkins University Press, 1981.

Johnson, Barbara. *The Critical Difference: Essays in the Contemporary Rhetoric of Reading*. Baltimore: Johns Hopkins University Press, 1980.

―――. *A World of Difference*. Baltimore: Johns Hopkins University Press, 1988.

Leitch, Vincent B. *Deconstructive Criticism: An Advanced Introduction*. New York: Columbia University Press, 1983.

Miller, J. Hillis. *Ariadne's Thread: Story Lines*. New Haven, CT: Yale University Press, 1992.

―――. *Fiction and Repetition: Seven English Novels*. Cambridge, MA: Harvard University Press, 1982.

―――. *The Linguistic Moment: From Wordsworth to Stevens*. Princeton, NJ: Princeton University Press, 1985.

―――. *Theory Now and Then*. Durham, NC: Duke University Press, 1991.

Norris, Christopher. *Deconstruction: Theory and Practice*. 3rd ed. London: Routledge, 2002. An excellent introduction.

Ryan, Michael. *Marxism and Deconstruction: A Critical Articulation*. Baltimore: Johns Hopkins University Press, 1982.

Psychoanalysis

Bowie, Malcolm. *Lacan*. Cambridge, MA: Harvard University Press, 1991.

Brenner, Charles. *An Elementary Textbook of Psychoanalysis*. Rev. ed. New York: International Universities Press, 1973. A short summary of classical psychoanalysis.

Chodorow, Nancy. *The Reproduction of Mothering: Psychoanalysis and the Sociology of Gender*. Berkeley: University of California Press, 1978.

Fenichel, Otto. *The Psychoanalytic Theory of Neurosis*. New York: Norton, 1945. A comprehensive reference for classical psychoanalytic ideas.

Freud, Sigmund. *The Freud Reader*. Ed. Peter Gay. New York: Norton, 1989.

Gallop, Jane. *Reading Lacan*. Ithaca, NY: Cornell University Press, 1985.

Grosz, Elizabeth. *Jacques Lacan: A Feminist Introduction*. London: Routledge, 1990.

Horney, Karen. *Feminine Psychology*. New York: Norton, 1967.

Jones, Ernest. *Hamlet and Oedipus*. New York: Norton, 1949.

Malcolm, Janet. *Psychoanalysis: The Impossible Profession*. London: Gollancz, 1981. An excellent introduction to clinical psychoanalysis.

McCannell, Juliet Flower. *Figuring Lacan: Criticism and the Cultural Unconscious*. Lincoln: University of Nebraska Press, 1986.

Mellard, James M. *Using Lacan, Reading Fiction*. Urbana: University of Illinois Press, 1991.

Mitchell, Juliet. *Psychoanalysis and Feminism: A Radical Reassessment of Freudian Psychoanalysis*. 2nd ed. New York: Basic Books, 2000.

Lacan, Jacques. *Ecrits: A Selection*. Trans. Alan Sheridan. New York: Norton, 1977.

———. *Ecrits: The First Complete Edition in English*. Trans. Bruce Fink. New York: Norton, 2007.

Muller, John P., and William J. Richardson, eds. *The Purloined Poe: Lacan, Derrida, and Psychoanalytic Reading*. Baltimore: Johns Hopkins University Press, 1988.

Ragland-Sullivan, Ellie. *Jacques Lacan and the Philosophy of Psychoanalysis*. Urbana: University of Illinois Press, 1986.

Rose, Jacqueline. *Sexuality in the Field of Vision*. London: Verso, 1986.

Wollheim, Richard. *Sigmund Freud*. New York, Viking, 1971.

Wright, Elizabeth. *Psychoanalytic Criticism: A Reappraisal*. 2nd ed. London: Routledge, 1998. A comprehensive survey.

Zizek, Slavoj. *Looking Awry: An Introduction to Jacques Lacan through Popular Culture*. Cambridge, MA: MIT Press, 1991.

———. *The Zizek Reader*. Ed. Elizabeth Wright and Edmond Wright. Oxford: Blackwell, 1999.

Feminism

Baym, Nina. *Feminism and American Literary History: Essays*. New Brunswick, NJ: Rutgers University Press, 1992.

Beauvoir, Simone de. *The Second Sex*. 1949. Trans H. M. Parshley. New York: Knopf, 1952.

Carby, Hazel V. *Reconstructing Womanhood: The Emergence of the Afro-American Woman Novelist*. Oxford: Oxford University Press, 1987.

Célestin, Roger, Eliane DalMolin, and Isabelle de Courtivron, eds. *Beyond French Feminisms: Debates on Women, Politics, and Culture in France, 1981–2001*. New York: Palgrave Macmillan, 2003.

Cixous, Hélène. *The Hélène Cixous Reader*. Ed. Susan Sellers. New York: Routledge, 1994.

Collins, Patricia Hill. *Black Feminist Thought: Knowledge, Consciousness, and the Politics of Empowerment*. New York: Routledge, 1990.

de Lauretis, Teresa. *Technologies of Gender: Essays on Theory, Film, and Fiction*. Bloomington: Indiana University Press, 1987.

Ellmann, Mary. *Thinking about Women*. New York: Harcourt, Brace & World, 1968.

Felski, Rita. *Literature after Feminism*. Chicago: University of Chicago Press, 2003.

Friedan, Betty. *The Feminine Mystique*. New York: Norton, 1963.

Fuss, Diana. *Essentially Speaking: Feminism, Nature, and Difference*. New York: Routledge, 1989.

Gilbert, Sandra M., and Susan Gubar. *The Madwoman in the Attic: The Woman Writer and the Nineteenth-Century Literary Imagination*. New Haven, CT: Yale University Press, 1979.

Haraway, Donna Jeanne. *Simians, Cyborgs, and Nature: The Reinvention of Nature*. New York: Routledge, 1991.

Hirsch, Marianne, and Evelyn Fox Keller, eds. *Conflicts in Feminism*. New York: Routledge, 1990.

hooks, bell. *Feminist Theory from Margin to Center*. Boston: South End Press, 1984.

Irigaray, Luce. *The Irigaray Reader*. Ed. Margaret Whitford. Cambridge, MA: Basil Blackwell, 1991.

———. *This Sex Which Is Not One*. 1977. Trans. Catherine Porter with Carolyn Burke. Ithaca, NY: Cornell University Press, 1985.

Kaplan, E. Ann, ed. *Feminism and Film*. Oxford: Oxford University Press, 2000.

Kristeva, Julia. *The Kristeva Reader*. Ed. Toril Moi. Oxford: Basil Blackwell, 1986.

Marks, Elaine, and Isabelle de Courtivron, eds. *New French Feminisms: An Anthology*. Amherst: University of Massachusetts Press, 1980.

Millett, Kate. *Sexual Politics*. Garden City, NY: Doubleday, 1970.

Mohanty, Chandra Talpade. *Feminism without Borders: Decolonizing Theory, Practicing Solidarity*. Durham, NC: Duke University Press, 2003.

———, Ann Russo, and Lourdes Torres, eds. *Third World Women and the Politics of Feminism*. Bloomington: Indiana University Press, 1991.

Moi, Toril. *Sexual/Textual Politics: Feminist Literary Theory*. 2nd ed. London: Routledge, 2002.

Mulvey, Laura. *Visual and Other Pleasures*. Bloomington: Indiana University Press, 1989.

Newton, Judith, and Deborah Rosenfelt, eds. *Feminist Criticism and Social Change: Sex, Class, and Race in Literature and Culture*. New York: Methuen, 1985.

Oliver, Kelly, and Lisa Walsh, eds. *Contemporary French Feminism*. Oxford: Oxford University Press, 2004.

Russ, Joanna. *How to Suppress Women's Writing*. Austin: University of Texas Press, 1983.

Showalter, Elaine. *A Literature of Their Own: British Women Novelists from Brontë to Lessing*. 2nd ed. Princeton, NJ: Princeton University Press, 1999.

Silverman, Kaja. *Male Subjectivity at the Margins*. New York: Routledge, 1992.

Thornham, Sue, ed. *Feminist Film Theory: A Reader*. New York: New York University Press, 1999.

Walker, Alice. *In Search of Our Mothers' Gardens: Womanist Prose*. San Diego: Harcourt Brace Jovanovich, 1983.

Warhol, Robyn R., and Diane Price Herndl, eds. *Feminisms: An Anthology of Literary Theory and Criticism*. 2nd ed. New Brunswick, NJ: Rutgers University Press, 1997.

Wittig, Monique. *The Straight Mind and Other Essays*. Boston: Beacon, 1992.

Woolf, Virginia. *A Room of One's Own*. London: Hogarth Press, 1929. A classic.

Queer Studies

Abelove, Henry, Michèle Aina Barale, and David M. Halperin, eds. *The Lesbian and Gay Studies Reader*. New York: Routledge, 1993.

Butler, Judith. *Bodies That Matter: On the Discursive Limits of "Sex."* New York: Routledge, 1993.

Castle, Terry. *Gender Trouble: Feminism and the Subversion of Identity*. New York: Routledge, 1990.

———. *The Apparitional Lesbian: Female Homosexuality and Modern Culture*. New York: Columbia University Press, 1987.

Dollimore, Jonathan. *Sex, Literature, and Censorship*. Cambridge, Eng: Polity Press, 2001.

———. *Sexual Dissidence: Augustine to Wilde, Freud to Foucault*. Oxford: Oxford University Press, 1991.

Duggan, Lisa, and Nan D. Hunter. *Sex Wars: Sexual Dissent and Political Culture*. 2nd ed. New York: Routledge, 2006.

Edelman, Lee. *Homographesis: Essays in Gay Literary and Cultural Theory*. New York: Routledge, 1994.

Eng, David, and Alice Y. Hom, eds. *Q & A: Queer in Asian America*. Philadelphia: Temple University Press, 1998.

Faderman, Lillian. *Surpassing the Love of Men: Romantic Friendship and Love between Women from the Renaissance to the Present*. New York: William Morrow, 1981.

Foucault, Michel. *The History of Sexuality, Volume One: The Will to Knowledge*. 1976. Trans. Robert Hurley. New York: Pantheon Books, 1978.

Halberstam, Judith. *Female Masculinity*. Durham, NC: Duke University Press, 1998.

———. *In a Queer Time and Place: Transgender Bodies, Subcultural Lives*. New York: New York University Press, 2005.

Jagose, Annamarie. *Queer Theory: An Introduction*. New York: New York University Press, 1996.

Johnson, E. Patrick, and Mae G. Henderson, eds. *Black Queer Studies: A Critical Anthology*. Durham, NC: Duke University Press, 2005.

Martin, Robert K. *The Homosexual Tradition in American Poetry*. 2nd ed. Iowa City: University of Iowa Press, 1998.

Munt, Sally, ed. *New Lesbian Criticism: Literary and Cultural Readings*. New York: Columbia University Press, 1992.

Rich, Adrienne. *Blood, Bread, and Poetry: Selected Prose, 1979–1985*. New York: Norton, 1986.

———. *On Lies, Secrets, and Silence: Selected Prose, 1956–1978*. New York: Norton, 1979.

Rubin, Gayle. "The Traffic in Women: Notes on the 'Political Economy' of Sex." *Toward an Anthropology of Women*. Ed. Rayna R. Reiter. New York: Monthly Review Press, 1975. 157–210.

Sedgwick, Eve Kosofsky. *Between Men: English Literature and Male Homosocial Desire*. New York: Columbia University Press, 1985.

———. *Epistemology of the Closet*. Berkeley: University of California Press, 1990.

———. *Tendencies*. Durham, NC: Duke University Press, 1993.

Sinfield, Alan. *Cultural Politics—Queer Reading*. 2nd ed. London: Routledge, 2005.

———. *Gay and After*. London: Serpent's Tail, 1998.

———. *On Sexuality and Power*. New York: Columbia University Press, 2005.

———. *The Wilde Century: Effeminacy, Oscar Wilde, and the Queer Moment*. London: Cassell, 1994.

Smith-Rosenberg, Carroll. "The Female World of Love and Ritual: Relations between Women in Nineteenth-Century America." *Disorderly Conduct: Visions of Gender in Victorian America*. New York: Knopf, 1985. 53–76.

Stryker, Susan, ed. *The Transgender Studies Reader*. New York: Routledge, 2006.

Warner, Michael, ed. *Fear of a Queer Planet: Queer Politics and Social Theory*. Minneapolis: University of Minnesota Press, 1993.

Marxism

Adorno, Theodor W. *Aesthetic Theory*. 1970. Trans. Robert Hullot-Kentor. Ed. Gretel Adorno and Rolf Tiedemann. London: Athlone Press, 1997.

———. *Negative Dialectics*. 1966. Trans. E. B. Ashton. New York: Seabury Press, 1973.

Althusser, "Ideology and Ideological State Apparatuses." 1970. *Lenin and Philosophy and Other Essays*. Trans. Ben Brewster. New York: Monthly Review Press, 1971.

Arato, Andrew, and Eike Gebhardt. *The Essential Frankfurt School Reader*. New York: Urizen Books, 1978.

Belsey, Catherine. *Critical Practice*. 2nd ed. London: Routledge, 2002.

Benjamin, Walter. *Illuminations*. Ed. Hannah Arendt. Trans. Harry Zohn. New York: Harcourt, Brace & World, 1968.

———. *Reflections: Essays, Aphorisms, Autobiographical Writings*. Ed. Peter Demetz. Trans. Edmund Jephcott. New York: Harcourt Brace Jovanovich, 1978.

Bourdieu, Pierre. *Distinction: A Social Critique of the Judgment of Taste*. Trans. Richard Nice. 1979. Cambridge, MA: Harvard University Press, 1984.

Brecht, Bertolt. *Brecht on Theatre*. Ed. and trans. John Willett. London: Methuen, 1964.

Eagleton, Terry. *Criticism and Ideology: A Study in Marxist Literary Theory*. London: NLB, 1976.

————. *Ideology: An Introduction.* London: Verso, 1991.

Gramsci, Antonio. *Prison Notebooks.* Trans. Joseph A. Buttigieg. 2 vols. New York: Columbia University Press, 1991.

Habermas, Jürgen. *The Structural Transformation of the Public Sphere: An Inquiry into a Category of Bourgeois Society.* 1968. Trans. Thomas Burger with Frederick Lawrence. Cambridge, MA: MIT Press, 1989.

————. *The Theory of Communicative Action.* 1981. Trans. Thomas McCarthy. 2 vols. Boston: Beacon Press, 1984, 1987.

Horkheimer, Max, and Theodor Adorno. *Dialectic of Enlightenment.* 1944. Trans. John Cumming. New York: Continuum, 1982.

Jameson, Fredric. *Marxism and Form: Twentieth-Century Dialectical Theories of Literature.* Princeton, NJ: Princeton University Press, 1971.

————. *The Political Unconscious: Narrative as a Socially Symbolic Act.* Ithaca, NY: Cornell University Press, 1981.

————. *Postmodernism, or, the Cultural Logic of Late Capitalism.* Durham, NC: Duke University Press, 1991.

Lukács, Georg. *The Meaning of Contemporary Realism.* 1958. Trans. John and Necke Mander. London: Merlin, 1963.

————. *Studies in European Realism: A Sociological Survey of the Writings of Balzac, Stendhal, Zola, Tolstoy, Gorki, and Others.* 1948. Trans. Edith Bone. London: Hillway, 1950.

The Marx-Engels Reader. Ed. Robert C. Tucker. 2nd ed. New York: Norton, 1978.

Nelson, Cary, and Lawrence Grossberg, eds. *Marxism and the Interpretation of Culture.* Urbana: University of Illinois Press, 1988.

Williams, Raymond. *Marxism and Literature.* Oxford: Oxford University Press, 1977.

New Historicism and Cultural Studies

Bérubé, Michael. *Public Access: Literary Theory and American Cultural Politics.* London: Verso, 1994.

Clifford, James. *Predicament of Culture: Twentieth-Century Ethnography, Literature, and Art.* Cambridge, MA: Harvard University Press, 1988.

Cultural Studies. Ed. Lawrence Grossberg, Cary Nelson, and Paula A. Treichler. New York: Routledge, 1992.

The Cultural Studies Reader. Ed. Simon During. 2nd ed. London: Routledge, 1999.

Dollimore, Jonathan, and Alan Sinfield, eds. *Political Shakespeare: Essays in Cultural Materialism.* 2nd ed. Ithaca, NY: Cornell University Press, 1994.

Foucault, Michel. *The Foucault Reader.* Ed. Paul Rabinow. New York: Pantheon Books, 1984.

Fiske, John. *Reading the Popular.* Boston: Unwin, Hyman, 1989. See also other works by Fiske.

Frith, Simon. *Sound Effects: Youth, Leisure, and the Politics of Rock'n'Roll*. New York: Pantheon Books, 1981. See also other works by Frith.

Frow, John, and Meaghan Morris, eds. *Australian Cultural Studies: A Reader*. Urbana: University of Illinois Press, 1993.

Gallagher, Catherine, and Stephen Greenblatt. *Practicing New Historicism*. Chicago: University of Chicago Press, 2000.

Gilroy, Paul. *"There Ain't No Black in the Union Jack": The Cultural Politics of Race and Nation*. 2nd ed. Chicago: University of Chicago Press, 1991.

Grady, Hugh, and Terence Hawkes, eds. *Presentist Shakespeares*. London: Routledge, 2007.

Greenblatt, Stephen Jay. *Renaissance Self-Fashioning: From More to Shakespeare*. Chicago: University of Chicago Press, 1980.

———. *Shakespearean Negotiations: The Circulation of Social Energy in Renaissance England*. Berkeley: University of California Press, 1988.

Grossberg, Lawrence. *We Gotta Get Out of This Place: Popular Conservatism and Postmodern Culture*. New York: Routledge, 1992. See also other books by Grossberg.

Hall, Stuart, and Tony Jefferson, eds. *Resistance through Rituals: Youth Subcultures in Post-War Britain*. 2nd ed. London: Routledge, 2006.

Hebdige, Dick. *Subculture: The Meaning of Style*. Rev. ed. London: Routledge, 2003.

hooks, bell. *Outlaw Culture: Resisting Representations*. New York: Routledge, 1994.

———. *Teaching to Transgress: Education as the Practice of Freedom*. New York: Routledge, 1994.

———. *Where We Stand: Class Matters*. New York: Routledge, 2000.

McRobbie, Angela. *Feminism and Youth Culture*. 2nd ed. London: Routledge, 2000. See also other books by McRobbie.

Montrose, Louis Adrian. *The Purpose of Playing: Shakespeare and the Cultural Politics of the Elizabethan Theatre*. Chicago: University of Chicago Press, 1996.

Morris, Meaghan. *Pirate's Fiancée: Feminism, Reading, Postmodernism*. London: Verso, 1988.

Ross, Andrew. *No Respect: Intellectuals and Popular Culture*. New York: Routledge, 1989.

Sinfield, Alan. *Faultlines: Cultural Materialism and the Politics of Dissident Reading*. Berkeley: University of California Press, 1992.

———. *Literature, Politics, and Culture in Postwar Britain*. Oxford: Blackwell, 1989.

Stallybrass, Peter, and Allon White. *The Politics and Poetics of Transgression*. London: Methuen, 1986.

Veeser, H. Aram, ed. *The New Historicism*. London: Routledge, 1989.

Williams, Raymond. *The Country and the City*. New York: Oxford University Press, 1973.

———. *Culture and Society, 1780–1950*. London: Chatto & Windus, 1958.
———. *The Long Revolution*. London: Chatto & Windus, 1961.

Postcolonial and Race Studies

Achebe, Chinua. "An Image of Africa: Racism in Conrad's *Heart of Darkness*." 1977. *Hopes and Impediments: Selected Essays, 1965–1987*. London: Heinemann, 1988. 1–20.

Anzaldúa, Gloria. *Borderlands/La Frontera: The New Mestiza*. 2nd ed. San Francisco: Aunt Lute Books, 1999.

Ashcroft, Bill, Gareth Griffiths, and Helen Tiffin, eds. *The Post-Colonial Studies Reader*. 2nd ed. London: Routledge, 2006.

Baker, Houston A., Jr. *Blues, Ideology, and Afro-American Literature: A Vernacular Theory*. Chicago: University of Chicago Press, 1984.

Bernabé, Jean, Patrick Chamoiseau, and Raphaël Confiant. *Eloge de la créolite*. Paris: Gallimard, 1989.

Bhabha, Homi K. *The Location of Culture*. London: Routledge, 1994.

Brennan, Timothy. *At Home in the World: Cosmopolitanism Now*. Cambridge, MA: Harvard University Press, 1997.

Calderon, Hector, and José David Saldívar, eds. *Criticism in the Borderlands: Studies in Chicano Literature, Culture, and Ideology*. Durham, NC: Duke University Press, 1991.

Césaire, Aimé. *Discourse on Colonialism*. 1950. Trans. Joan Pinkham. New York: Monthly Review Press, 1972.

Chatterjee, Partha. *The Nation and Its Fragments: Colonial and Postcolonial Histories*. Princeton, NJ: Princeton University Press, 1993.

Crenshaw, Kimberlé, et al., eds. *Critical Race Theory: The Key Writings that Formed the Movement*. New York: New Press, 1995.

Fanon, Frantz. *Black Skin, White Masks*. 1952. Trans. Charles Lam Markmann. New York: Grove Press, 1967.

———. *The Wretched of the Earth*. 1961. Trans. Constance Farrington. New York: Grove Press, 1963.

Gates, Henry Louis, Jr., ed. *"Race," Writing, and Difference*. Chicago: University of Chicago Press, 1986.

———. *The Signifying Monkey: A Theory of African-American Literary Criticism*. New York: Oxford University Press, 1988.

Gilroy, Paul. *The Black Atlantic: Modernity and Double Consciousness*. Cambridge, MA: Harvard University Press, 1993.

Glissant, Edouard. *Caribbean Discourse: Selected Essays*. Trans. J. Michael Dash. Charlottesville: University Press of Virginia, 1989.

Hill, Mike, ed. *Whiteness: A Critical Reader*. New York: New York University Press, 1997.

hooks, bell. *Black Looks: Race and Representation*. Boston: South End Press, 1992.

————. *Yearning: Race, Gender, and Cultural Politics*. Boston: South End Press, 1990.

Loomba, Ania. *Colonialism/Postcolonialism*. 2nd ed. London: Routledge, 2005.

Lott, Eric. *Love and Theft: Blackface Minstrelsy and the American Working Class*. New York: Oxford University Press, 1993.

Lowe, Lisa. *Immigrant Acts: On Asian American Cultural Politics*. Durham, NC: Duke University Press, 1996.

McClintock, Anne. *Imperial Leather: Race, Gender, and Sexuality in the Colonial Contest*. New York: Routledge, 1993.

Morrison, Toni. *Playing in the Dark: Whiteness and the Literary Imagination*. Cambridge, MA: Harvard University Press, 1992.

Napier, Winston, ed. *African American Literary Theory: A Reader*. New York: New York University Press, 2000.

Ngugi wa Thiong'o. *Decolonising the Mind: The Politics of Language in African Literature*. London: James Currey, 1986.

Omi, Michael, and Howard Winant. *Racial Formation in the United States: From the 1960s to the 1990s*. 2nd ed. New York: Routledge, 1994.

Said, Edward W. *Culture and Imperialism*. New York: Knopf, 1993.

————. *Orientalism*. New York: Pantheon Books, 1978.

————. *The World, the Text, and the Critic*. Cambridge, MA: Harvard University Press, 1983.

Saldívar, José David. *Border Matters: Remapping American Cultural Studies*. Berkeley: University of California Press, 1997.

Shen Wu, Jean Yu-wen, and Min Song, eds. *Asian American Studies: A Reader*. New Brunswick, NJ: Rutgers University Press, 2000.

Smith, Linda Tuhiwai. *Decolonizing Methodologies: Research and Indigenous Peoples*. London: Zed Books, 1999.

Spillers, Hortense J. *Black, White, and in Color: Essays on American Literature and Culture*. Chicago: University of Chicago Press, 2003.

Spivak, Gayatri Chakravorty. "Can the Subaltern Speak? Speculations on Widow-Sacrifice." *Wedge* 7/8 (Winter/Spring 1985): 120–30. Longer version in *Marxism and the Interpretation of Culture*. Ed. Laurence Grossberg and Cary Nelson. Urbana: University of Illinois Press, 1985. 271-313.

————. *A Critique of Postcolonial Reason: Toward a History of the Vanishing Present*. Cambridge, MA: Harvard University Press, 1999.

————. *In Other Worlds: Essays in Cultural Politics*. London: Methuen, 1987.

————. *Outside in the Teaching Machine*. New York: Routledge, 1993.

————. *The Post-Colonial Critic: Interviews, Strategies, Dialogues*. Ed. Sarah Harasym. London: Routledge, 1990.

————. "Three Women's Texts and a Critique of Imperialism." *Critical Inquiry* 12 (Autumn 1985): 243–61.

Trask, Haunani-Kay. *From a Native Daughter: Colonialism and Sovereignty in Hawai'i*. Rev. ed. Honolulu: University of Hawai'i Press, 1999.

Vizenor, Gerald. *Fugitive Poses: Native American Indian Scenes of Absence and Presence*. Lincoln: University of Nebraska Press, 1998.

———. *Manifest Manners: Postindian Warriors of Survivance*. Hanover, NH: University Press of New England, 1994.

Williams, Patrick, and Laura Chrisman, eds. *Colonial Discourse and Postcolonial Theory: A Reader*. New York: Columbia University Press, 1994.

Young, Robert J. C. *White Mythologies: Writing History and the West*. 2nd ed. London: Routledge, 2004.

Reader Response

Bérubé, Michael. *Marginal Forces/Cultural Centers: Tolson, Pynchon, and the Politics of the Canon*. Ithaca, NY: Cornell University Press, 1992.

Bleich, David. *Readings and Feelings: An Introduction to Subjective Criticism*. Urbana, IL: National Council of Teachers of English, 1975.

———. *Subjective Criticism*. Baltimore: Johns Hopkins University Press, 1978.

Bobo, Jacqueline. *Black Women as Cultural Readers*. New York: Columbia University Press, 1995.

Eco, Umberto. *The Role of the Reader: Explorations in the Semiotics of Texts*. Bloomington: Indiana University Press, 1978.

Fetterley, Judith. *The Resisting Reader: A Feminist Approach to American Fiction*. Bloomington: Indiana University Press, 1978.

Fish, Stanley. *Is There a Text in This Class? The Authority of Interpretive Communities*. Cambridge, MA: Harvard University Press, 1980.

———. *Surprised by Sin: The Reader in "Paradise Lost."* 2nd ed. Cambridge, MA: Harvard University Press, 1998.

Flynn, Elizabeth A., and Patrocinio P. Schweickart, eds. *Gender and Reading: Essays on Readers, Texts, and Contexts*. Baltimore: Johns Hopkins University Press, 1986.

Freund, Elizabeth. *The Return of the Reader: Reader-Response Criticism*. London: Methuen, 1987.

Holland, Norman N. *5 Readers Reading*. New Haven, CT: Yale University Press, 1975.

———. *The Dynamics of Literary Response*. New York: Oxford University Press, 1968.

Holub, Robert C. *Reception Theory: A Critical Introduction*. London: Methuen, 1984.

Iser, Wolfgang. *The Act of Reading: A Theory of Aesthetic Response*. Baltimore: Johns Hopkins University Press, 1978.

———. *The Implied Reader: Patters of Communication in Prose Fiction from Bunyan to Beckett*. Baltimore: Johns Hopkins University Press, 1974.

Jauss, Hans Robert. *Toward an Aesthetic of Reception*. Trans. Timothy Bahti. Minneapolis: University of Minnesota Press, 1982.

Mailloux, Steven. *Interpretive Conventions: The Reader in the Study of American Fiction*. Ithaca, NY: Cornell University Press, 1982.

McHenry, Elizabeth. *Forgotten Readers: Recovering the Lost History of African-American Literary Societies*. Durham, NC: Duke University Press, 2002.

Radway, Janice A. *Reading the Romance: Women, Patriarchy, and Popular Literature*. 2nd ed. Chapel Hill: University of North Carolina Press, 1991.

Suleiman, Susan, and Inge Crosman, eds. *The Reader in the Text: Essays on Audience and Interpretation*. Princeton, NJ: Princeton University Press, 1980.

Tompkins, Jane P., ed. *Reader-Response Criticism: From Formalism to Post-Structuralism*. Baltimore: Johns Hopkins University Press, 1980.

PHOTOGRAPHIC CREDITS

➻ Index ➻

Key terms appear in bold along with the numbers for the pages that introduce and explain them.

A

absence, 81, 86, 127–28, 130, 134
Achebe, Chinua, 247, 276, 277
Adorno, Theodor W., 196
affective fallacy, the, 28–29, 279
affective stylistics, 280
agency, *passim*; defined, **204.**
   See also subject, the
Agrarians, the, 24
Alien, 129
alienation effect, the, 208
alienation of labor, the, 190–91,
   193, 213
All in the Family, 50
Allison, Dorothy, 166
Althusser, Louis, 130, 198–203,
   207, 227, 230
always already, defined, **46, 80**
ambiguity, 16, 17–19, 20, 22, 25,
   35, 36, 83
American Psychological
   Association, 173
anal stage, the, 108
Anderson, Benedict, 130
antifeminism, 138, 139, 143, 150
antillanité, **263–64**
Anzaldúa, Gloria, 263, 271
aporia, 81, 258, 260

arbitrary link between signified and
   signifier, the, **43, 44**
archetypal criticism, 127
Aristotle, *Poetics*, 14
As the World Turns, 114
aura, 197
Austen, Jane, 12, 61–63, 270, 276–77
—works: *Mansfield Park*, 276–77;
   Pride and Prejudice, 12, 61–63
authenticity, 81, 100, 243
authority, 81, 110, 140–41
authority of experience, the, 140–41

B

Bacall, Lauren, 159–60
Baker, Houston A., 272
balance, 18–19, 37, 83, 85, 225,
   238–39
Balzac, Honoré de, 193
baring the device, 59
Barker, Pat, *Regeneration* trilogy, 13
Barthes, Roland, 41, 52–53, 56, 226
base, 188, 197–98, 204, 208
Baym, Nina, 148
Beardsley, Monroe C., 28–29, 31,
   279
Beckett, Samuel, 193

307

competence, 48, 50, 55, 283

compromise, 117–19

compulsory heterosexuality, 163–65

condensation, 117–19, 120, 132

congealing, 201, 211, 214

Conrad, Joseph, *Heart of Darkness,* 65, 275, 276–77

consent, 194

considerations of representation, 117–19

construction, *passim*; defined, **45–46.** *See also* gender; gender and psychoanalysis; sex

conventions, 43–44, 49–50, 52, 70–71, 114, 122

countertransference, 105

creolization, 263–64, 265

critical legal studies, 267–68

critical race studies, critical race theory, vii, 262, 267–71, 276

critical spectators, 157–59, 286

critical theory, defined, 10; Frankfurt School, 196

criticism, defined 3–4

crossblood, 265

cross-cultural poetics, 264

The Crying Game, 169–71

Cry, the Beloved Country (Alan Paton), 253

Culler, Jonathan, 48, 283

cultural capital, 209–10

cultural feminism, 137

cultural materialism, 232, 234

cultural poetics, 222

cultural studies, *passim. See esp.* 89, 97–98, 231–39

cummings, e. e., 34

D

daily residue, the, 119

"Danielle," 206–07, 234

Daughters of the Dust, 286

Davis, Rebecca Harding, "Life in the Iron Mills," 211

death of the author, 52–53, 113, 116

decentering, 79, 81

decolonization, 246–47, 266

deconstruction, 75–100 and *passim*

deep structure, 45, 48

defamiliarization, 58–59, 150

defenses, 104, 106, 117–19, 120, 124–25

de Man, Paul, 89–91

Derrida, Jacques, 77–78, 80, 82, 85–91, 127–28, 144–46, 226, 228, 255, 257–58, 261, 272

Desai, Anita, 276

detective novel, the, 53–58

diachronic, the, 53–55, 58, 69

dialectic, 189–90

dialectical materialism, 190

diaspora, 243, 271

Dickens, Charles, 13, 17, 65

—works: *Great Expectations,* 17, 65; *Hard Times,* 13

Dickinson, Emily, 12, 17, 30–31, 58–59, 270

—works: "Further in summer than the birds," 12, 31; "Much Madness is divinest Sense," 17

Dietrich, Marlene, 159–60

différance, 81, **86–88,** 100, 128, 130, 132

difference, 40–41, 44

difference feminism, 137

direct discourse. *See* discourse (direct, indirect, and free indirect)

Dirty, Pretty Things, 274–76

disability studies, 287

discipline, 230, 253

Index